The Talmudic Argument

THE TALMUDIC ARGUMENT

A study in Talmudic reasoning and methodology

LOUIS JACOBS

Rabbi of the New London Synagogue
Visiting Professor at Harvard Divinity School

The right of the University of Cambridge to print and sell all manner of books was granted by Henry VIII in 1534. The University has printed and published continuously since 1584.

CAMBRIDGE UNIVERSITY PRESS

Cambridge
London New York New Rochelle
Melbourne Sydney

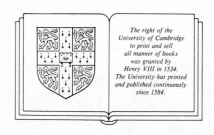

Published by the Press Syndicate of the University of Cambridge
The Pitt Building, Trumpington Street, Cambridge CB2 1RP
32 East 57th Street, New York, NY 10022, USA
296 Beaconsfield Parade, Middle Park, Melbourne 3206, Australia

First published 1984

Printed in Great Britain by
the University Press, Cambridge

Library of Congress catalogue card number: 84-4351

British Library Cataloguing in Publication Data

Jacobs, Louis
The Talmudic argument.
1. Talmud—Criticism, interpretation, etc.
I. Title
296.1′2 BM501

ISBN 0 521 26370 0

FOR DANIEL

ON THE OCCASION OF HIS BARMITZVAH

Contents

Preface

This book seeks to combine the methodological and the literary approach to the study of the reasoning and argumentation typical of the Babylonian Talmud. In the great, traditional Yeshivot, most of which today are influenced by the methods of the Lithuanian Talmudic giants – R. Hayyim Soloveitchik and his son R. Velvel; R. Simeon Skopf; R. Moshe Mordecai Epstein of Slabodka; R. Baruch Baer of Kamenitz; R. Joseph Judah Laib Bloch of Telz; R. Meir Simhah of Dvinsk; R. Elhanan Wasserman and others too numerous to mention – the Talmud is subjected to acute, logical analysis of the utmost rigour, to yield important results for the full understanding of the work. But, in these institutions, historical and literary questions are virtually ignored. Modern critical investigation is considered not so much to be taboo as irrelevant. As the old Yeshiva gibe has it, the Professor of Semitics can tell you what kind of clothes Abbaye wore but the *lamdan* ('traditional scholar') can tell you what Abbaye said. Modern critical scholars, on the other hand, in addition to their massive historical researches, have, in recent years, subjected the Talmudic texts to keen literary analysis, in which the pre-history of the Talmudic pericopae and their later formulation have been studied in order to shed fresh light on how the literary traditions have emerged and to try to solve the mystery of how the Babylonian Talmud came to assume its present form, who its authors were and how they went about their task. One thinks of scholars like I. H. Weiss; Isaac Halevy; C. Albeck; Abraham Weiss; David Halivni; Saul Lieberman; Hyman Klein; J. N. Epstein; Benjamin De Friess; Shamma Friedman; Jacob Neusner and his pupils. Quite naturally, these scholars, in their concentration on context, tend to leave content to take care of itself to some extent. Whatever originality this book may possess lies in its attempt to combine the two methods by analysing both the logic of the arguments and their literary form.

The first two chapters are introductory: one on Talmudic argumentation in general, its nature, terms and history; the other on the central literary problem of how the Babylonian Talmud was composed. The bulk of the work consists of the analytical treatment of a number of typical *sugyot* (plural of *sugya*, the name for a complete Talmudic unit). Each *sugya* is paraphrased, the thrust of the argument noted and an attempt made to subject the material to literary analysis. The passages in smaller type call attention to further points requiring elucidation and provide some information regarding the discussion of the same theme in other parts of the Talmud as well as in the post-Talmudic works. For this purpose the two works: *Kesef Nivḥar* and the *Entziklopedia Talmudit* have proved invaluable. The final chapter seeks to tie all the material together and to suggest the conclusions which have been reached in the investigation.

In reply to the question, allegedly put by the combative person who witnessed two men fighting: 'Is this a private quarrel or can anyone join in?', I hope that the answer, so far as this book is concerned, is that non-professional students of the Talmud and, for that matter, anyone interested in Jewish thought, will gain something from reading the book. At the same time, I am sufficiently presumptuous to offer the work as a small contribution towards the solution of the kind of problems faced by full-time Talmudic scholars.

Note on transliteration

This is not a work on Hebrew and Aramaic philology. The transliteration from these languages has, consequently, been kept as simple as possible. In the main the scheme followed is that of the *Encyclopedia Judaica* (vol. 1, p. 90), e.g. *ḥet* is represented by *ḥ* and *hey* by *h* (without the dot) but *k* represents both *kof* and *kaf*. However, for the sake of greater accuracy, the sign ʻ is used for ʻ*ayin*, to distinguish it from *alef* (which is not marked). The letter *e* is used to represent both the *segol* and the *tzeri* (*eh* and *ay*) but where otherwise the *e* might be read as part of a single syllable the *tzeri* is marked *ē*, e.g. *nosē* reads *no-say*, the mark denoting that it is not to be read as *nose*. The sign ´ is placed over a vowel letter to denote that the letter has to be sounded on its own and is not part of a diphthong or a single syllable with previous letters, e.g. *le-hoíl* is to be read as *le-ho-il*, *kanésu* is to be read as *ka-ne-su* not *kane-su*.

NOTE ON BIBLICAL TRANSLATIONS

Quotations are usually from the Authorised Version of the Bible. In certain cases, however, a free translation is given, where the particular exegesis of the Talmud requires it.

Where alternative verse numbers are given, they are quoted from *The Torah: A New Translation*, Philadelphia, 1962.

Note on the Babylonian Talmud

For readers totally unfamilar with the Talmud this brief outline gives the essential facts. Three easily remembered (but only approximate) dates are: 200 C.E. when the Mishnah was compiled; 400 C.E. when the Palestinian Talmud (also known as *Yerushalmi*, the Jerusalem Talmud) was compiled; and 500 C.E. when the Babylonian Talmud was compiled. The Mishnah ('Teaching') is a digest of what the Rabbis call 'the Oral Torah', i.e. the detailed expositions, as these developed in the Palestinian schools, of 'the Written Torah', the Pentateuch and the rest of the Hebrew Bible. The teachers whose views are recorded in the Mishnah and in other works from the same period are known as Tannaím ('teachers'). The Mishnah is divided into six Orders and these are subdivided into tractates and chapters. Each chapter contains a number of smaller units, each of which is also called a Mishnah. Thus Mishnah is the term for the smallest unit as well as for the work as a whole. The Mishnah is in Hebrew, this being the scholarly language in Palestine in the first two centuries.

In the schools of Palestine and Babylon the Mishnah became accepted as a sacred text, taking its place by the side of the Bible. In these schools the Mishnah was discussed and interpreted so that the name given to the post-Mishnaic teachers is Amoraím ('interpreters'). Around the year 400 C.E. the debates and discussions of the Palestinian Amoraím were collected and edited to form the Palestinian Talmud. (The word 'Talmud' also means 'teaching' or 'study'.) Around the year 500 the material from the Babylonian schools was collected and edited to form the Babylonian Talmud. Both the Palestinian and the Babylonian Talmuds are in Aramaic (the language of discourse even among the scholars in this period) but the former is in the Western dialect of Aramaic, the latter in the Eastern. The Babylonian Talmud is far more comprehensive than the Palestinian and is often referred to as *the* Talmud, although, strictly speaking, there are two Talmuds. Although the Mishnah exists both in manuscript and in print on its own, it is always presented, too, as part of the Talmud. Thus the Babylonian Talmud in its present form consists of the Mishnah together with the Talmud proper, the material from the Babylonian schools.

There was constant scholarly exchange between the two centres of Palestine and Babylon with the result that teachings of the Babylonian Rabbis are found in the Palestinian Talmud and teachings of the Palestinian Rabbis in the Babylonian Talmud. Eventually, out of fear of the censor (for whom the Talmud was suspect as allegedly containing attacks on Christianity), a substitute name for 'Talmud' was used. This is the term 'Gemara' (also with a meaning of 'teaching' but here of a particular text). This term is used in the Talmud frequently for a particular passage or text but is now used for the Talmud as a whole. Thus, nowadays, and in all printed versions, the Babylonian Talmud is called 'The Gemara', consisting, as above, of the Mishnah and the Gemara.

The complete Talmud was first printed in Italy in the sixteenth century, since when it has gone into numerous editions. The standard edition of the Babylonian Talmud is that printed and reprinted (and now frequently photocopied) in Vilna by the printing house of Romm. There is a uniform pagination in all editions of the Babylonian Talmud. Each folio page has two sides – a and b. The method used to quote a passage from the Talmud is to refer to the tractate, the page and the side; thus *Bava Kama* 11a means tractate *Bava Kama*, page 11, side a; *Yoma* 23b means tractate *Yoma*, page 23, side b. The Babylonian Talmud has been translated into English, under the editorship of Dr I. Epstein, and published by the Soncino Press.

The following is a list, in order, of the tractates of the Babylonian Talmud. (There is no Babylonian Talmud on a number of tractates of the Mishnah.) The list gives the name of the tractate, its translation and a brief description of its subject matter.

Berakhot: 'Blessings'; the Shema' and the daily prayers
Shabbat: 'Sabbath'; the Sabbath laws
'Eruvin: 'Mixtures'; the laws of Sabbath boundaries

Pesaḥim: 'Passovers'
Yoma: 'The Day'; the laws of the Day of Atonement, *Yom Kippur*
Sukkah: 'Booth', the laws of Tabernacles
Betzah: 'Egg' (after the opening word); the laws of the Festivals
Rosh ha-Shanah: 'Beginning of the year'; the laws of the New Year festival
Ta'anit: 'Fast'; the laws of Fast Days
Megillah: 'Scroll (of Esther)'; the laws of the Purim Festival
Mo'ed Katan: 'Minor Festival'; the laws of the intermediate days of the Festivals
Ḥagigah: 'Festival offering'; the special offering for the Pilgrim Festivals
Yevamot: 'Sisters-in-law'; the laws of levirate marriage
Ketubot: 'Marriage settlements'
Nedarim: 'Vows'
Nazir: 'Nazirite'
Sotah: 'Wife suspected of adultery'
Gittin: 'Divorces'
Kiddushin: 'Marriage'
Bava Kama: 'First gate', dealing with torts
Bava Metzi'a: 'Middle gate', dealing with civil law
Bava Batra: 'Last gate', dealing with property law
Sanhedrin: procedures of the Sanhedrin and other Law Courts
Makkot: 'Floggings', dealing with criminal law
Shevu'ot: 'Oaths'
'Avodah Zarah: 'Strange worship'; laws concerning idolatry
Horayot: 'Court decisions', given in error
Zevaḥim: 'Sacrifices', of animals in the Temple
Menaḥot: 'Meal offerings'
Ḥullin: 'Non-sacred', animals, and their preparation as food
Bekhorot: 'First-borns'
'Arakhin: 'Assessments', of gifts to the Temple
Temurah: 'Exchange', of a sacred animal
Keritot: 'Extirpations'
Me'ilah: 'Trespass-offering'
Niddah: 'Menstruant'

Abbreviations

ARN	*Avot de-Rabbi Natan*
b.	ben, 'son of'
BSOAS	*Bulletin of the School of Oriental and African Studies*
C.E.	Common Era
Dor	*Dor Dor ve-Doréshav* by I. H. Weiss
DS	*Dikdukey Soférim* by R. Rabbinovicz
EJ	*Encyclopedia Judaica*
ET	*Entziklopedia Talmudit*
Gilyon ha-Shas	Notes of R. Akiba Eger (1761–1837)
ha-Gra	Notes of Elijah Gaon of Vilna (1720–97)
HUCA	*Hebrew Union College Annual*
JE	*Jewish Encyclopedia*
JJS	*Journal of Jewish Studies*
JQR	*Jewish Quarterly Review*
JSS	*Journal of Semitic Studies*
Kesef Nivḥar	by Baruch Benedict Goitein (*c.* 1770–1842)
Maggid Mishneh	Commentary on Maimonides' *Yad* by Vidal Yom Tov of Tolosa (fourteenth century)
Maharsha	Novellae of R. Samuel Edels (1555–1631)
Meíri	*Bet ha-Beḥirah* by Menahem Meíri of Perpignan (1249–1316)
Mevuot	*Mevuot le-Sifrut ha-Amoraím* by J. N. Epstein
R.	Rabbi
R.	(after Genesis, Exodus etc.) Midrash *Rabbah*
Raábad	R. Abraham ben David of Posquirês (*c.* 1125–98)
Ramban	R. Moses ben Nahman, Nahmanides (1194–1270)
Ran	R. Nissim Gerondi (d. *c.* 1375)

Rashba	R. Solomon Ibn Adret (*c.* 1235–*c.* 1310)
Rashi	R. Solomon Yitzhaki (1040–1105)
Riban	R. Judah ben Nathan, son-in-law of *Rashi*
Ritba	R. Yom Tov Ishbili (*c.* 1250–1330)
Rosh	R. Asher ben Yehiel (*c.* 1250–1327)
SM	*Shitah Mekubbetzet* by Bezalel Ashkenazi (*c.* 1520–91)
Soncino	*The Babylonian Talmud*, translated into English, Soncino Press
Tosafists	Glosses to the Talmud by the French and German schools, twelfth to fourteenth century
Tur	The *Turim* of Jacob ben Asher (d. *c.* 1340)
Yad	*Yad ha-Ḥazakah*, Code of Maimonides (1135–1204)

I

The Talmudic argument

The Babylonian Talmud consists almost entirely of arguments having as their aim the elucidation of the law, ruling, religious teaching or ethical idea. Theories are advanced and then contradicted. They are examined from many points of view and qualified where necessary. One argument leads to another when logic demands it. The claims of conflicting theories are investigated with great thoroughness and much subtlety. Fine distinctions abound between apparently similar concepts. The whole constitutes reasoning processes which have received the most careful study on the part of generations of Jewish scholars and have contributed more to the shaping of the Jewish mind than any other factor.

No serious student of the Babylonian Talmud can be unaware that, for all the variety of topics discussed in the work, there is a formal pattern to the argumentation. Whatever the subject matter, the moves open to the debaters are comparatively few in number and these are always expressed in the same stereotyped formulae. There is much originality in Talmudic argumentation but this consists in the application to new situations of conventional responses, not in the invention of new responses. The game is always played according to the rules.

These formal methods of argumentation occur with the utmost frequency in the Babylonian Talmud yet, although there is to be observed a complete consistency in their use, nowhere in the Talmud itself is any attempt made at their enumeration and classification. Part of this task was left to the famous post-Talmudic methodologies, largely concerned with the classification of Talmudic method. However, in the main, the Talmudic methodologies deal with the precise definition of the terms used rather than with the actual types of argument. Of these there has been very little detailed, systematic treatment.

For Talmudic methodology see W. Bacher, *Exegetische Terminologie der jüdischen Traditionsliteratur*, Hebrew translation by A. Z. Rabbinowitz under title '*Erkhey Midrash* (Tel-Aviv, 1924); H. Strack, *Introduction to the Talmud and Midrash* (Philadelphia, 1945), pp. 135–9; M. Meilziner, *Introduction to the Talmud*, 4th edn with new bibliography by A. Guttmann (New York, 1968), part III: 'Talmudic terminology and methodology', pp. 190–280; and I. H. Weiss' survey of the methodological literature in *Bet Talmud*, vol. I (Vienna, 1881) and vol. II (Vienna, 1882). The most important of the methodologies are: *Mevo ha-Talmud* attributed to Samuel ha-Naggid (d. 1055), printed with commentaries in the Vilna edition of the Talmud after tractate *Berakhot; Sefer Keritut* by Samson of Chinon (end of thirteenth century), ed. J. Z. Roth with commentary (New York, 1961), and by S. B. D. Sofer with commentary (Jerusalem, 1965); *Halikhot 'Olam* by Joshua ha-Levi of Tlemcen (compiled in Toledo *c.* 1467), edition Warsaw, 1883, with commentaries: *Kelaley ha-Gemara* by Joseph Karo (1488–1575) and *Yavin Shem'va* by Solomon Algazi (seventeenth century); *Sheney Luḥot ha-Berit* by Isaiah Horowitz (d. *c.* 1630) (Amsterdam, 1649), section *Torah she-be-'al Peh; Yad Malakhi* by Malachi Ha-Kohen of Leghorn (early eighteenth century) (Jerusalem, 1976).

In every complete Talmudic unit – the *sugya* – the differing views are presented in the form of a debate. The protagonists may be actual teachers expressing their opinions, Rav and Samuel, R. Johanan and Resh Lakish, Rabbah and R. Joseph, Abbaye and Rava and so forth. Very frequently, however, the thrust and parry of the debate is presented anonymously. It has long been conventional among students of the Talmud to give a kind of fictitious personality to the arguments by attributing questions to an alleged 'questioner' (the *makshan*) and answers to an alleged 'replier' (*tartzan*). In a particular *sugya* different types of argument may be produced as the course of the debate demands, e.g. an appeal to authority, the detection of flaws in an analogy, the readmission of a rejected plea and so forth. The unit as a whole consists of all the arguments, together with any extraneous material which may arise as the discussion proceeds.

On the use of the terms *makshan* and *tartzan* see e.g. *Rashi*, *Shabbat* 104a top; *Kiddushin* 2a, s.v. *ve-khesef minalan; Tosafists* to *Berakhot* 44a s.v. *inhu* and *Yoma* 43b s.v. *amar R. Yehudah.* Cf. ben Yehudah's *Thesaurus*, vol. VII, p. 3295 and vol. XVI, p. 7923.

The sustained argument, particularly in the form of question and answer, as presented in the Babylonian Talmud, has strong antecedents in the earlier sources. There are numerous instances in the Pentateuch and in the historical books of the Bible: Eve's debate with the serpent (Genesis 3: 1–5); God's accusation of Adam (Genesis 3: 9–13); God's interrogation of Cain (Genesis 4: 9–15); Abraham's plea to God to spare Sodom (Genesis 18: 23–33); Abimelech's upbraiding of Abraham (Genesis 20: 9–17); Abraham's reproof of Abimelech (Genesis 21: 22–30); Abraham's purchase of the field and bargaining with Ephron (Genesis 23: 3–16); Jacob's dialogue with his wives (Genesis 31: 4–16) and with Laban (Genesis 31: 26–53); the arguments presented by Schechem and Hamor (Genesis 34: 4–23); the arguments and counter-arguments in the Joseph saga (Genesis 42: 7–38; 43: 2–14; 44: 6–34); Joseph's bargain with the Egyptians (Genesis 47: 15–25); Pharaoh's complaint against the midwives (Exodus 1: 15–19); Moses' confrontation with God (Exodus 3: 4 to 4: 17); Moses' dialogue with Pharaoh (Exodus 10: 1–11); Jethro's plea for reforms (Exodus 18: 13–23); Moses' entreaty on behalf of his people (Exodus 32: 7–14 and 33: 12–23); Moses' questioning of Aaron and his sons (Leviticus 10: 16–20); Moses' complaint (Numbers 11: 11–23); the episode of Moses, Aaron and Miriam (Numbers 12: 1–14); the debate between Caleb and the spies (Numbers 13: 27 to 14: 10); the rebellion of Korah (Numbers 16: 1–19); Moses and the King of Edom (Numbers 20: 14–21); Balaam and the ass (Numbers 22: 28–35); the account of the sons of Reuben and Gad (Numbers 32: 1–32); the two lawsuits concerning the daughters of Zelophehad (Numbers 27: 1–7 and 36: 1–10). The major portion of the book of Deuteronomy consists of a sustained argument in which Moses reminds the people of their history and their obligations in the future. Among arguments of this type in the historical books are: Rahab and the spies (Joshua 2: 1–21); the debate between the other tribes and the sons of Reuben and Gad (Joshua 22: 13–14); Jotham's argument (Judges 9: 7–20); Jephthah and the sons of Ammon (Judges 11: 12–28); Samuel against the appointment of a king (I Samuel 8: 10–21); his rebuke of the people in this matter (I Samuel 12: 1–24); his castigation of Saul (I Samuel 13: 10–14); Eliab and David (I Samuel 17: 28–37); Jonathan and Saul (I Samuel 20: 21–32); David at Nob (I Samuel 21: 2–7); David and Saul (I Samuel 24: 9–22); David and Abigail (I Samuel 25: 23–35); David and Uriah (II Samuel 11: 10–12); David and the death of his child (II Samuel 12: 17–23); the woman of Tekoa

(II Samuel 14: 4–24); Barzillai and David (II Samuel 19: 32–40); Bath-sheba and David (I Kings 1: 11–27); Solomon and the two harlots (I Kings 3: 16–27); Obadiah and Elijah (I Kings 18: 7–15); Elijah and the prophets of Baal (I Kings 18: 21–7); the four lepers (II Kings 7: 3–4); Rab-shakeh and Eliakim (II Kings 18: 19–35).

As for the prophetic books, the whole of the prophetic message is in the form of a sustained argument. The passages especially to be noted are: Isaiah 40: 12–26; 44: 9–20; 49: 14–26; 51: 12–13; 58: 2–14; 66: 1–2; Jeremiah 2: 4–37; 12: 1–13; Ezekiel 18: 1–29; Amos 3: 3–8; 6: 1–2; 9: 7; Jonah 1: 6–15; 4: 2–11; Micah 6: 3–8; Zechariah 4: 1–7; Malachi 1: 2–14; 2: 10–17; 3: 13–16.

The same type of sustained argument is found in the book of Psalms. Psalm 10 in its entirety is a plea for the salvation of the righteous from the hands of the wicked. In both Psalm 15 and Psalm 24 the way of righteousness is prescribed and expressed as a reply to a question. Psalm 23 draws the conclusion that man should trust in God from the premiss that the Lord is his Shepherd. Psalm 50 is an argument in favour of the view that it is righteousness that God wants, not sacrifices. Psalm 96 is a mighty plea that God be praised and Psalm 100 that He is to be thanked. These themes are repeated in Psalms 104 and 105. Psalm 112 is an argument for righteous living and Psalm 115 against idolatry. Psalm 119 exhausts the letters of the alphabet eight times in calling attention to the need for man to be loyal to God's law. In Psalm 136 there are a number of 'proofs' that God's mercy 'endureth for ever'. Psalm 139 argues that it is impossible to escape from God. Psalm 146 argues that it is better for man to put his trust in God than in princes. And the book of Psalms in general is mainly an appeal by argument to God, expressed in poetry, that He should pay heed to the cry of the poor and oppressed.

In the other books of the Hagiographa the same phenomenon is to be observed. In Proverbs we find arguments for the cultivation of wisdom (3: 13–23); against harlotry (5: 1–20; 7: 5–23); against sloth (6: 6–15); against wickedness (10: 2–32); and for the worth of a good wife (31: 10–31). The book of Job has the arguments of Satan (1: 6 to 2: 6); of Job's friends and his replies (4: 1 to 37: 24); of God to Job (38 to 41) and Job's reply (42: 1–6). The book of Ruth contains Naomi's argument to her daughters-in-law (1: 8–170) and that of Boaz with his kinsman (4: 1–12). In addition to the argument for pessimism, the general theme of Ecclesiastes, there are arguments in favour of melancholia (7: 2–6); of wisdom (7: 10–12); of mirth (8: 15); and of effort (11:1–8). Esther contains the arguments advanced by Memucan for deposing Vashti (1: 16–22); Haman's arguments for destroying the Jews (3: 8–11); Esther's dialogue with Mordecai (4: 10–14) and Esther's plea for her people (7: 3 to 8: 6).

The dialectical tone of the above passages was no doubt familiar to the Babylonian Amoraím and, for that matter, to many of their fellow-Jews, from infancy. In addition, so far as we can tell, the hermeneutical principles laid down by the Tannaím were widely discussed and accepted by all the Amoraím. These principles are themselves largely ways of argumentation and references to them abound in the Babylonian Talmud.

It should be noted that it is acknowledged in the Rabbinic literature itself that the argument from the minor to the major is found in the Bible; see my article: 'The "*qal va-ḥomer*" argument in the Old Testament', *BSOAS*, 35: 2 (1972), 221–7. A. Schwarz, in *Der Hermeneutische Syllogismus in der Talmudischen Litteratur* (Karlsruhe, 1901); *Die Hermeneutische Antinomie in der Talmudischen Litteratur* (Vienna, 1913); *Die Hermeneutische Quantitätsrelation in der Talmudischen Litteratur* (Vienna, 1913) and in other works, has examined the thirteen principles of R. Ishmael with the utmost attention to detail. These principles are found in *Sifra*, Introduction. The seven principles attributed to Hillel are found in *Sifra*, Introduction, end; *ARN* 37; *Tosefta Sanhedrin*, 7, end. The twelfth-century Karaite author Judah Hadassi argued for Greek influence on the hermeneutic principles and this matter has been discussed by David Daube, 'Rabbinic methods of interpretation and Hellenistic rhetoric', *HUCA*, 22 (1949), 239–64 and by Saul Lieberman, *Hellenism in Jewish Palestine* (New York, 1950), pp. 47–82. Cf. J. Z. Lauterbach 'Talmud hermeneutics', *JE*, vol. XII, pp. 30–3; Chaim Hirschensohn, *Berurey ha-Middot* (New York, 1929–31); M. Ostrowsky, *ha-Middot she-ha-Torah Nidreshet ba-Hem*, (Jerusalem, 1924); and my article 'Hermeneutics', *EJ*, vol. VIII, pp. 366-72. The Palestine Talmud uses some of the methods of argument that are found in the Babylonian Talmud but these are in a much less finished form in the Palestinian Talmud; see I. H. Taviob, '*Talmudah shel Bavel ve-Talmudah shel Eretz Yisrael*' in his *Collected Writings* (in Hebrew) (Berlin, 1923), pp. 73–88 and the Introduction, *Ḥomat Yerushalayim* by S. Feigensohn (*Shafan ha-Sofer*), based on Z. Frankel's work, in the Vilna edition of the Palestinian Talmud.

The Babylonian Amoraím thus had a long tradition behind them of skill in debate and argument. The study of the Torah was their consuming purpose in life to which they applied themselves with ruthless devotion and dedication. Over the years, the exercise of their minds in these dialectics seems to have produced an automatic response to the problems they were concerned to solve. Naturally, it is necessary to distinguish between the use of argument by the Amoraím themselves and the use by the final editors. This problem will be considered in the following chapter. But even if, as seems extremely probable and as we shall see there, the final form of these arguments owes much to the redactors or compilers of the Talmud, the methods must have had a history and some were almost certainly used even by the earliest of the Babylonian Amoraím.

On the more general question of attitudes towards skill in debating matters of Torah, it is clear that such skill was highly praised. In the Mishnah (*Avot* 2: 8) we find a report that Rabban Johanan b. Zakkai praised his disciple R. Eliezer b. Hyrcanus, saying that he was 'a plastered cistern which loses not a drop', i.e. he had an extraordinarily retentive memory and was able to recall everything he had been taught. He praised another disciple, R. Eleazar b. Arakh, saying that he was 'an ever-flowing spring', i.e. he had the ability to advance fresh, original arguments and theses. Two versions are then recorded. According to one of these, the master declared that if all the Sages of Israel were in one scale of the balance and Eliezer b. Hyrcanus in the other he would outweigh them all. The other version, in the name of Abba Saul, is: if all the Sages of Israel were in one scale of the balance, together with Eliezer b. Hyrcanus, and Eleazer b. Arakh was in the other scale, he would outweigh them all. A Talmudic report (*'Erwin* 13b) about the second-century teacher R. Meir says that no one in his generation could be compared to him in brilliance but that, none the less, the law does not follow his opinions because his colleagues were incapable of penetrating to the depths of his mind and the law always follows the majority opinion. Of R. Meir it is also said that he was able to produce arguments to render the clean unclean and the unclean clean. This statement was puzzling to the *Tosafists* to the passage. 'What is so meritorious', they ask, 'in arguing against the laws of the Torah?' Is it possible that we have here an echo of an institution in which disciples were taught to test their skills in argumentation by arguing for positions known to be false because contradicted by the Torah? In the same Talmudic passage it is stated, R. Judah the Prince declared that the reason his intellect was sharper than his colleagues' was because he had had the privilege of sitting in the lecture-hall behind R. Meir. Had he sat in front of the master when he taught, his brilliance would have been even greater; no doubt a reference to the use of gestures and facial expressions by the teacher in order to convey the teachings more effectively. In support the verse is quoted: 'But thine eyes shall see thy teachers' (Isaiah 30: 20). In the legend told (*Shabbat* 33b) regarding R. Meir's contemporary, R. Simeon b. Yohai, it is said that this teacher spent twelve of privation in a cave, which had the effect of heightening his intellectual powers. Before that time, when R. Simeon suggested a problem his son-in-law was able to provide 12 different solutions, but after the experience in the cave the roles were reversed: to every problem set by his son-in-law R. Simeon was able to offer 24 different solutions. It is said (*Bava Metzi'a* 84a) of the two third-century Palestinian Amoraím, R. Johanan and R. Simeon b. Lakish, that 'Resh Lakish' was able to produce 24 objections to every statement made by R. Johanan. When Resh Lakish died, the Sages sent R. Eleazar b. Pedat as a substitute for Resh Lakish, but R. Johanan found him very unsatisfactory. R. Eleazar was able to do no more than produce 24 proofs in support of R. Johanan's statements and this was of no help to the master, who preferred to be challenged, as he was by Resh Lakish.

To be noted is the number 24, in this narrative and the one about R. Simeon b. Yohai and his son-in-law. In the latter story the number is perhaps a play on the number 12, the period of years R. Simeon spent in the cave. The number 24 is a formal number, almost certainly corresponding to the 24 books of the Bible with which the scholar is expected to be familiar; see Exodus R. 41: 5 and *Tanḥuma*, ed. Buber, to Exodus 31: 18 and Buber's notes. Cf. the number 48 (twice 24) in the account of Symmachus' reasoning powers in '*Eruvin* 13b and the 48 days in which the Torah is acquired, *Avot* 6: 5 (*Kinyan Torah*). Cf. *Ta'anit* 8a: 'R. Adda b. Ahavah used to arrange his lessons in proper order 24 times, corresponding to the number of books of the Torah, Prophets and Hagiographa, before he appeared in the presence of Rava.'

The two types of scholar referred to, as above, as 'the plastered cistern' and 'an everflowing spring' were called, in the Amoraic period (*Berakhot* 64a), 'Sinai' (one who knows the whole Torah as it was given at Sinai) and '*oker harim* ('uprooter of mountains'). In an age when teachings were transmitted orally, the scholar with vast stores of information was highly regarded but his claim to pre-eminence was hotly contested by admirers of the less knowledgeable but more original and brilliant scholar. Rabbah was such a scholar while his colleague, R. Joseph, belonged to the other type. The scholars of Palestine, when asked for their advice, sent a message that R. Joseph was to be preferred as the Sinai type (*Horayot* 14a). This same Rabbah, it is said, was fond of encouraging his disciples to cultivate sharpness of mind by appearing, on occasion, to act contrary to the law in order to see whether the disciples would be sufficiently alert to spot his mistakes (*Berakhot* 33b; *Ḥullin* 43b; *Niddah* 4b). This method of 'alerting the mind of the disciples' (*le-ḥadded et ha-talmidim*) is also said to have been practised by Samuel ('*Eruvin* 13a); by R. Akiba (see *Niddah* 45a); and by the latter's teacher, R. Joshua (*Nazir* 59b). In another passage (*Zevaḥim* 13a) the method is attributed to Rabbah's teacher, R. Huna. This idea of sharpening the wits of the disciples must not be confused with the demand that words of Torah should be 'sharp' in the scholar's mouth (*Kiddushin* 30a) even though the same term (*meḥuddadim*) is used, since there the meaning is a sharp clear utterance ('when someone asks you a question do not stammer when you tell him the answer'; cf. *Sifre* to Deuteronomy 6: 7, where the reading is *mesudarim*, 'well-ordered', see edn. Friedmann, p. 74a and Friedmann's note).

The Talmudic debate and argument reached its apogee in the work of Abbaye and Rava, Rabbah's disciples. Hundreds of debates between these two are recorded in the Babylonian Talmud. Later generations considered the work of these two to be so typical of Rabbinic learning that when they wished to list the many themes with which Rabban Johanan b. Zakki was conversant they referred, anachronistically, to his being familiar with 'the arguments of Abbaye and Rava' (*havayot de-Abbaye ve-Rava*), though these are described as a 'small thing' in comparison with the 'great thing', the mystical study of the Heavenly Chariot seen by Ezekiel (*Sukkah* 28a; *Bava Batra* 134a).

A study of Abbaye and Rava, listing every reference to them in the Talmud, is: *Abbaye ve-Rava* by J. L. Maimon (Jerusalem, 1965). In the twelfth century, Maimonides identified 'the arguments of Abbaye and Rava' with the typical approach of the whole range of Talmudic study, *Yad, Yesodey ha-Torah* 4: 13. David Kimhi remarked in a letter (*Kovetz Teshuvot ha-Rambam*, ed. A. Lichtenberg (Leipzig, 1859), part III, pp. 4c–d) that, for all his love of philosophy, he was thoroughly familiar with *havayot de -Abbaye ve-Rava*. Cf. Frank E. Talmage, *David Kimhi The Man and His Commentary* (Harvard University Press, 1975), pp. 37–8. In later ages this identification became a commonplace so that the term *havayot de-Abbaye ve-Rava* was used as a synonym for the Halakhic discussions of the Talmud.

Some time before the Amoraic period, the debate in Torah matters was described in military terms – *milḥamtah shel Torah*

(*Sanhedrin* 111b). On the verse: 'And he carried away all Jerusalem, and all the princes, and all the mighty men of valour' (II Kings 24: 14) the *Sifre* (to Deuteronomy 32: 25) comments: 'What mighty deeds could have been accomplished by men taken into captivity and what kind of warfare could men bound in chains have engaged in? But "all the mighty men of valour" means, in the warfare of the Torah.' This enabled the Rabbis to interpret Biblical verses glorifying military prowess as referring to the battles of the mind. For instance, on the verse: 'Happy is the man that hath his quiver full of them: they shall not be ashamed, but they shall speak with the enemies in the gate' (Psalm 127:5), a Rabbi commented: even father and son, master and disciple, become enemies of one another when they are on opposing sides in the Torah debates (*Kiddushin* 30b). The debates were said to take place even in Heaven, the scholars in the Yeshivah on High having the right to disagree even with God Himself (*Bava Metzi'a* 86a). Both motifs, of military metaphor and debate in Heaven, are present in the comment (*Bava Kama* 92a) on: 'Hear, Lord, the voice of Judah, and bring him unto his people; let his hands be sufficient for him; and be thou an help to him from his enemies' (Deuteronomy 33: 7). Moses prayed that Judah be admitted to the Heavenly Yeshivah but Judah was unable to understand the debates in order to participate in them. Moses' prayer for Judah to participate was granted, but a further plea by Moses was required before Judah was able to argue so convincingly that his decisions in matters of law could be followed. In the same vein are the statements regarding King David when he rendered legal decisions (*Berakhot* 4a). R. Judah, in the name of Rav, interprets (*Sanhedrin* 93b) the verse praising David's qualities (I Samuel 16: 18) as referring to his skill in debate: 'that is cunning in playing' – knowing the right questions to ask; 'a mighty valiant man' – knowing the correct answers; 'a man of war' – knowing how to give and take in the battle of the Torah; 'prudent in matters' – knowing how to deduce one thing from another; 'and a comely person' – who demonstrates the proofs for his opinions; 'and the Lord is with him' – the ruling is always in accordance with his views.

Skill in Torah debate was also compared to the skill exhibited by a competent craftsman. The 'craftsmen and smiths' carried away into captivity (II Kings 24: 14) were identified with scholars gifted with great reasoning powers (*Sifre* to Deuteronomy 32: 25). On the basis of this the keen debater was compared to a carpenter.

Of a text presenting severe problems of interpretation it was said that neither a carpenter nor his apprentice could remove the difficulties (*'Avodah Zarah* 50b, cf. Palestinian Talmud *Yevamot* 8: 2, 9b). In similar vein scholars were compared to builders (*Berakhot* 64a), possibly because scholars 'built up' their arguments, as in the very frequent *binyan av*, 'father construction', for an argument by inference where the premiss is the 'father' to the conclusion reached by a process of 'building'. The expression: 'Do you weave them all in the same web' (*Berakhot* 24a; *Shabbat* 148a; *Pesaḥim* 42a; *Ḥullin* 58b) suggests that scholars were compared to weavers, as does the use of *massekhet*, 'web', for a tractate. The purveyor of the difficult Halakhic teachings was compared to a dealer in precious stones for the connoisseur whereas the more popular but less profound Aggadic teacher was compared to the retailer of cheap tinsel goods which all can afford to buy (*Sotah* 40a).

The keen scholar was called a *ḥarif*, 'sharp one'. Thus there is a discussion as to which is the superior scholar, the *ḥarif*, capable of raising objections, or the more cautious debater who is less quick in refutation but can arrive more readily at a correct solution (*Horayot* 14a). When a particularly pungent argument was seen to solve a problem far more effectively than more learned but pedestrian attempts, it was said that one grain of sharp (*ḥarifta*) pepper is worth more than a basket-full of pumpkins (*Megillah* 7a). The acuteness of a scholar's reasoning process was spoken of as his 'sharp knife' (*Ḥullin* 77a, cf. *Yevamot* 122a). The scholars of Pumbedita were especially renowned for their sharpness. Among these were Efa and Avimi, described as 'the sharp ones of Pumbedita' (*Sanhedrin* 17b; *Kiddushin* 39a; *Menaḥot* 17a). The brilliance of the Pumbeditans was, however, somewhat suspect in that it bordered on the eccentric, so that they acquired the reputation of 'causing an elephant to pass through the eye of a needle', i.e. of producing far-fetched, improbable arguments (*Bava Metzi'a* 38b, cf. *Berakhot* 55b).

There are found in the Babylonian Talmud a number of formal terms for the moves in an argument and for the argument itself, some of them of earlier usage. The earlier term for argumentation and debate is *nosē ve-noten*, 'give and take' (*Sifre* to Deuteronomy 32: 25). This term is also used (e.g. in *Shabbat* 31a) for business dealings, 'buying and selling', as in the idiomatic English expression 'selling an idea'. The Aramaic equivalent is *shakla ve-taria* (*Bava*

Kama 92a; *Sotah* 7b). The reasoning by means of which an argument is supported is *sevara* ('theory', 'reasoning', 'common-sense') with a root meaning of 'to think'. Very frequently in the Talmud one finds the expression: '*mar savar . . . u-mar savar . . .*', 'this master holds . . . and this master holds . . .'. The term Saboraím, for the post-Talmudic teachers is derived from this term; perhaps 'expounders'. An objection is a *kushia* (*Bava Kama* 117a; *Bava Metzi'a* 84a and very freq.), from a root meaning of 'hardness', hence, a difficulty. A stronger term, used when the difficulty is insurmountable, is *tiyuvta*, 'refutation' (*Bava Kama* 15b and freq.). The term *metevē*, 'an objection was raised' (from the same root) and similar expressions are used when the refutation is from a Tannaitic source. When the objection is based on Amoraic reasoning, the term used is *matkif*, from a root meaning 'to seize', i.e. A seized hold of B's theory and sought to refute it. The reply to an objection raised is *tirutz*, 'an answer', from a root meaning of 'to make straight' (*Gittin* 4b; *Bava Metzi'a* 14b and freq.), generally used when a difficulty is 'straightened out', e.g. by emending a text and the like. A more direct reply is *piruka*, 'a reply', from a root meaning of 'to break', i.e. to shatter the objection (*Bava Kama* 117a; *Bava Metzi'a* 84a; '*Avodah Zarah* 50b and freq.). The term for a proof advanced in support of a theory is found in the Mishnah ('*Eduyot* 2: 2) and used by the Amoraím (*Pesaḥim* 15a). The term is *raáyah*, literally 'a seeing'. The Aramaic equivalent is *sa'ya*, 'a support', with a root meaning of 'to assist' (*Sanhedrin* 71b; *Ḥullin* 4a and very freq.). The unit of argument and counter argument is *shema'ta*, from a root meaning 'to hear' (*Kiddushin* 50b; *Sanhedrin* 38b). The *shema'ta* generally consists of the text, *gemara*, and its exposition, the *severa*. The bringing of an argument to a successful conclusion so that it results in a correct application of the law is '*asukey shema'ta aliva de-hilkheta*, i.e. bringing the argument to a final ruling, to the *halakhah*, the actual ruling in practice (e.g. in *Bava Kama* 92a). An abstract problem of definition in which the two ways of looking at the matter are so equally balanced that, without proof from some authority, it is impossible to decide which is correct, is known as a *ba'ya*, from a root meaning of 'to request', i.e. to request a solution to the problem (*Berakhot* 2b; *Pesaḥim* 9b and very frequently throughout the Talmud). Solutions to this kind of problem are described by terms taken from the root *pashat*, 'to make clear', 'to smooth out' a difficulty (*Berakhot* 26b; *Kiddushin* 9b and very freq.).

Where no solution is forthcoming the term used is *teyku*, 'it remains standing', i.e. the two possibilities are so equally balanced and, in the absence of proof from authority, there is no solution to the problem; it is by nature insoluble (*Berakhot* 8a; 25b; and very freq.). There are over 300 instances of this phenomenon in the Babylonian Talmud but none in the Palestinian. A doubt about the facts used in an argument or about the correctness of a theory that has been advanced is *safek*, 'a doubt' (*Berakhot* 3b; *Bava Metzi'a* 83b; *Keritot* 21b and freq.).

On the *teyku* phenomenon see my study: (London–New York, 1981), in which all the instances are noted. The debate between scholars is called a *maḥaloket*, 'division', 'controversy', e.g. the debates between the House of Shammai and the House of Hillel are described in the Mishnah (*Avot* 5: 7) as: 'controversy for the sake of Heaven', *maḥaloket le-shem shamayyim*. The whole subject of the *maḥaloket* is treated by B. De Friess, *Meḥkarim be-Sifrut ha-Talmud* (Jerusalem, 1968), pp. 172–8. The *locus classicus* for the problem is *Tosefta Sanhedrin* 7: 1 (ed. Zuckermandel, p. 425). This reads: 'R. Jose said: "At first there was no controversy (*maḥaloket*) in Israel except in the Court of the Seventy in the Chamber of Hewn Stones... When the disciples of Hillel and Shammai who had not served (their masters) sufficiently increased, controversy increased and there were two Torot in Israel."' In the Babylonian Talmud (*Sanhedrin* 88b) this is quoted as: 'R. Jose said: "At first they did not increase controversy in Israel... When the disciples of Shammai and Hillel, who had not served sufficiently, increased, controversy increased and Torah became as if it were two Torot."' Thus, according to the reading in the *Tosefta*, controversy between the Sages is said to have been completely unknown before the rise of the disciples of Shammai and Hillel, whereas according to the reading in the Babylonian Talmud it is said that controversy was known before this period, but not to any large extent. De Friess discusses how far R. Jose's view is historical. In any event, the term *maḥaloket* became in our literature the normal one for the controversy or debate with its Aramaic equivalent, *pelugta*. When, for instance, the Talmud states, as it does very frequently, that A and B disagree on this or that point, it is usually expressed as: *be-mai ka-mippalgi*, 'on what point do they disagree?'

Two terms are, at times, ambiguous. These are: *ve-ha-tanya*, 'and we have learnt in a *Baraita*' and *peshita*, 'it is obvious'. In the majority of instances these are questions: 'But have we not learnt?'; 'Is it not obvious?' Occasionally, however, they are statements: 'We have learnt'; 'It is obvious that'. *Rashi* usually helps the student by pointing out when these terms are used as simple statements. There are no punctuation marks in the Talmud so that the reader has to supply these by inflections of the voice. To obtain the best results in detecting the various moves in a Talmudic *sugya* the

Talmud has to be 'sung', as it is in Yeshivot today with the traditional 'Gemara *niggun*'. There can be no doubt that melody was used in Talmud study from the earliest times and it seems certain that the compilers themselves relied on melody as a means of punctuation. There is even some evidence for a system of cantillation with musical notes as in the Biblical books.

The various kinds of arguments found in the Babylonian Talmud can be classified according to a number of formal types or patterns. All the main moves will be found to belong to one or other of these categories. The *argument from authority* consists of a proof or support of the correctness of a theory by an appeal to an incontrovertible source, i.e. Scripture or a Tannaitic source; a Mishnah or a *Baraita*. Where the attempted proof is from Scripture the only way to refute it is to interpret the relevant verse or verses differently. Where the attempted proof is from a Tannaitic source two moves are open to the contestant who wishes to engage in refutation. He can either demonstrate that an alternative interpretation is possible, or, perhaps, necessary, or he can adduce another Tannaitic source which disagrees with the one quoted by his opponent and on which he can now rely. This is based on the generally accepted view, at least by the later Amoraím, that an Amora cannot disagree with a Tanna unless he can find support for so doing in the opinions of another Tanna.

The terms used to introduce a proof from authority are: *minalan*, 'How do we know this?' (*Berakhot* 7a; *Pesaḥim* 7b; *Kiddushin* 3b and freq.); *mena hanney miley*, 'How do we know these things?' (*Ḥullin* 24b and very freq.); *mina ha milta*, 'How do we know that?' (*Ḥullin* 10b; 11a); *mina amina lah?*, 'How do I know this?' (*Sanhedrin* 61b); *Mai ta'ama*, 'What is the reason? (*Bava Batra* 173b and very freq.); *ta shema'*, 'Come and hear' (*Bava Kama* 22a and very freq.); *dikhetiv*, 'For it is written in Scripture' (*Sanhedrin* 61b and very freq.); *diténan*, 'For we have learnt in a Mishnah', *Yevamot* 57a and very freq.); *de-tono rabbanan*, 'For our Rabbis have taught' (*Ḥullin* 24b and very freq.) introducing a *Baraita*; *de-tanya*, 'For we have learnt in a *Baraita*' (*Bava Kama* 30a and very freq.); *she-neémar*, 'For it is said in Scripture' (*Berakhot* 7b and very freq.); *ve-ha-tenan*, 'But we have learnt in a Mishnah' (*Bava Batra* 30a and very freq.); *af anan nami teninan*, 'We have also been taught this' (*Berakhot* 27a and freq.); *tenituha*, 'We have learnt it in a Mishnah' (*Bava Kama* 22a and freq.); *amar kera*, 'Scripture said' (*Kiddushin* 3b and freq.); *amar raḥamana* 'The All-Merciful said', used for a Scriptural proof (*Bava Metzi'a* 3b and very freq.); *de-amar R*..., 'For Rabbi...said' (*Pesaḥim* 7b and very freq.). This last term is sometimes used even for a proof from an Amora, provided the Amora is an established authority.

The *argument by comparison* is the deduction of a rule, not stated explicitly, from an accepted teaching to which it bears a strong resemblance. The refutation of this consists in demonstrating that although the two cases do appear to be analogous they are, in fact, different. This can be termed an *argument by differentiation*. The *either/or argument* seeks to demonstrate that whichever one of two possible interpretations of a given premiss is adopted, it will lead to the desired conclusion. The *on the contrary argument* seeks to demonstrate that, far from the premiss yielding the suggested conclusion, it yields the exactly opposite conclusion. The *acceptance of an argument in part* seeks to demonstrate that a particular conclusion will follow from one construction of the phenomenon under consideration but not from a different construction. The *argument based on an opponent's position* seeks to demonstrate that even if the suggested premiss is true, which, in fact, it is not, the suggested conclusion does not follow from it. The *argument exposing the flaws in an opponent's argument* is a suggestion to the opponent that if he will only examine carefully the steps in his argument he will see for himself that his case is faulty. An argument is, at times, put forward only to be rejected.

The following are the terms used: (a) *Argument by comparison: hainu*, 'that is', i.e. 'this is the same as that' (*Pesaḥim* 9b–10a and freq.); *yalfinan*, 'we learn' (this from that) (*Yevamot* 57 and freq.); *shema'minah*, 'hear from this', i.e. compare that to this (*Pesaḥim* 5b and very freq.). (b) *Argument by differentiation: shani hatam*, 'there it is different' (*Kiddushin* 50a and very freq.); *ve-R.*, 'and what will R . . . say in reply?' (*Kiddushin* 51a and freq.); *mi damey*, 'are the two cases alike?' (*Pesaḥim* 14b and freq.); *hakhi hashta*, lit. 'how now', i.e. 'what is the comparison?' (*Ḥagigah* 13b and freq.). (c) *Either/or argument: mi-mah nafshakh*, 'whichever way you see it' (*Ḥullin* 29a and freq.). (d) *On the contrary argument: ipkha mistabbera*, 'it is more plausible to see it in the opposite way' (*Pesaḥim* 28a and freq.); *aderabbah*, 'on the contrary' (*Pesaḥim* 28a and freq.). Sometimes, as in *Pesaḥim* here, the two terms are combined: *aderabbah ipkhah mistabbera*; sometimes they are used separately. In J. S. Roth's edition of Samson of Chinon's *Sefer Keritut*, p. 434, note 2, there is a fairly comprehensive list of the instances of *aderabbah* in the Babylonian Talmud. (e) *Acceptance of an argument in part: bishel-ama . . . ela . . .*, 'This is correct according to . . . but . . .' (*Pesaḥim* 7a and very freq.); *haniḥah*, 'this is appropriate' (*Bava Kama* 12a and very freq.). (f) *Argument based on an opponent's position: u-le-ta 'amekh*, 'and according to your reasoning' (*Berakhot* 43a and very freq.); *li-devarav de-R. . .*', 'according to the opinion of R . . .' (*Kiddushin* 51a and freq.). (g) *Argument exposing a flaw in an opponent's argument: ve-tisbera*, 'and even according to your theory' (*Bava Kama* 32a and freq.); *mi sabbarit*, 'do you hold' (*Berakhot* 27a and freq.). (h) *Argument put forward only to be rejected: mahu de-tema*, 'it might have been said' (*'Arakhin* 21b and freq.); *saleka da'atekh amina*, 'I might have argued' (*Kiddushin* 34b; *Sotah* 44a and very freq.); *ka-saleka da'atekh*, 'you might have supposed' (*Pesaḥim* 26a and very freq.).

In addition to arguments based on pure reason there are to be found arguments based on the facts of the case or the interpretation of the facts. An example of this is the *argument based on historical or geographical conditions*, in which an attempt is made to demonstrate that these conditions affect the law and limit its application. Another example is the *argument based on the analysis of states of mind*, in which the law is said to depend on how human beings normally react psychologically in a given situation.

The terms are: (a) *Argument based on historical or geographical conditions: bimey R. nishnet...*, 'this was (only) taught in the days of R...' (e.g. *Bava Kama* 94b); *ha lan ve-ha le-hu*, 'this is according to us (the Babylonians) and that according to them (the Palestinians)' (*Berakhot* 5b; *Kiddushin* 29b and freq.). (b) *Argument based on analysis of states of mind: ḥazakah*, 'it is an established fact that' (*Bava Metzi'a* 3a; *Bava Batra* 6b and freq.). For a full treatment of this argument see *ET*, vol. XIII, s.v. *ḥazakah 3*, pp. 693–713.

At times there occurs the *readmission of an argument that has been previously rejected.* An argument that has been rejected in favour of what seemed to be a more convincing argument is now reinstated as offering, after all, the best solution of the difficulty, the reason for the original rejection then being shown to be unsound. The *argument against a statement of the obvious* is presented whenever a statement is made that appears to be quite superfluous since no one would have thought otherwise. The defence is to demonstrate that what seemed so obvious is not so at all. Reasons are given why it might have been thought otherwise and the statement requires, therefore, to be stated.

The terms are: (a) *Readmission of an argument that has been previously rejected: le-'olam...*, 'in reality', 'actually' (*Berakhot* 3a–b and very freq.); *ela meḥavrata ke...*, 'but it is better to say' (*Pesaḥim* 55b and freq.). (b) *Argument against a statement of the obvious: mai ka-mashma' lan*, 'what does he tell us?' (*Shabbat* 108a and freq.); *peshita*, 'is it not obvious?' (*Bava Batra* 137a and freq.).

The *argument to resolve a contradiction between sources* occurs where two Scriptural verses or two Tannaitic sources appear to contradict one another. Where the contradiction appears to be between two Scriptural verses the only way open is to show that, rightly understood, there is no contradiction, that it is only apparent not real. Where two Tannaitic sources appear to be in contradiction this solution is open but here, on occasion, the argument may proceed to demonstrate that there is, indeed, a contradiction and we must conclude that there is a debate on the matter between Tannaím. The attempt is then made to identify the Tannaím involved by referring to other Tannaitic sources. The *argument by textual emendation* seeks to demonstrate that the text of a Mishnah or *Baraita* cannot possible be accepted as it stands, that it is obviously corrupt. The correct text is then established by means of emendation. The *argument from the principle of literary economy* proceeds on the assumption that the earlier, classical texts have been so carefully worded that any apparently superfluous statement is not coincidental or due to mere literary style but is contrived and the text is then examined in order to discover what the apparently superfluous statement intends to teach.

The terms are: (a) *Argument to resolve a contradiction between sources: mar amar ḥada u-mar amar ḥada ve-lo feligey*, 'this master says one thing and the other master another and they are not in disagreement' (*Ḥullin* 105a and freq.); *terey tannai*, 'there are two Tannaím' (i.e. who disagree on the matter (*Berakhot* 3a and freq.). (b) *Argument by textual emendation: ḥesurey meḥasara ve-hakhi ka-teni*, 'something is missing and this is how it should read' (*Pesaḥim* 10b; *Bava Kama* 16a and very freq.). The standard methodologies differ as to whether the intention in such instances is really to emend the text or is simply a way of explaining the text, i.e. the text does not really have to be read differently but this is what it means. For the first view see *Rashi* to *Berakhot* 11b, s.v. *af li-gemara; Rashi* to *Megillah* 28b, s.v. *hey tzana* and the other sources quoted by M. Higger, *Otzar ha-Baraitot*, vol. x (New York, 1948), pp. 130–1. For the opposite view see Isaiah Horowitz: *Shelah, Torah she-be-'al Peh* s.v. *be-khamah mekomot.* Other terms for the same device are: *meshabeshta hi*, 'the text is erroneous' (*Gittin* 73a); *al tinney*, 'do not learn thus' (*Sotah* 49b); *teni*, 'learn it thus' (*Bava Kama* 4a–b and freq.). (c) *Argument from the principle of literary economy: tzerikhey*, 'both are necessary', generally after *lama li le-mitney*, 'why do I have to state?' (*Gittin* 8a and very freq.).

Frequently in the Talmudic debate a statement is presented in more than one form. The *different versions of an argument* are due to the difficulties in transmitting accurately reports of what the earlier teachers actually said. Similarly, there is the *argument presented by different teachers* where the statement itself is not in doubt but the doubt is about who made the statement. In both these instances there is generally an attempt to demonstrate the *consequences of different arguments*, i.e. the practical differences which result from looking at the matter in one way rather than another. The

Talmudic debate also frequently calls attention to the *limited application of an argument*. The suggestion here is that the argument is sound so far as it goes but when examined turns out to be limited in scope.

The terms are: (a) *Different versions of an argument: ika de-amrey*, 'others say' (*Ḥullin* 3b and very freq.). (b) *Argument presented by different teachers*: 'R... says... and R... says' (*Berakhot* 3b–4a and very freq.); *ve-ibbayit ema*, 'and if you want I can say' (*Berakhot* 3b and very freq.). (c) *The consequences of different arguments: mai beynayhu... ika beynayhu...*, 'what is the difference between them? The difference between them is...' (*Kiddushin* 50a; *Bava Kama* 23a; *Bava Batra* 174b and freq.). (d) *Limited application of an argument: haney miley*, 'when are these words applied?' (*Berakhot* 15a and very freq.); *lo nitzrekha*, 'it is not necessary (to state it except in the following instance)' (*Bava Metzi'a* 30b and very freq.); *lo amaran ela*, 'we do not state it except...' (*Berakhot* 8b and freq.).

A large portion of the Talmudic debate is taken up with the posing of purely academic problems. These are either set by individual Amoraím or anonymously and the aim of the exercise is to discuss theoretically the principles upon which the law is based. As we have noted in connection with the term *ba'ya* (see p. 11), in this type of problem the two halves are so equally balanced that no reason exists for favouring one over the other. There are more than a thousand of these problems scattered through the Talmud. It is highly probable that such contrived problems were set consciously as an intellectual exercise, especial skill being required to see that the two halves were, in fact, equally balanced.

M. Guttman, '*Sheélot Akademiot ba-Talmud*' in *Dvir*, 1 (Berlin, 1923), 38–87; 2 (Berlin, 1924), 101–64, has assembled all the material in the Talmud on the purely academic question – the *ba'ya* – which he compares to mathematical puzzles or philosophical conundrums such as Zeno's problem of Achilles and the tortoise.

It has to be said that there is no actual classification of the different types of argument in the Talmud itself and the names for them are our invention. Nevertheless a close study of the Talmud reveals that the patterns we have noted are there. Certain 'ploys' are always used as the occasion demands. These are strictly limited but the richness and variety of the Talmudic debate are nevertheless preserved, because these depend not on the number of the moves available but on the ingenuity of the protagonists in making the right move at the right time.

2

The literary form of the Babylonian Talmud

How was the Babylonian Talmud compiled and by whom? These are among the most intractable problems in Jewish literature. This many-volumed work, bearing all the marks of a finished literary product, replete with the names of Amoraím and with their opinions and debates, from the beginning of the third to the end of the fifth century, remains completely silent on the questions every student feels bound to ask: Who recorded all these opinions? Is it a literary work at all or was it originally a verbal compilation, committed to writing at a later date? Is it correct to speak of 'editors' of the Talmud, or did the work simply grow by stages? What are we to make of the mediaeval tradition that R. Ashi and Ravina were the compilers of the Talmud, in view of the immense portion of the work that must have been added, at least, after these teachers? Assuming that there were editors, what principles guided them in their selection of the material and how did they shape it? Is there evidence of different hands shaping the material in different tractates or even in the same tractate? Why is there no Talmud to many of the tractates of the Mishnah? Mediaeval and modern scholars down to the present day have tried to supply answers to these and similar questions, but the basic problem remains as stubborn as ever.

The basic mediaeval text around which much of the question has centred is the famous letter of Sherira Gaon which dates from the tenth century, i.e. some five centuries after the 'close of the Talmud'. Moreover this letter is in two recensions, a Spanish and a French, which contradict one another on some of the most important issues, e.g. when the Talmud was committed to writing. The best edition of the *Iggeret De-Rav Sherira Gaon* is that of B. M. Lewin (Haifa, 1921), J. N. Epstein's *Prolegomena Ad Litteras Amoraiticas* (*Mevuot*), ed. E. Z. Melamed (Jerusalem, 1972), has a full discussion on the implications of the letter (Appendix, pp. 610–15), and this work as a whole deals with our problem. A very full treatment of the letter is in M. A. Tenenblatt's *The Formation of the Babylonian Talmud* (in Hebrew, Tel-Aviv, 1972), chapter 15, pp. 276–94. Tenenblatt's work is an admirable summary of all the views on our question, relying heavily on the very fine study by Julius Kaplan, *The Redaction of the Babylonian Talmud* (New York, 1933). Tenenblatt refers to the work of S. M. Rubinstein, *le-Ḥeker Siddur ha-Talmud* (Kovno, 1932), a work which I have not been able to consult but which is extensively quoted by Tenenblatt (chapter 5, pp. 81–111). Kaplan's very thorough work opens with an analysis and critique of the view of the earlier scholars: Graetz, Frankel, Rapoport, Brüll, I. H. Weiss, Halevy and W. Jawitz. Other works on the subject are those of Hyman Klein (see works cited in the bibliography); C. Albeck, *Introduction to the Talmud* (in Hebrew, Tel-Aviv, 1969); David Halivni, *Sources and Traditions* (in Hebrew, Tel-Aviv, 1968); B. M. Lewin, *Rabbanan Savorai ve-Talmudan* in *Azkarah* (in memory of Rabbi A. I. Kook), vol. IV (Jerusalem, 1937), pp. 145–208; Abraham Weiss, *Hithavut ha-Talmud Bishlemuto* (New York, 1943) and *le-Ḥeker ha-Talmud* (New York, 1954); Louis Jacobs: *Studies in Talmudic Logic and Methodology* (London, 1961); Jacob Neusner, ed., *The Formation of the Babylonian Talmud: Studies in the Achievements of Late Nineteenth and Twentieth Century Historical and Literary-Critical Research* (Leiden, 1970); Shamma Friedman, *Perek ha-Ishah Rabbah be-Bavli* (Jerusalem, 1978).

The three periods relevant to the problem are: (1) the Amoraic; (2) that of the Saboraím (the meaning of which term is itself very problematical); (3) the Geonic. While there are very few Geonic additions to the Talmud the degree of Saboraic participation is hotly debated. Some scholars hold that the Talmud in its present form is the work of the Amoraím, the Saboraím only adding occasional notes and the like. Others look upon the Saboraím as the real editors of the Talmud. Others again see a lengthy process of editorial work, beginning with the Amoraím and completed by the Saboraím. Abraham Weiss' is a lone voice. Weiss denies that the Talmud was ever 'edited' at all. In his view there are strata of Talmudic material, the earliest of which belong to the early Amoraic period, one being added to the other until, eventually, the Talmud emerged in the form in which we have it now.

Hardly any of the scholars who have discussed the question, with great subtlety and profound understanding, and whose work is indispensable, have noted adequately the feature to which this book repeatedly calls attention – the literary structure of the Talmudic *sugya*. It is hoped that, after a careful study of the material as presented here, the reader will become convinced not only that the

Talmud was put together by a series of anonymous editors, in the post-Amoraic period, but that these men were, in fact, far more than mere editors or compilers. They were literary artists of a high order who, undoubtedly, used earlier material and actual statements of the Amoraím, but who worked this material into shape. There has been hardly any detailed literary analysis of the Talmudic *sugya* as a whole. When such analysis is undertaken, it becomes abundantly clear that the *sugya* is presented in such a way that argument leads on to further argument, in neat and logical sequence. We have referred in this connection repeatedly to the 'final editors' but, in reality, the compilers were creative artists, reshaping all the earlier material to produce a literary work.

Our thesis does not seek to deny that there are earlier strata to be detected in the *sugya*. It is obvious that the final editors did use much earlier material and there is a considerable body of evidence, marshalled by J. N. Epstein and Abraham Weiss in particular, for the existence of such strata. Our thesis calls attention, however, to the re-working of all this material, in the process of which some of the material has been left in its original form. Nor can we deny that there are later additions, i.e. made after the bulk of the work had been completed. Sherira Gaon and other mediaeval writers report a tradition that, for example, the first *sugya* in tractate *Kiddushin* is Saboraic and the different style of this passage supports the tradition. Abraham Weiss has succeeded in detecting other opening passages of tractates that are late and here again, though Weiss does not stress this, the style is revealingly different. Our concern is with what the mediaeval scholars referred to as *setama de-gemara*, 'the anonymous Gemara', i.e. the framework of the *sugyot*. This anonymous material, comprising the bulk of the Talmud, is, we maintain, not merely a framework provided for the earlier material but embraces that material as well, which has been re-shaped. Shakespeare, for example, used earlier chronicles and the like, but was far less interested in conveying these verbatim and with regard to historical truth than in using them as bricks with which to construct his completely literary product. We maintain that the Babylonian Talmud is a work of this order.

If we are correct the following three positions will have to be maintained. First, the Talmud is a literary work, contrary to the opinion of some mediaeval and some modern scholars that it was not at first written down. It is impossible for a literary work of this nature, in which there are such things as literary device and the working up of the material to a carefully calculated climax, to be carried by successive generations only in the mind and expressed by word of mouth. True, even today, there are those who do know the whole Talmud by heart, but that is because they know the completed work. The shaping of the material in this way can only have been done, originally, in writing.

Secondly, this framework is, as we have already suggested, far more than a mere framework. It *is* the Talmud, in a very real sense. It is difficult, perhaps impossible, at this late hour, to know how much of the material put into the mouth of the Amoraím is authentic, how much their own reported words; but it is clear from our analysis that some, at the very least, of 'their' words have been put into their mouths so as to promote the on-going argument of the *sugya*. Some of it, at least, is 'fictitious', contrary to Abraham Weiss, who disagrees with the *Tosafists* who pointed out long ago the existence of fictitious *sugyot*.

Thirdly, since the framework is uniform in style and literary form and embraces the teachings of even the latest of the Amoraím, it follows that the final editors were post-Amoraic; 'Saboraic', in fact, though this, after all, is only a convenient term for the remarkable body of men who, for whatever reason, preferred to remain anonymous.

It would seem that something of this kind happened towards the end of the fifth and the beginning of the sixth century, possibly even later in the sixth century. A number of teachers felt themselves obliged to collect the Amoraic material and to shape it so that a coherent work on the Mishnah would result. Although, no doubt, their concern was also with practical law – there are many instances of case law in the Babylonian Talmud – their main aim was purely academic. They evidently wished to provide argument and debate as an intellectual exercise, precisely because, as stated in the previous chapter, the study of the Torah was by this time the established and acknowledged supreme way of worship. From this point of view the nature of the raw material they used was irrelevant. The only condition necessary for its inclusion was that it should have to do with one or other aspect of Jewish teaching. In all probability there were a number of centres in which these men flourished. An indication of this is the different style and language of the tractates *Nedarim*, *Nazir*, *Temurah* and *Me'ilah*, as has frequently been noted. But even here, and for all the differences in style, basically the method was the same. A comparison of the Babylonian Talmud with the Palestinian demonstrates that the flavour of the former is all its own: the use of keen questioning and reply, of the thrust and parry of debate, of the liveliness of the arguments, especially of the stock framework into which lengthy discussions have been fitted. Had the writing of Introductions been in vogue at that time we would, no doubt, have had an Introduction in which the aim of the work was stated. But, as with the Biblical books, the Talmud gives all the appearance of having dropped down from Heaven complete, as it were. The very problem of how and by whom the Talmud was compiled is itself the most eloquent testimony to the teachers' skill. Instead of introducing us to their own work they introduce us into the world of the Amoraím, in some respects an imaginary world, but one in which the spirit of the Amoraím actually lived on.

On the pseudepigraphic nature of a good deal of the Talmudic material, ie. on the conscious attempt to use earlier teachers as figures in a truth-conveyed-through-fiction narrative, cf. my 'How much of the Babylonian Talmud is pseudepigraphic?', *JJS*, 28, 1 (Spring, 1977), 46–59. From the evidence adduced there, it emerges that in a large number of instances the editors clearly reveal their intention of writing this kind of material and in an even larger number of instances the pseudepigraphic nature can easily be detected. The majority of scholars who have dealt so comprehensively with our problem have concentrated in the main on those Talmudic passages which purport to give some information on the scope of the work of the teachers, Amoraic for the most part, who feature as the heroes of the work. But this is to miss the point that they are the 'heroes' not the authors of the work. It seems to me that the closest analogy to the genre of much of the Babylonian Talmud is that of an historical novel, where the novelist may well draw on actual events of the past and even use the recorded words of real historical characters and yet, for all that, what happened in the past was not quite like that. The work of fiction tries to succeed in bringing the past to life but in a way really larger than life. Unless this is appreciated and if one persists, as some do, in seeing the Babylonian Talmud as the 'Hansard' of the Amoraic debates, the whole point is missed. One may even hazard a guess that some of the confusions regarding Amoraic chronology are due to this peculiar nature of the Talmudic material in which the argument counts for practically all, the historical details for very little; though one should not be so sceptical as to deny the usual, conventional reconstruction, in broad outline at least, of the history of the Amoraic period. Cf. David Goodblatt's *Rabbinic Instruction in Sassanian Babylon* (Leiden, 1975), for a very helpful reminder of how precarious it is to reconstruct the actual conditions obtaining in the Babylonian 'schools' on the basis of alleged 'traditions' first mentioned hundreds of years after the events. The correct method for all inquiries of this kind is to see what the sources themselves say, always bearing in mind that in the Babylonian Talmud we have a very unusual type of literary product.

3

Berērah: Retrospective specification

The following (from *Gittin* 25a–26a) is one of the main Talmudic passages in which the *berērah* theme is developed.

The term *berērah* is Amoraic. The root meaning of *brr* is 'to choose'; here the meaning is: a choice, among possibilities, which determines an act, the choice being made not when the act is performed but subsequently. The legal problem is whether the later 'choice' validates the original act as if the choice had been made at the time of the act. For this reason it is best to paraphrase *berērah* as 'retrospective specification', i.e. the subsequent 'choice' or specification operates retrospectively. In the Talmudic debate, when an authority is said to accept the *berērah* principle, this is formulated as: 'he holds *berērah*' (*it lēh berērah*) and when an authority is said to reject the *berērah* principle, this is formulated as: 'he does not hold *berērah*' (*let lēh berērah*).

Our *sugya* opens with a problem set by the third-century Babylonian Amora, R. Hoshea, and presented to his teacher, R. Judah. The rule is that a *get* ('bill of divorce') to be valid requires to be written specifically for that husband and wife. If, for instance, a man had two wives with the same name and the *get* has been written for the purpose of divorcing wife A, that *get* is invalid as a bill of divorce for wife B, even though the name is the same. R. Hoshea's problem is as follows. The husband instructed the scribe to write out the *get* 'for the wife who will first come out through the door', i.e. the *get* is written for that particular wife, the one who subsequently does emerge first, but at the time of writing it is not known whether it is wife A or wife B who will in fact, emerge first. Is such a *get* invalid, since at the time of writing it cannot be said to have been written specifically for that wife, or do we rather say that since it later became clear that wife A or B did, in fact, emerge first this operates retrospectively, so that the *get* is considered to have been written for her and is valid? In other words, is the *berērah* principle accepted?

R. Judah replies that the solution to the problem is to be found in the Mishnah (*Gittin* 3: 1, 24b, to which this passage is appended). The Mishnah rules that if the husband instructs the scribe to write the *get* 'for the wife I will decide to divorce', the *get* is invalid since at the time of writing the husband has not yet decided which of the two he will divorce. This is, suggests R. Judah, exactly analogous to R. Hoshea's case. Just as in the case dealt with in the Mishnah ('for the wife I will decide to divorce') the *get* is invalid because, evidently, the *berērah* principle is rejected, so, too, in R. Hoshea's case ('for the wife who will first come out through the door') the *get* is invalid because the *berērah* principle is rejected.

To this R. Hoshea objects that he has discovered another Mishnah (*Pesaḥim* 8: 3) from which it appears that the *berērah* principle is accepted. This Mishnah deals with the Paschal lamb. Before the Paschal lamb is slaughtered those who are to eat of it must be 'counted' or 'numbered' for that lamb; i.e. a man cannot fulfil his obligation to eat of the meat of the Paschal lamb unless he has been allotted a share in that lamb at the time of its slaughtering. Now the Mishnah rules: 'If a man says to his sons: "Behold I will slaughter the Paschal lamb for whichever of you arrives first in Jerusalem", the first one to enter with his head and most of his body acquires thereby his portion and with it he acquires on their behalf the portions of his brothers.' From this Mishnah it appears that, although at the time when the lamb was slaughtered it was not known which of the sons would, in fact, be the first to enter Jerusalem, the son who did reach Jerusalem first acquires his portion in the lamb. Hence it is clear that the Mishnah does accept the *berērah* principle.

To this R. Judah retorts: 'Hoshea, my son! What has *Pesaḥim* to do with *Gittin*?', i.e. the two cases are not analogous. A comment of the third-century Palestinian Amora is then quoted. R. Johanan, commenting on the *Pesaḥim* Mishnah, explains it as 'in order to encourage the sons to be energetic in the performance of the precepts', i.e. the Mishnah does not deal, as R. Hoshea thought, with the case of a father who had not 'counted' his sons before the lamb had been slaughtered but rather with the case of a father who had, in fact, 'counted' all his sons for the lamb before it had been slaughtered. The father only pretended to make his 'counting' depend on the son who first entered Jerusalem and this pretence was for the sake of encouraging his sons to be energetic in the performance of the precepts. Thus the reason why the son who first enters Jerusalem acquires his share is not at all because of the *berērah* principle, as R. Hoshea imagined, but because the son had been 'counted' from the beginning. It is not at all a question of *retrospective* specification. The specification, albeit unknown to the sons, had been made by the father from the beginning, from the time of the slaughtering when it was required to become operative.

The Talmud proceeds to demonstrate that this interpretation must be correct. For the Mishnah rules that the other sons, too, acquire their portion. But how can they acquire the lamb, if the reason why the son who enters Jerusalem first acquires it is because of the *berērah* principle? This principle can only operate in favour of the son who enters first. No *berērah* principle can operate on behalf of the other sons and we have learnt (Mishnah *Pesaḥim* 8:3, the same Mishnah) that once the lamb has been slaughtered there can be no further 'counting'. It must follow that the Mishnah deals with the case of a father who had previously 'counted' all his sons so that the *berērah* principle is entirely irrelevant to the issue. A *Baraita* is then quoted in further support of the contention that the issue is not one of *berērah* but of prior 'counting' and a pretence of the father in order to encourage his children to be energetic. The *Baraita* states: 'It once happened that daughters entered Jerusalem before the sons so that the daughters were found to be energetic and the sons lazy.' This *Baraita* supports the argument that the whole purpose of the father's declaration is in order to encourage his children to be energetic and is not for the purpose of having them 'counted' i.e. since the 'counting' had already been done on their behalf.

Thus far we have had the debate between R. Hoshea and R. Judah and the discussion around this. The comments of the Babylonian Amoraím Abbaye and Rava are now introduced. These lived a century after R. Hoshea and R. Judah but were evidently familiar with the earlier debate. From an analysis of this debate it emerges that neither R. Hoshea nor R. Judah draws a distinction which, according to Abbaye, can legitimately be drawn. Three cases have so far been considered:

(1) R. Hoshea's: *The wife who will first come out through the door*
(2) The *Gittin* Mishnah: *The wife I will decide to divorce*
(3) The *Pesaḥim* Mishnah: *The son who will first enter Jerusalem*

Throughout the whole of the previous discussion it is assumed that the three cases are analogous, but Abbaye perceives a clear distinction between (1) and (3) on the one hand and (2) on the other. In cases (1) and (3)the required specification depends on another – the wife who will first come out through the door in (1) and the son will first enter Jerusalem in (3). But case (2) depends on the husband's own decision. It is the husband himself who will eventually specify which wife he wishes to divorce. Why should we not say, argues Abbaye, that the *berērah* principle does operate in cases (1) and (3) – where the man concerned makes the specification depend on another (*toleh be-da' at aḥerim*) – but does not operate in case (2) – where the man concerned makes the specification depend on his own ultimate decision (*toleh be-da' at ' atzmo*)? If this distinction is accepted all difficulties are removed. In case (2) the *berērah* principle does not operate – hence the ruling of the *Gittin* Mishnah that the *get* is invalid; whereas in cases (1) and (3) it does operate – hence the ruling in the *Pesaḥim* Mishnah that the son who first enters Jerusalem does acquire his portion in the Paschal lamb and hence the solution of R. Hoshea's problem fails to be contradicted by the *Gittin* Mishnah.

We are helped by *Rashi*, the great French commentator, to appreciate the distinction drawn by Abbaye. It must be postulated that the less uncertainty there is in the original specification, i.e. at the time of the act, the more readily can the final specification operate retrospectively. So much has been achieved, as it were, at the beginning that the *berērah* principle requires no severe application for the final specification to be achieved. Conversely, the greater the degree of uncertainty there is at the beginning the less readily can the *berērah* principle be put to work so as to achieve retrospective specification. So much has already been specified in the first instance that even a weak specification such as that provided by *berērah* will suffice, whereas so little has been achieved in terms of specification in the second instance that the *berērah* principle is called upon to do practically all the work, and this it cannot do. Now where, as in cases (1) and (3), the final specification is made to depend on another this very fact means that the man concerned has, at the time of his act, virtually made up his mind, leaving only the final clarification to another. The man who states his intention of divorcing whichever wife will first come out through the door has decided definitely to divorce that wife; the lack of clarity in the specification being due solely to ignorance of which wife will eventually emerge first. Similarly, the father has already decided quite definitely that the portion of the Paschal lamb is to be acquired by the son who first enters Jerusalem. In case (2), on the other hand, the husband is himself uncertain whether he will divorce wife A or wife B. In *Rashi*'s words: 'he halts between two opinions'. Consequently, at the time of the act, the writing of the *get*, the degree of specification is exceedingly weak. In the famous words of Sam Goldwyn, it is only 'a definite maybe'. Here all depends on the final specification operating retrospectively and it may well be that even though in instances (1) and (3) the *berērah* principle operates here it does not.

Rava, however, defending R. Hoshea and R. Judah, refuses to draw Abbaye's distinction. According to Rava the issue is simple: does the *berērah* principle operate or does it not? No distinction is to be made regarding *berērah*, so that it is accepted as operative in some instances and not in others. As our *sugya* puts it: 'Rava said: What is the difficulty? Possibly, whoever accepts the *berērah* principle does so whether it depends on his own decision or on the decision of others, whereas whoever does not accept the *berērah* principle rejects that principle whether it depends on his own decision or on the decision of others.'

In the next stage of the *sugya* R. Mersharsheya addresses Rava, seeking to prove to him that Abbaye's distinction is well-founded and that he, Rava, is ill-advised to refuse to make the distinction. This R. Mesharsheya seeks to do by quoting two opinions of the second-century Tanna, R. Judah (not, of course, to be confused with the Babylonian teacher of R. Hoshea mentioned at the beginning of the *sugya*). An examination of R. Judah's views as recorded (a) in a *Baraita* and (b) in a Mishnah (*Gittin* 7: 4) seems to show that in the case recorded in the *Baraita* he does not accept the *berērah* principle, whereas in the case recorded in the Mishnah he accepts it. Thus R. Judah seems to contradict himself. But the case in the *Baraita* is one in which the final specification depends on the person himself, whereas in the case of the Mishnah it depends on others. This shows the correctness of Abbaye's distinction and refutes Rava.

First the *Baraita* is quoted. The case recorded here is of one who buys wine from Samaritans who are suspected of failing to tithe their wine. The buyer is obliged to separate the tithes before being allowed to drink the wine. Supposing he wishes to drink from the jar of wine he has bought and has no vessels to hand into which he can pour the separated tithes. What remedy is there for him, to allow him to drink the wine? Is he allowed to declare that the wine he will later separate as the tithes, is now separated as tithe wine, to be removed later from the jar, even though the actual separation will not have taken place until later? In other words, does the *berērah* principle operate so that the subsequent separation of the tithe wine operates retrospectively and the wine he drinks from the jar before the actual separation is wine from which the tithes have been separated? The *Baraita* states that R. Meir permits it but R. Judah, R. Jose and R. Simeon forbid it. Thus it is clear that R. Judah does not accept here the *berērah* principle and here the subsequent specification depends not on others but on himself; it is the buyer himself who will be responsible for the later specification when he eventually separates the tithes by pouring them out into his vessels. It is the buyer himself who decides ultimately which part of the wine he will separate as his tithes.

In the Mishnah in question there is a ruling of R. Judah regarding a law recorded in the previous Mishnah (*Gittin* 7:3). The case considered in this previous Mishnah is that of a sick man who delivers a *get* to his wife (in order to release her from the levirate bond – Deuteronomy 25: 5–10 – in the event of his death), stipulating that the *get* will only be valid if he dies from the illness from which he is at present suffering, but that in the event of his death the *get* will be valid retrospectively, i.e. from the time of its delivery (as it must be if the wife is to avoid the levirate bond). Now R. Judah in the following Mishnah discusses what the status of the wife will be during the period of the illness and rules that until the man actually dies she has the full status of the married woman. But R. Judah, by discussing the status of the wife *during* the period of the husband's illness, clearly implies his agreement with the previous ruling of the Mishnah that when the husband does eventually die from that illness the *get* is valid retrospectively. Now for the *get* to be retrospectively valid the principle of *berērah* must be invoked and this shows that R. Judah does accept the *berērah* principle. How, then, can we square this with his opinion as recorded in the *Baraita*? We must perforce accept Abbaye's distinction. In the Mishnah the later specification depends on 'others' (i.e., as *Rashi* comments, on God in whose hand is life and death). Thus we see that there is an authority, namely, R. Judah, who accepts the *berērah* principle when the subsequent specification depends on others, but who rejects that principle when the subsequent specification depends on the person himself.

R. Mesharsheya (so in current editions, variant reading, as in marginal note, Ravina) proceeds further to refute Rava and to support Abbaye's distinction. In the Samaritan *Baraita* it is stated that R. Simeon, too, as well as R. Judah, forbids the drinking of the wine and so evidently rejects the *berērah* principle. But another *Baraita* records the following case. A man cohabits with a woman (the act of cohabitation can effect a valid marriage if performed for that purpose) declaring that the act is for the purpose of effecting a valid marriage, but only if his father will subsequently approve of the match. R. Simeon here rules that if subsequently the father is pleased with the match the marriage is retrospectively valid. Thus, although R. Simeon rejects the *berērah* principle in the case of the wine, here he accepts it. The solution must surely be on the basis of Abbaye's distinction. In the case of the wine the subsequent specification depends on the man himself and here R. Simeon refuses to accept the *berērah* principle. But in the case of the marriage the subsequent specification depends on 'others', i.e. on the father and here R. Simeon does accept the *berērah* principle.

Rava has now been forced into a corner, but manages to extricate himself. In reply to R. Mesharsheya, Rava stoutly persists in his refusal to draw the distinction suggested by Abbaye. No such distinction, argues Rava, is made by any authority. Those who reject the *berērah* principle do so even when the subsequent specification depends on others. Those who accept the *berērah* principle do so even when the subsequent specification depends on the person involved himself. In that case why do R. Judah and R. Simeon forbid the drinking of the wine and so evidently refuse to accept the *berērah* principle? To this Rava replies that the reason why R. Judah and R. Simeon prohibit the wine is not because the tithing is invalid. It is perfectly valid because the *berērah* principle is accepted. The reason why they prohibit the wine is out of fear that the jar may split before the buyer returns home to separate the tithes. If that were to happen no tithes would have been given, the wine having been lost, and this would mean that he had imbibed untithed wine. Rava suports this interpretation by quoting the conclusion of the *Baraita* in which R. Judah and R. Simeon, in fact, ask R. Meir why he is not apprehensive that the jar will split and R. Meir retorts that he has no such apprehensions. Thus, argues Rava, all three authorities, R. Judah, R. Simeon and R. Meir, accept the *berērah* principle, the sole matter on which they disagree being whether the buyer is allowed to take the risk of the jar splitting before he can pour out the tithe wine.

The commentators are puzzled by the implications of our passage, that the validity of the *get* in R. Judah's case and of the marriage in R. Simeon's depend on the *berērah* principle. Surely all authorities accept the validity of a conditional declaration. The rule of condition (*tennai*) is treated everywhere in the Talmudic literature with unqualified acceptance. Nowhere else is there the slightest suggestion that *tennai* depends on *berērah*, so that those authorities who reject *berērah* reject *tennai*. And yet here the proof that R. Judah and R. Simeon reject *berērah* is from cases that deal with *tennai*. In order to cope with this difficulty, *Rashi* draws a distinction between a condition the fulfilment of which depends solely on the person who makes it (e.g. 'Be betrothed to me on the condition that I give you 200 *zuz*') and a condition the fulfilment of which is beyond his control ('This is your *get* if I die from this illness' and 'Be betrothed to me if my father will be pleased with the match'). In the former case the act is complete from the beginning, since the intention to satisfy the requirements of the condition and the fulfilment of the condition depend entirely on the person who makes the condition. This does not depend at all on the principle of *berērah*. The condition is here treated as something external to the act so that the validity of the act depends on no retrospective specification. But in those cases where the fulfilment of the condition depends on others the act itself is indeterminate until the condition has been fulfilled and this does depend on *berērah*, although, as a specification which depends on others, it can possibly operate more readily than when *berērah* depends solely on the person's own decision. Thus, as *Rashi* sees it, there are three cases of doubtful validity in descending order:

(1) A condition the man can fulfil himself ('on condition that I give you 200 *zuz*'). This does not depend on *berērah* and is valid, if the condition is fulfilled, even according to those authorities who reject the *berērah* principle.

(2) A condition the man cannot fulfil himself ('on condition that I die of this illness' and 'on condition that my father is pleased with the match'). This does depend on *berērah*, but here the principle can be the more readily employed precisely because all the indefiniteness is due to the decision of others, not to the indecisiveness of the person himself.

(3) 'Let the *get* be written for whichever wife I shall decide to divorce.'

This is not a *condition*. The act itself is indecisive and so depends on *berērah*. It is, moreover, a form of *berērah* less easily applied since all the uncertainty is in the mind of the man himself. Other commentators (see e.g. *Meíri*) offer different interpretations, but *Rashi*'s seems entirely satisfactory.

In the form we now have it this *sugya* is a complete unit, evidently built up by the final editors out of earlier material extending from the second century in Palestine (Mishnah and *Baraita*) down to the second half of the fourth century (R. Mesharsheya) in Babylon, In schematic form the *sugya* can be thus presented:

(1) R. Hoshea's problem: *get* written for wife who first emerges
(2) R. Judah's reply: Mishnah: 'For wife I shall decide to divorce'
(3) 'From which we see that *berērah* is not accepted' (this is in Aramaic)
(4) R. Hoshea's objection from Mishnah *Pesaḥim*
(5) R. Judah's reply: What has *Pesaḥim* to do with *Gittin*
(6) Elaboration: R. Johanan: to encourage them to be energetic
(7) Proof that this is correct from latter part of the same Mishnah (this is in Aramaic)
(8) Further support from the *Baraita*: daughters energetic (introduced in Aramaic)
(9) Abbaye's objection: distinction between *toleh be-daʿat ʿatzmo* and *toleh be-daʿat aḥerim*
(10) Rava: possibly no distinction should be made
(11) R. Mesharsheya's objection to Rava from R. Judah in Mishnah and *Baraita*
(12) R. Mesharsheya's second objection to Rava from R. Simeon
(13) Rava's reply: not because of *berērah* but fear that jar may split

It can be seen from the above that the framework of the *sugya* has been provided by the final editors, who shaped the earlier material in order to provide a carefully constructed progression of thought, working it all up into a complete unit in which argument follows on argument in the right order. No doubt the debate between R. Hoshea and R. Judah is authentic but (3), (7) and (8), and probably (6), do seem to have been added by the final editors as part of their framework. There is no conclusive evidence that the term *berērah* itself was used by R. Hoshea or R. Judah. Even allowing, however, for editorial reworking of the arguments of Abbaye and Rava, it would seem probable that in the original debate between these two Amoraím the term *berērah* was actually used. In any event the term *berērah* belongs to the Amoraic period and is one of the many examples of Amoraic abstractions by means of which the views of the Tannaím were summarised.

For *berērah* as an Amoraic formulation and as part of the general Amoraic thrust towards abstraction see *EJ*, vol. II, p. 867. *ET*, vol. IV, p. 216 defines *berērah* as: 'Of something unspecified (*she-eyno mevurar*) now but which becomes specified at a later date; whether or not we say that the specification operates retrospectively.' Cf. pp. 216–46 for a comprehensive account of all the legal discussions on the subject. *Kesef Nivḥar*, no. 33, 1–37, pp. 46a–54b, lists all the Talmudic references to *berērah* as well as the comments of the major post-Talmudic authorities. The main Talmudic passages, in addition to the above, in which the *berērah* theme is considered are: *Gittin* 25a (the *sugya* which precedes ours); 47a–48b; '*Eruvin* 36b–38a; 71b; 82a; *Yoma* 55b–56b; *Sukkah* 24a; *Betzah* 10a–b; 37b–38a; 39a–b; *Sotah* 18a; *Bava Kama* 51b; 69a–b; *Bava Batra* 27b; *Ḥullin* 14a–b; 135b; *Bekhorot* 56b–57a. A classic analysis of the *berērah* theme is given by *Ran* to *Nedarim* 45b.

4

Yeúsh she-lo mi-da'at: unconscious abandonment of property

This *sugya*, one of the best-known in the Talmud, is found in *Bava Metzi'a* 21a–22b. The basis of the *sugya* is a debate between the two fourth-century Babylonian Amoraím, Abbaye and Rava.

Yeúsh is the technical term for abandonment of property when it has been stolen or lost without hope of recovery. The basic meaning of *yeúsh* is despair. Although in some circumstances *yeúsh* of stolen property gives title to the thief, this matter is dealt with at length elsewhere in the Talmud. In our *sugya* the reference is to *yeúsh* of lost property. The legal principle here is that if a man who has lost some of his property despairs, i.e. gives up all hope of ever recovering that property, the property is held to have become ownerless and the finder may keep it. According to the rule as stated in the Mishnah (*Bava Metzi'a* 2:1 and further) the normal procedure when one finds lost property is to have the find proclaimed in a public place such as a synagogue. This serves as a kind of lost-property office. There finders and losers repair, the loser stating any distinguishing marks – *siman*, 'sign', 'means of identification' – and if this tallies with the *siman* of the lost article the article is restored to its owner. Thus, since there is a procedure for its recovery, it is assumed that there has been no *yeúsh* where the lost article has a *siman*. Why should the loser despair of recovering his article since he knows of the procedure and stands a good chance of identifying his property and having it returned to him? Yet if he, none the less, did declare in the presence of witnesses that he had abandoned all hope of ever recovering his property, then *yeúsh* does come into operation and the finder, subsequent to the act of *yeúsh* by the owner, may keep what he finds. Thus the general rule is that finding is keeping if the article has no *siman* (because it can then be assumed that *yeúsh* has taken place), but finding is not keeping if the article does have a *siman* (because here *yeúsh* cannot be assumed) unless, as above, there is evidence of an explicit declaration of *yeúsh*.

The debate between Abbaye and Rava concerns *yeúsh she-lo mi-da'at*, literally, 'unconscious abandonment of property'. Translated thus baldly into English the term makes no sense. How can abandonment of property be otherwise than conscious? The meaning of this technical term is, as *Rashi* explains it, 'the status of a lost article, of which it can be assumed that when the owner will become aware that he has lost it he will abandon it but of whose loss the owner is unaware at the time when the article is found'. The point here is that *yeúsh* only operates to give title to the finder if it takes place *before* the finder takes possession of the article. If there had been no *yeúsh* beforehand, the finder, when he takes the article, is held to have become a bailee acting on behalf of the owner since, in the absence of any prior *yeúsh*, the finder has no legal title to the article. An article held in trust for its owner by a bailee is legally held to be still in the owner's possession so that *yeúsh* cannot come into effect. *Yeúsh* only takes effect when an article has been lost, not when it is still in the owner's possession. If, for instance, a man has an article in his house which he imagines to have been lost, any *yeúsh* he may express will be ineffective and it would obviously be wrong for another, hearing of the *yeúsh* declaration, to enter the owner's house and appropriate the article for himself. The debate between Abbaye and Rava concerns, as we have noted, an article which the owner would abandon when he becomes aware that he has lost it but of whose loss the owner is unaware at the time when the finder takes it. Abbaye argues that there has been no actual, positive *yeúsh* before the finder took it and hence the finder becomes a bailee and any subsequent *yeúsh* is inoperative. Rava argues that, since if the owner had been aware of his loss he would certainly have abandoned all hope of recovery, it is treated as if there had been *yeúsh* when he lost it. There is, for Rava, a kind of *yeúsh* state, even though there is no conscious awareness on the part of the loser. The loser's lack of awareness of his loss is irrelevant, according to Rava, since when he does become aware of his loss he will certainly engage in *yeúsh*. Thus our *sugya* opens: '*Yeúsh she-lo mi-da'at*: Abbaye said: It is not *yeúsh* but Rava said: It is *yeúsh*.'

After this bare statement of the opinions of Abbaye and Rava, there is an anonymous Talmudic elaboration which seeks both to explain the views held by the two Amoraím and to delineate the boundaries of their debate. This addition reads: 'With regard to an article that has a *siman* no one in the world [the usual technical term for both protaganists, i.e. here Abbaye and Rava] disagrees that it is not *yeúsh*. And even though we did eventually hear that he engaged in *yeúsh* it is still not *yeúsh*. For when it came into his hand [i.e. into the finder's possession], it came into his hand at a time when it was prohibited to him, since when he [the loser] becomes aware of his loss he does not engage in *yeúsh*, for he says: "I have a *siman* so I will state the *siman* [at the 'lost-property office'] and take it." Where the article has been found after it has been swept away by the sea tides or by the overflow of a river, the Torah permits it even if it has a *siman*, as we shall have occasion to state later on. When do they [Abbaye and Rava] disagree? It is with regard to an article that has no *siman*. [Here] Abbaye said: It is not *yeúsh*. For he [the loser] does not know that he has lost it. Rava said: It is *yeúsh*. For as soon as he becomes aware that he has lost it he engages in *yeúsh*, saying: "I have no *siman*" Hence it is from now [from the time of his loss] that he engages in *yeúsh*.'

The meaning of this addition is that there are in all three distinct cases. In one of these Rava agrees with Abbaye that there is no *yeúsh*; in another Abbaye agrees with Rava that there is *yeúsh*; and in the third there is a debate between Abbaye and Rava. The case where both agree that there is no *yeúsh*, i.e. that *yeúsh* is inoperative, is where the lost article has a *siman*. Such an article is not normally abandoned (since it can be reclaimed). Hence even Rava will agree that *yeúsh she-lo mi-da'at* will be inoperative and the finder may not keep it even if the owner eventually did engage in *yeúsh*. The reason is obvious. Here there is, in fact, no 'unconscious *yeúsh*' at all. When *yeúsh* does eventually take place the article is already in the finder's possession. He has acquired it illegally and is a bailee for whom *yeúsh* is inoperative. There is not the slightest reason for suggesting that the loser's subsequent *yeúsh* should operate retrospectively.

This has nothing to do with the *berērah* principle, considered in the previous chapter; see *Raábad* quoted by *SM* who states that the discerning will note the difference between our case and *berērah*. The difference appears to be this. In the case of *berērah* the act takes place *now*. It is only the exact *specification* that is required to work retrospectively. For instance, in the case of: 'Write a *get* for the wife who will first come out through the door', the act, the writing of the *get* with that intention, takes place at once. All that *berērah* has to do is to clarify the significance of the act. But here there was no act of *yeúsh* at all at the time the owner lost his article. A subsequent act of *yeúsh* is in no way connected with the status of the article at the time it was lost and there is no reason whatever for holding that the subsequent act of *yeúsh* should operate retrospectively.

The case where both Abbaye and Rava agree that there is *yeúsh* is where the sea or a river has swept away an article and that article is subsequently deposited elsewhere by the sea or river. Here there is an express permission of the Torah (to be described later on in the *sugya*, hence 'as we shall have occasion to state later on') for the finder to keep the article. The principle here would appear to be that once the article has been swept away beyond human ken it becomes automatically ownerless; it is as if it had vanished from the owner's possession. The finder may here keep the article even if it has a *siman*, since the whole purpose of a *siman* is for the identification and here there is no point in the identification, the Torah having declared the article to be ownerless. Consequently, if the owner is unaware that his article has been swept away, it is still permitted and even Abbaye would agree. Abbaye only demands that the owner be aware of his loss where the right of the finder to keep the lost article depends on *yeúsh*. Here Abbaye demands an actual *yeúsh*, not an 'unconscious' one. But the right of the finder to keep an article swept away by the sea is not because of the *yeúsh* principle but because the Torah has permitted it. Hence the owner's awareness of his loss is entirely irrelevant and Abbaye will agree that the finder may keep the article. Thus there are three cases where the owner is ignorant of his loss at the time:

(1) Where there is a *siman* – even Rava agrees – because there is no *yeúsh state*

(2) Where the sea has swept it away – even Abbaye agrees – because *yeúsh* is irrelevant

(3) Where there is no *siman*: Abbaye forbids, because there is no actual *yeúsh*; Rava permits, because there is a *yeúsh state*

The Talmud now seeks to prove the case one way or another, in favour of Rava or of Abbaye. First there is a series of attempted proofs from the Mishnah to which this *sugya* is appended (*Bava Metzi'a* 21 : 1). Here a number of items are listed which, if lost, may be kept by the finder, evidently because they have no *siman*, so that *yeúsh* can be assumed. The point behind this series of proofs is that according to Abbaye's reasoning the finder is only allowed to keep a lost article that has no *siman* if he knows for certain that the loser has become aware of his loss before he, the finder, takes possession of the article. If it is doubtful whether or not the loser has become aware of his loss it is illegal for the finder to keep the article, since there may not have been the positive *yeúsh* Abbaye demands if the finder is to keep the article. Now first in the list recorded in the Mishnah are scattered sheaves (literally, 'scattered fruit'). These have no *siman*; there are no means of identification. But presumably these sheaves have fallen off the owner's cart and he will not become aware of his loss until a considerable time has elapsed. Why, then, according to Abbaye, is the finder allowed to keep them? The Mishnah appears to support Rava and refute Abbaye. The reply given on Abbaye's behalf is that the fourth-century Babylonian Amora, Ukba bar Hama, has in any event previously (*Bava Metzi'a* 21a) explained the Mishnah as referring not to sheaves that have been lost but to sheaves left scattered at the threshing floor. The Mishnah means, on Ukba bar Hama's interpretation, that if sheaves are found stacked up at the threshing floor, it is proper to assume that their owner will return to fetch them; but where the sheaves are found scattered at the threshing floor it is safe to assume that they have been intentionally abandoned there by the owner after he had completed his threshing. The owner evidently attached no significance to these scattered sheaves and will not bother to gather them up. They are thus in the category of 'articles that have been lost intentionally' (*avēdah mi-da'at*), i.e. it has nothing whatsoever to do with the *yeúsh* question. The reason why the finder may keep the sheaves is because the owner has left them there intentionally for whoever wishes to take them. (*Rashi* used the expression, 'they are *hefkeri*', *hefker* being 'ownerless property', property over which the owner has intentionally relinquished his ownership.)

The second proof is from another item in the Mishnaic list – 'scattered money'. Money has no *siman* (even if, for instance, coins have a mark denoting that they belonged to a particular person, this cannot count as a means of identification since money is not kept by the owner but is used for purchasing goods). But according to Abbaye, who requires positive *yeúsh*, the owner may not have been aware that he has lost the money. The reply is given that the Palestinian Amora, R. Isaac, has stated that it is in the nature of men constantly to be examining their money-bags to see if these are intact and it can therefore be assumed that the loser has become aware of his loss before the money has come into the possession of the finder.

The third attempted proof from the Mishnah is from two further items in the list: 'cakes of figs and baker's loaves'. These, to be sure, have no *siman* but the owner is unlikely to have become aware of his loss before the finder takes them, which supports Rava and refutes Abbaye. To this the reply is given that it is safe to assume that the loser does know of his loss almost at once because they are 'heavy' and he quickly senses the lessening of the load he carries.

The fourth attempted proof is from another item in the Mishnah: 'strips of purple wool'. Surely here the owner does not become aware of his loss until much later (i.e. since these are mere 'strips' and are not 'heavy')? The reply is that these are valuable so that a similar principle to that stated by R. Isaac applies. Just as men constantly check their money-bags to see whether or not anything is missing so do they check these valuable strips of wool. The owner will have become aware of his loss almost immediately.

There is a difficulty with regard to this series of attempted proofs from the Mishnah (see *SM* and the marginal note of the Vilna Gaon). The Mishnah gives the following list of items the finder may keep: (1) scattered fruit; (2) scattered money; (3) small ears of corn in the public domain; (4) cakes of figs; (5) baker's loaves; (6) strings of fish; (7) pieces of meat; (8) bundles of wool shearings; (9) bundles of flax; (10) strings of purple wool. The Talmud in our passage refers only to the (1), (2) and (4) and (5) treated together, and then (10). Why are the others omitted? The Vilna Gaon explains the omission of (3) on the grounds that, in any event, the Talmud later on (*Bava Metzi'a* 22b) understands item (3) as referring to ears of corn that have been left there *intentionally*. As for the omission of the other items in the list, the Gaon refers to a variant reading adopted by the *Rosh*. If our text is correct, however, the explanation of the omission would seem to be that when the Talmud quotes (4) and (5) together, not as separate items, as they are in the Mishnah, the meaning is: 'cakes of figs, baker's loaves *etc.*' There is no equivalent in Talmudic language for 'etc.' and it is plausible to suggest that it is here implied. The progress of thought would thus be: You have dealt adequately with 'scattered fruit' by saying that it is 'fruit' left at the threshing floor, but what will you do with 'scattered money'? The reply is given, because of R. Isaac's principle. But what of cakes of figs, baker's loaves *etc.* (i.e. items (6) to (9)) where this does not apply? Reply: all these are heavy and their loss is known. But what of (10) 'strips of wool', which are not 'heavy'? Reply: they are valuable and so R. Isaac's principle applies.

A further proof is now attempted from a *Baraita*. This reads: 'If one finds coins ['monies'] in synagogues, houses of study or any public place, they belong to him [the finder] because the original owners give up all hope of recovery.' This seems to refute Abbaye, since the owner may not have been aware of his loss. The reply is, as above, that R. Isaac has said that men are in the habit of constantly examining their money-bags and hence the loser will have become aware of his loss.

The obvious difficulty here is that we have already been given R. Isaac's principle in reply to the first objection regarding scattered money in the Mishnah. Why repeat it in connection with the *Baraita*? Moreover, from the expressions used ('As R. Isaac said' in the Mishnaic instance; 'R. Isaac said' in the instance of the *Baraita*) it would appear that R. Isaac made his original statement not on the Mishnah but on the *Baraita*, from which it was later applied to the Mishnah. Why? (See *Tosafists* s.v. *ta shema*'.) It should be noted that R. Isaac's principle is quoted, too, in *Bava Kama* 118b, but there also as a quote. From all this it would appear (see *Ritba* quoted by *SM*) that, indeed, once one knows of R. Isaac's principle one knows that the same reply can be given when the attempted refutation is from the *Baraita*, but that originally the questions were put at different times and owe their present arrangement to the final editors (*Ritba* calls them: R. Ashi and Ravina, the traditional editors of the Talmud) who presented them in this order so as to work down, as it were, from the Mishnah to a *Baraita*.

An attempt is now made to support Rava from another Mishnah (*Peah* 8: 1). Here the ruling is given that once the 'stragglers' (*namoshot*) have been in a field, any gleanings left behind are permitted to anyone who cares to appropriate them even if he is not a poor man. The gleanings, the sheaves which fall during the reaping, belong to the poor by the law of the Torah (Leviticus 23: 22) but once the 'stragglers' have been through the field the gleanings belong to whoever wishes to take them. The third-century Palestinian Amoraím, R. Johanan and Resh Lakish, are quoted as defining *namoshot* either as 'old men who walk [slowly] with the aid of their sticks' (and so are able to see all the gleanings that are available, *Rashi*) or as 'gatherers after gatherers'. In any event, the Mishnah states that there is a stage at which all the poor of that town have had their choice of the gleanings. Whatever remains is the result of *yeúsh* on the part of these poor to whom the gleanings belong. But the gleanings really belong, as it were, to all the poor everywhere. Now it is true that if the poor of other towns were to know that the *namoshot* had passed through that field they would engage in *yeúsh*, but they cannot know this and hence, according to Abbaye, the gleanings ought to be prohibited as *yeúsh she-lo mi-da'at*. The reply is given, the poor of other towns engage in *yeúsh* beforehand, since they know full well that the gleanings in that field will be gathered by the poor of the town in which it is found.

Another Mishnah (*Ma'aserot* 3:4) is now quoted: 'If dried figs are found by the wayside, even if they are found beside a field in which figs have been laid out to dry, and so, too, if a fig tree overhangs a road and figs are found underneath it, they are permitted and there is no prohibition because of the laws against theft and [as ownerless property that has been appropriated] they are exempt from tithing. In the case of olives and carobs, however, they are forbidden.' The Talmud observes that the first law recorded in this Mishnah, that the dried figs and the figs underneath the tree are permitted, affords no refutation of Abbaye. These dried figs are valuable and, as in R. Isaac's principle, the owner constantly examines his field and soon becomes aware of his loss. So, too, with regard to the figs underneath the tree, the owner is aware that figs do constantly fall from the tree and hence engages in *yeúsh* from the beginning. But the second law in the Mishnah appears to refute Rava. It is at present assumed that the reason why the olives and carobs are forbidden is because these do not drop so easily from the tree and so there has been no actual, positive *yeúsh*. But when the owner does become aware of his loss it is assumed that he does engage in *yeúsh*. We thus have here an instance of *yeúsh she-lo mi-da'at*. The reply is given by the late-third-century Palestinian Amora, R. Abbahu. (The chronology is here somewhat odd. R. Abbahu could hardly have replied to a difficulty presented on the debate between Abbaye and Rava. The meaning is either that the issue debated by Abbaye and Rava was known in the time and place of R. Abbahu or, more probably, that R. Abbahu made his comment independently on the Mishnah and this fortuitously was of help to Rava in his debate with Abbaye.) According to R. Abbahu the reason why the olives and carobs are forbidden is because everyone can see that they belong to the owner of the tree underneath which they are found and hence there is no *yeúsh* at all, even when the owner discovers his loss. The owner will not despair because he knows that people will appreciate that the olives and carobs are his and will not take them for themselves. In that case, it is objected, why not say the same with regard to figs? To this the reply is given by Rava's disciple, R. Pappa, that when figs fall from the tree onto the ground they become repulsive and uneatable and hence there is *yeúsh*.

A further attempt at proof is from another *Baraita*: 'If a *ganav* ['thief'] took from one man and gave to another and so, too, if a *gazlan* ['robber'] took from one and gave to another and so, too, if the River Jordan took from one and gave to another, that which has been taken has been taken and that which has been given has been given', i.e. and the one to whom it has been given may keep it, presumably because the owner has engaged in *yeúsh*. Now a *ganav* is a sneak-thief who steals by stealth while a *gazlan* is a robber who snatches property from its owner with the owner's knowledge but under protest. Hence, the Talmud remarks, there is no refutation of Abbaye from the cases of *gazlan* and the Jordan because the owner is aware of his loss. But in the case of the *ganav* the owner in unaware at the time of his loss and this is a refutation of Abbaye. The reply is given that R. Pappa has 'interpreted' (*tirgemah*) this clause as referring not to a sneak-thief, the usual meaning of *ganav*, but to an armed robber. In that case, the Talmud objects, it is the same as the *gazlan*, to which the reply is given that the *Baraita* is recording two kinds of *gazlan*, the one who snatches the object from its owner and the one who threatens the owner with violence if he does not surrender the object. In both cases the owner is aware of his loss. The point of this discussion is, it is assumed that when an object has been stolen the owner will engage in *yeúsh* so that even if the object has a *siman* it is treated here like an object which has no *siman* with regard to the law of lost property (see *Tosafists* s.v. *mah she-natan*).

Another *Baraita* is now quoted: 'If a river swept away a man's beams, wood or stones and deposited these in a neighbour's field, they are his [the neighbour's] because the owners have engaged in *yeúsh*', i.e. it can be assumed that there has been *yeúsh* right from the beginning, when the river swept the goods away. But according to Rava, since it is evidently a case where the owner does engage in *yeúsh* when he becomes aware of his loss, why does he have to be aware of it *at the time*? The Talmud replies that the *Baraita* deals with the case of an owner who can save his goods, hence they are only permitted when it is known that he has engaged in *yeúsh* from the beginning. But in that case, the Talmud objects, why does the *Baraita* go on to state: 'If the owners were running after them [the beams etc.] they are forbidden'? Why are they only forbidden then? Since we are dealing with objects that can be rescued, they ought to be forbidden in any event. The reply is that the objects can be rescued but only if great effort is taken. Consequently, where the owners are running after them this demonstrates that there is no *yeúsh*, otherwise *yeúsh* can be assumed.

The discussion now takes a new turn. A *Baraita* is quoted which does not deal with *yeúsh* at all and is yet said to be relevant to the debate between Abbaye and Rava. This *Baraita* deals with the separation of *terumah*, the tithe given to the priest (Numbers 18: 12). The *Baraita* reads: 'In what manner did the Sages say that when one separates *terumah* without the knowledge of the owner the *terumah* becomes such? If a man went into the field of his neighbour and gathered sheaves and separated *terumah* without the owner's permission, then, if the owner suspects theft [i.e. if the owner is displeased, imagining that the one who has separated *terumah* is robbing him in being too generous to the priest] it is not *terumah*, otherwise it is *terumah*. How can he know whether or not the owner is suspicious of theft? If the owner came along and said: "Why did you not go to the better ones?", then, if there are better ones there it is *terumah*, otherwise it is not *terumah* [the owner is being sarcastic]. If the owner himself gathered further sheaves and added these to the ones gathered it is in any event *terumah*.' From this *Baraita* it follows that when the owner of the field *later* declares: 'Why did you not go to the better ones?', it is *terumah* because this demonstrates that he is the sort of person who is only too pleased that his *terumah* has been separated on his behalf. Thus, as it were, there is a state of willingness with regard to *terumah* and hence the separation is valid even though at the time of separation there was no positive awareness by the owner of what was being done on his behalf. This refutes Abbaye who holds that for *yeúsh* to be effective positive awareness is required at the time.

On the face of it, what has *terumah* to do with *yeúsh*? The real point of this stage of the discussion is as follows. It is here being suggested that the debate between Abbaye and Rava is not specifically about *yeúsh* but about 'knowledge' or 'awareness' where the law requires these. Their debate does not revolve around the legal definition of *yeúsh* but rather around the legal definition of 'knowledge' or 'awareness', wherever these are required by a particular law. In both cases – *yeúsh* and *terumah* – awareness is required on the part of the person involved. By definition both *yeúsh* and separation of the *terumah* depend on the person's awareness of what is being done. Now Rava does not demand a positive awareness for *yeúsh* to be effective but, as it were, only an awareness *state*. It follows that since Abbaye does require positive awareness for *yeúsh* to become effective he will require positive awareness for *terumah* to be effective and, conversely, since the *Baraita* evidently does not require it in the case of *terumah* it will not require it in the case of *yeúsh*, which refutes Abbaye.

The reply is given by Rava himself – 'Rava interprets [*tirgemah*] it on behalf of Abbaye'; as if to say, Rava admits that Abbaye can easily find his way out of the difficulty through a reinterpretation of this *Baraita*. Rava suggests that the *Baraita* does not deal, as was first thought, with a man who goes into the field of his neighbour to separate *terumah* without the owner's permission but with a man who has been delegated by the owner to separate his *terumah*. 'Without the knowledge of the owner' in the *Baraita* does not mean that the owner is totally unaware but simply that the owner, when he delegated the other man to separate his *terumah*, did not inform him of the quality of the sheaves he should separate. The Talmud adds that this interpretation must be given in any event since according to a Rabbinic understanding of Numbers 18:28 an agent cannot act without the knowledge of his principal, i.e. without being authorised by the principal to act as such. Thus, the Talmud continues, the *Baraita* refers to an owner who did instruct his agent to separate *terumah* on his behalf. The owner, however, failed to give his agent instructions regarding the quality of the sheaves he intended him to separate. Normally a man gives average quality for his *terumah*, neither bad nor good, but here the agent took it upon himself to give the better quality. Here the statement: 'Why did you not go to the best?' suffices to demonstrate that this was the owner's intention right from the beginning, that he left it entirely to the agent to determine which quality he will separate and that whatever is done is done with the full approval of the owner.

This is followed by a digression from the main theme in the form of a narrative. The fifth-century Babylonian Amoraím, Amemar, Mar Zutra and R. Ashi, paid a visit to the orchard of one Mari bar Isak, whose tenant-farmer brought dates and pomegranates for the Rabbis to eat. The other two Rabbis saw no harm in eating but Mar Zutra, renowned for his scrupulous piety, refused to eat since Mari was unaware of the gift. When Mari did come along he remarked to his tenant: 'Why did you not give the Rabbis those better fruits?' When Mar Zutra still refused to eat, his colleagues reminded him of the ruling in the *Baraita*. Mar Zutra, however, quoted a ruling of Rava that the principle, stated in the *Baraita*, of 'Why did you not go to the better ones?' applies only to *terumah*, the giving of which is a religious obligation, whereas Mari may really have been displeased and only said what he did in order to avoid being embarrassed.

The Talmud now reverts to the main theme. Another *Baraita* is quoted, dealing with the following. Leviticus 11: 38 reads: 'But if any water be put upon the seed, and any part of their carcase fall thereon, it shall be unclean unto you.' The Rabbinic understanding of this verse is that food only becomes contaminated, through contact with a source of ritual contamination such as a dead reptile, if the food has first been in contact with some liquid. Fruit while still on the tree cannot become contaminated. If the fruit has been plucked from the tree it only becomes susceptible to contamination if it has first been 'prepared' (*hekhshar*) by coming into contact with liquid after it has been plucked from the tree. This is sometimes referred to as the law of 'be put' – *ki yuttan* – after the verse in Leviticus. There is the further law that in order for the liquid to 'prepare' the food the owner of the food must be willing for the liquid to be there. We are now in a position to understand the relevance of the *Baraita* quoted to our discussion. The *Baraita* reads: 'if the dew is still on them [some fruit] and he was pleased [that the fruit should be moistened] then it is a case of *be put*. But if the dew had dried, then even though he was pleased [that the fruit had been moistened] it is not a case of *be put*.' In other words, the owner of the fruit must be pleased with the moisture while it is still there. But if Rava is correct, the fact that the owner was later pleased demonstrates that there was a state of 'unconscious awareness' at the time, when the dew was on the fruit. This supports Abbaye. As the Talmud spells it out: 'What is the reason? Is it not because we do not say: since it has become evident that he is now pleased he is pleased from the beginning?'

This section, too, has to be understood on the basis of our

previous remarks regarding the 'awareness' issue between Abbaye and Rava. It has to be said once again that the Talmud understands our debate as not specifically about *yeúsh* but about any law in which 'awareness' is required for something to take effect. Does 'unconscious awareness', i.e. a state of 'willingness' but no actual, positive 'willing' suffice. According to Rava it does but according to Abbaye it does not. The *Baraita* thus supports Abbaye and refutes Rava.

To this the Talmud replies by referring to the words 'be put' in our text. Traditionally this is written without the *vav*, although it is read as *ki yuttan*. Now according to this traditional way of writing the words can be read not as *ki yuttan*, 'be put', but as *ki yitten*, '*he* puts'. Hence here even Rava will agree that positive awareness – as when *he* actually *puts* it there – is required. The Talmud asks, in that case, even if he is pleased, it ought not to be effective since we require him actually to put it there and in this case the dew came onto the fruit without human agency. In reply to this a piece of exegesis by R. Pappa is quoted. R. Pappa contrasts the traditional *reading* – 'be put' – with the traditional *writing* – '*he* puts' In order to reconcile the two, the rule is stated that it is effective even if the liquid came onto the food by itself (as in 'be put') but (like '*he* puts') it is only effective if he knows about it. Thus even though as a general principle Rava holds that 'unconscious awareness' suffices, it does not suffice with regard to the law of *hekhsher* because of the special implications of the 'be put' and '*he* puts' verse. The *Baraita* of *hekhsher* thus deals with an exceptional case.

A final proof is quoted to support Abbaye and refute Rava. This is from an exposition by R. Johanan in the name of the Tanna R. Ishmael (variant reading R. Simeon) ben Yehozadok. This reads: 'Whence do we know that a lost article swept away by a river is permitted? Because it is written: "And so shalt thou do with his ass; and so shalt thou do with his garment; and so shalt thou do with every lost thing of thy brother's, which is lost from him, and thou hast found" (Deuteronomy 22: 3). When it is "lost from him" but "found" so far as other men are concerned but excluding this [where the river swept it away] where it is lost from him but is not found so far as others are concerned.' The Torah law only demands that a lost article be returned when it is only 'lost' so far as the loser is concerned. If it is 'lost' to all, i.e. when the river has swept it away, the Torah allows the eventual finder to keep it, it is treated by the Torah as ownerless property. (This is the reference at the beginning of our *sugya* where it says: 'as we shall have occasion to state later on'.)

Now the Talmud takes all this to mean that the Torah is recording two cases: (1) *issura* ('that which is forbidden'), when it is only *lost from him*; (2) *hetēra* ('that which is permitted'), when it is swept away by the river. Moreover, it is as if Scripture declares: *hetēra* is always permitted, whether or not the article has a *siman* and *issura* is always forbidden whether or not it has a *siman*. This is as if the Torah had stated explicitly that a lost article is forbidden, even if there is no *siman*, if the loser is unaware of his loss (as he is unaware in the case of *hetēra* when the river sweeps it away). This favours Abbaye.

The conclusion of the whole discussion is: 'The refutation [*tiyuvta*] of Rava is, indeed, a refutation. And the ruling is in accordance with Abbaye in the cases Y'AL KGM.' The latter is a mnemonic, referring to six disputes between Abbaye and Rava in the Talmud. Although, generally, where Abbaye and Rava debate an issue, the ruling follows the opinion of Rava, in these six cases it follows the opinion of Abbaye.

According to *Rashi* Y'AL KGM denotes:

(1) Y = *yeúsh she-lo mi-da'at*, our case
(2) 'A = *'ed zomem*, 'false witness', *Sanhedrin* 27a
(3) L = *leḥi ha-'omed me-elav*, 'a post put up accidentally', '*Eruvin* 15a
(4) K = *kiddushin she-lo nimseru le-viah*, 'betrothal which cannot lead to cohabitation', *Kiddushin* 51a
(5) G = *gilluy da'at-be-gittin*, 'revealing one's attitude indirectly in divorce', *Gittin* 34a
(6) M = *mumar okhel nevēlot lo-hakh'is*, 'an apostate who eats forbidden food out of spite', *Sanhedrin* 27a

The Talmud, in fact, only records Y'AL KGM in (1), (2) and (4), but for (5) see *Gittin* 34b top and *Rashi* ad loc. Cf. *Tosafists Kiddushin* 52a s.v. *be-y'al kgm* for other suggestions.

The *sugya* concludes with a note following on the ruling in favour of Abbaye. The fifth-century Babylonian Amora, R. Aha son of Rava, asked R. Ashi: 'Since Rava has been refuted, how can we eat dates the wind has blown from the tree?', i.e. the owner of the tree does not necessarily know of it at the time. R. Ashi replies that since the owner knows that any dates that will be blown off the tree will be eaten by vermin he engages in *yeúsh* right from the beginning, i.e. he knows that some dates will be blown off the tree to be eaten by vermin so he engages in *yeúsh* for these dates even while they are on the tree. But, R. Aha continues, what if the trees belong to orphans who are minors and, since a minor has no powers of consent in law, his *yeúsh* is ineffective. R. Ashi replies that we are not bound to assume, of all the trees on that large plot of ground, that the date-palms belong to orphans. R. Aha then asks, but what if we do know that the palms belong to orphans or what if there is a fence to keep out the vermin? In these cases, R. Ashi replies, the dates are indeed forbidden.

Note that Aha son of Rava states in his question: 'Since Rava has been refuted', not: 'Since my father has been refuted', which shows that this Amora is not the son of our Rava but of another Rava, see Hyman: *Toledot*, vol. 1, pp. 130–2.

In this *sugya* there is material from second-century Palestine (the Mishnah and *Baraita*) down to fifth-century Babylon (R. Ashi and his colleagues), all fitted into the framework by the later editors. Although in some instances of *tiyuvta*, 'it is a refutation', this is generally held to be the work of the post-Talmudic Saboraím, here it would seem to have been inserted prior to R. Aha son of Rava, who refers to it, though it is possible that these are not R. Aha's actual words and were added later. The mnemonic at the beginning of the *sugya*, found in our editions in brackets and listing the whole series of proofs, is undoubtedly Saboraic and supplied after our whole *sugya* had received its final form. There is some evidence of two successive editing processes, e.g. the words 'as we shall have occasion to state later on' seem to suggest that these were supplied when the main *sugya* had already been edited. It is, indeed, probable that this whole explanatory comment at the beginning of the *sugya*, describing in detail the limits of the debate, was supplied later and the same applies to the digression regarding Mari bar Isak, which is a unit on its own and seems to have been inserted by the later editors. The series of proofs are presented in a logical arrangement: first the Mishnah, then the *Baraitot* dealing with *yeúsh* directly, then the indirect *Baraitot* or *terumah* and *ki yuttan*, and, finally, the conclusive proof which is left to the end; all of which demonstrates clearly that the material has been given literary shape by the editors. It is to be noted that there are no references elsewhere in the Talmud to *yeúsh she-lo mi-da'at*, except for the Y in Y'AL KGM and this is almost certainly a later addition, made when the whole Babylonian Talmud had been completed. It is puzzling that Y'AL KGM only occurs in three instances. It is possible that it did originally occur in all six places.

5
Rubba: probability

The principle that the Torah allows reliance on probability in cases of doubt is found in numerous Talmudic passages. The *sugya* we here examine – *Ḥullin* 11a–12a – is concerned with the derivation of the principle from Scripture. What is the Scriptural warrant for relying on probability rather than demanding certainty? The term *rubba* is in Aramaic (Hebrew: *rov*) with the meaning of 'majority', hence the majority or most likely opinion. It can be translated literally into English as 'majority' but in most instances the word 'probability' comes nearest to the meaning. The *sugya* does not question the application of the principle. That is everywhere assumed. Its concern is solely with the question of Scriptural authority for the principle.

The *sugya* first sets the stage for the discussion. The opening words are: 'How do we know that which the Rabbis say: "Follow [lit. 'go after'] probability" [*rubba*]?' The Talmud immediately interjects: how can you ask, 'how do we know?'; surely there is no problem since Scripture states explicitly: 'Turn after the majority' (Exodus 23: 2)? That is to say, the Talmud is puzzled by the request for Scriptural warrant for the principle, as if this were unclear. There is an explicit verse which states that *rubba* is followed. (Actually, the plain meaning of the verse, in its context, is 'Do not turn after the majority to do evil' but in its traditional, Rabbinic, interpretation is: 'Do not follow a multitude to do evil (but otherwise) turn after the majority'.) The verse is applied by the Rabbis to a Court of Law, e.g. if two judges in a civil case declare a man to be liable and one judge declares him not to be liable or, in the case of a Lower Sanhedrin in a capital charge, if

12 declare him to be innocent and 11 guilty, the majority opinion is followed.

In the reply, three illustrations of *rubba* are given. One of these is that of the Sanhedrin, where the majority opinion is decisive. Another is that of nine butcher's shops selling meat that has been slaughtered properly by the method of *sheḥitah* and is hence *kasher* and one shop selling non-*kasher*. By the *rubba* principle any meat found in that town is *kasher* since a majority of the shops is *kasher*. The meat is assumed to have come from one of the shops belonging to the majority rather than from the single, minority shop. (The same law would apply if only two shops sold *kasher* meat and a third non-*kasher*, since there is still a simple majority.) The third illustration is from a case of levirate marriage (Deuteronomy 25: 5–10) debated by R. Meir and the Sages (*Yevamot* 61b). The purpose of levirate marriage is for the *levir* and the widow to have a child. Normally it is forbidden for a man to marry his deceased brother's wife but the Torah enjoins it where the brother has died without issue. It follows that if either the *levir* or the widow is sterile the prohibition of marrying a brother's wife applies. Now the condition of sterility, which in this context refers to physical defects in the generative organs of man or woman, cannot be determined while male or female are still minors. Consequently, the question arises, may levirate marriage take place where the *levir* is a boy under age or the widow a girl under age? It can be argued, and R. Meir does so argue, that this is forbidden since it may turn out later than the *levir* or the widow is really sterile. But the Sages disagree with R. Meir and permit the marriage on the grounds that the majority of persons are not sterile. It is improbable that either is sterile and the *rubba* principle is accepted. There are thus three cases of the application of *rubba*: (1) nine shops; (2) Sanhedrin; (3) minor boy or girl.

We now turn to the reply given in the Talmud to the question, why not derive *rubba* from the verse: 'Turn after the majority'? Indeed, the Talmud replies, one type of *rubba* – that represented by the nine shops and the Sanhedrin – requires no further Scriptural proof since it is derived from our verse. This is a case of '*rubba* before us'. Our question, however, is: what Scriptural warrant is there for relying on a different kind of *rubba*, that which is 'not before us', such as the case of the boy or girl?

Superficially, the distinction between the two types of *rubba* is clear. The Scriptural verse deals with the Sanhedrin, 12 members of which declare the man on trial to be innocent, 11 guilty. Because of the *rubba* principle he is declared innocent. Here the majority is 'before us', i.e. we can observe the majority which decided for acquittal. Similarly, in the case of the nine shops, we can observe the nine *kasher* shops on the basis of which the meat found is permitted to be eaten. But in the case of the boy or girl the majority is 'not before us'. We do not observe the majority on the basis of which we decide that the boy or girl is not sterile. So far so good. But what is the logical ground for the distinction? Why should it make any difference whether or not the majority is 'before us'? Much has been written on this question but the distinction would appear to be the following. In the case of the Sanhedrin the decision *comes* from the majority. It is basically a procedural matter, the Torah ruling that the majority opinion be followed. The man declared innocent by the majority is not said to be *innocent*, as if the majority were always right, but he is to be *acquitted*, since otherwise no case could be carried to a successful conclusion without a unanimous verdict, which the Torah does not demand. Thus if a majority decide that the man on trial is innocent he is acquitted, even if, in fact, as the minority holds, he is really guilty. He is innocent *in law*. Conversely, if the majority decides that he is guilty he is sentenced, even though, in fact, he may be innocent, as the minority holds. He is guilty *in law*. It is all a matter of legal procedure, not a determinative matter. From this case of the Sanhedrin that of the nine shops is derived. This, too, is a question of legal procedure in religious law. Since there is a doubt whether or not the meat is *kasher*, the procedure to be adopted is to resolve the doubt by relying on the probability principle, that the meat *comes* from the nine shops, though, in fact, it may well have come from the non-*kasher* shop. Here, too, the matter is procedural, not determinative. The meat is *kasher* in law no matter what its true nature, since the Torah allows us to rely on probability and that which the Torah allows is *kasher*. But in the case of the boy or girl it is not a procedural matter but one of determination arrived at by means of empirical investigation into the majority of instances. When we say that the marriage of the boy or girl is permitted because the majority of persons are not sterile, this does not mean that at any given moment there is an observable majority of non-sterile persons from which the boy or girl derive. That is nonsense. It is rather that we say, since our observation demonstrates that to be sterile is not the normal human state, it is safe to assume that the boy or girl will have the normal human nature and will not be sterile. We rely, in other words, on empirical investigation and the high degree of probability this affords. That this kind of *rubba* is to be relied on does not at all follow from the fact that the Torah permits us to rely on the very different kind of *rubba* that is 'before us', that is, purely procedural. From the fact that the Torah allows us to rely on a purely mathematical probability in the case of the Sanhedrin and the nine shops, as a matter of procedure, it cannot follow that where the laws of probability have to be relied on to determine the status of an individual they are so relied on. Consequently, the question in our passage is, what is the Scriptural warrant for relying on probability in such cases as that of the boy or girl which is an instance of '*rubba* that is not before us'?

Another illustration of '*rubba* that is not before us' is given in the *sugya* as it proceeds. If an animal has a defect in one of its vital organs, this is known as *terēfah*. Eighteen such defects are recorded (Mishnah *Ḥullin* 3: 1) that render the animal *terēfah*. If the internal organs of an animal that had had *sheḥitah* were left unexamined the animal would still be *kasher* on the grounds that 'the majority of animals are *kasher*' (*rov behemot kesherot*). This is another example of '*rubba* that is not before us', which is the concern of our *sugya*. Rabbi Hayyim Soloveitchik, R. Hayyim Brisker, is reported to have put the distinction between the two kinds of *rubba* neatly in this way. Even if all the animals in the world had died and only one animal were left, that animal would be *kasher* because of the principle 'the majority of animals are *kasher*'. An illustration based on the ideas of Rabbi Simeon Skopf of Grodno is the following. A coin has turned up heads three times. It would be a rash gambler who would bet on it turning up heads the fourth time. The mathematical probability is that it will turn up tails on the fourth toss, assuming that the coin is not loaded. But the reason that the odds are in favour of the coin turning up tails the fourth time is not because anything will happen to change the nature of the coin. But when a gambler bets on the favourite in a horse race he does so because the odds on the horse winning are determined by the horse itself, because of its previous performance which *demonstrates* that it is a 'winning' type of horse. The probability here is determinative, telling us something about the physical nature of the horse. All this can be compared with modern philosophical discussions on the theory of probability and with Hume's famous understanding of causality as empirical not metaphysical. The standard works on the theoretical discussion of doubt and *rubba* in the Talmudic and post-Talmudic literature are Aryeh Laib Heller's *Shev Shema'tata* and

Simeon Skopf's *Sha'arey Yosher*. Goitein's *Kesef Nivḥar*, no. 144 is also useful for a survey of most of the Talmudic and important post-Talmudic sources.

Having defined the scope of the inquiry – the Scriptural warrant for relying on *rubba* when it is 'not before us' – the Talmud proceeds to give a list of Amoraím, each of whom tries his hand at adducing conclusive proof from a Scriptural verse.

The first proof is attempted by R. Eleazar. We have noted that an animal with a serious defect is *terēfah* and forbidden to be eaten. It is also forbidden to offer such an animal as a sacrifice. (Some defects which render an animal *terēfah* can be detected while the animal is still alive.) R. Eleazar notes the verse dealing with a burnt-offering: And he shall cut it into its pieces (Leviticus 1: 6), one of the pieces mentioned being the head. Since the verse stresses 'cut *it* into *its* pieces' the traditional explanation is: 'but not its pieces into pieces', i.e. it is forbidden to cut up the head into smaller pieces. The head must be burnt on the altar while it is whole. Now if the membrane which covers an animal's brain is perforated, that animal is *terēfah* and cannot be offered as a sacrifice. How do we know that the burnt-offering is not *terēfah*, that its membrane has not been perforated? It cannot be that the head is cut open before it is burnt on the altar to see whether or not the membrane is intact, since Scripture forbids the cutting of the head into pieces. And yet the Torah does record this law of the head of the burnt-offering. It can only be that the principle of *rubba* is relied on and the majority of animals are not *terēfah*. R. Eleazar rests his case.

No, the Talmud retorts, this proof is invalid. It may be that *rubba* is not relied on and that, indeed, the head has first to be cut into in order to examine the membrane. As for the objection, it can be suggested that the Torah only prohibits the cutting of the head into two or more 'pieces', but there is no objection, if the head is kept whole, to cutting down into the head until one reaches the membrane.

Another proof is attempted by Mar son of Ravina. Of the Paschal lamb the Torah says: 'neither shall ye break a bone thereof' (Exodus 12: 46). But the membrane of the animal may have been perforated and the skull must not be broken into in order to conduct the examination to see whether the membrane is intact. This shows that the Torah does rely on the *rubba* principle, that the majority of animals are not *terēfah*. The Talmud invalidates this proof by suggesting that the examination can be carried out by burning through the skull with a hot coal until the membrane is reached. To do this would not offend against the law forbidding the breaking of its bones. A *Baraita* is quoted in which it is stated explicitly that there is no objection to burning through the bones of the Paschal lamb, only to breaking them.

The proof attempted by R. Nahman bar Isaac is then quoted. The verse regarding the offering of a sheep states: 'The fat thereof and the fat tail entire' (Leviticus 3: 9). Thus the fat tail has to be burnt *entire* on the altar and this implies that it must not be cut open before it is burnt. Now one of the *terēfot* is the severance of the spinal cord and the spinal cord goes into the tail. The tail cannot be cut open to see whether or not the spinal cord has been severed since the Torah ordains that the tail must be *entire.* If it be objected, the Talmud continues, that the tail is cut off lower down than that part of the spinal cord the severance of which renders the animal *terēfah,* this cannot be since Scripture states (in the same verse) that the tail must be removed 'hard by the rump bone' which is 'where the kidneys give counsel' (a pun on *'etzeh,* 'rump bone' and *'etzah,* 'counsel'), which means above the part of the spinal cord the severance of which makes the animal *terēfah.* To this the reply is given, there is no proof. It may be that the tail has first to be cut open to see whether or not the spinal cord is intact. As for the objection, 'entire' only excludes the complete division of the tail into parts but there is no objection to cutting into the tail until the spinal cord is reached, since the tail is still then 'entire', in one piece.

There follows the attempted proof of R. Sheshet son of R. Idi from the law of the heifer whose neck is broken (Deuteronomy 21: 1–9). Scripture states (verse 6) '*the* one whose neck was broken' (with the definite article). According to the traditional explanation, this means that when the heifer is buried it must still be in the state it was when it was beheaded. The only way to determine that the animal has no defects in its internal oregans is to examine these and here this is not possible since the heifer has to be as intact at the time of its burial as it was at the time of its beheading. This affords conclusive proof that the Torah does rely on *rubba* and the majority of animals are not *terēfah.* It may be objected, observes the Talmud further, that perhaps there is no need for the heifer to be *kasher* (and hence the proof would fall away) but this is not so. The heifer must not be *terēfah* since Scripture speaks of the heifer as producing 'forgiveness' (atonement', verse 8) and the same law that it has to be *kasher* applies to it as to the sacrifices which also produce 'forgiveness'. This comparison is stated as a teaching taught in the school of R. Jannai, i.e. there is, in any event, a rule that the heifer must not be *terēfah*. R. Sheshet's proof is not refuted.

Rabbah b. Shila seeks to prove it from the law of the red heifer (Numbers 19) of which Scripture states: 'And he shall slaughter it...and he shall burn it' (verses 3 and 5). The meaning is said to be that when the heifer is burnt it must be in the same state of 'wholeness' as it was when it was slaughtered and this implies that it must not be cut up in between, which means that no examination is possible to determine whether or not it is *terēfah*. If it be objected that there is no proof that the red heifer must not be *terēfah*, the proof is that Scripture calls the heifer 'a sin-offering' (verse 9) and, like the sin-offering, which is a sacrifice, it must be *kasher*. Rabbah b. Shila's proof is not refuted. The red heifer is valid even though no examination is possible, because the Torah relies on *rubba* and the majority of animals are *kasher*.

R. Aha bar Jacob seeks to prove it from the law of the scapegoat on the Day of Atonement. Scripture states: 'And he shall take the two goats' (Leviticus 16: 7), which means that both must be alike. (Some texts do not have this latter phrase.) But one of them might be *terēfah*? This proves that the *rubba* principle is accepted and the majority of animals are not *terēfah*. And if it be objected that there is no proof that the scapegoat has to be *kasher* (unlike the goat offered as a sacrifice), two lots have to be cast to determine which is the scapegoat and which the sacrifice, from which it follows that both goats must be *kasher* at the time of the casting of the lots since either may be chosen by lot for the sacrifice. If it be further objected that the scapegoat can be examined after it has been pushed off the mountain crag (Rabbinic understanding of Azazel in verse 8) this cannot be, because the Mishnah (*Yoma* 6: 6) informs us that the goat was broken into pieces before it reached half-way down the mountain. R. Aha bar Jacob's proof stands.

So far all the attempted proofs have been from the sacrificial system or matters connected with it. R. Mari's proof is from a different law, that of smiting a father or mother, the penalty for which is death by the Court (Exodus 21: 15). But the man smitten by the 'son' may not really be his father? It must be that paternity is established on the basis of *rubba*. The man is married to the smiter's mother and the majority of acts of cohabitation would be by the husband not by her lovers if she had had any. To this the Talmud objects that the law may only apply where husband and wife were imprisoned in a dungeon with no access to any other man from before the child's conception until the woman was seen to be pregnant. Paternity would here be established for certain and there would be no need to rely on *rubba*. To this the Talmud replies by quoting: 'There is no guarding against unchastity', i.e. even so it is only by probability that paternity is established since, despite its inaccessibility, another man may have gained access to the dungeon. R. Mari's proof stands. (However, some texts do not have the quote and on this reading R. Mari is refuted.)

R. Kahana's proof is from the law that a murderer is executed by the Court. Now just as an animal can be *terēfah* so can a man if he suffers from the same defects. A human *terēfah* is seen in law as a man already dead and though it is, of course, a serious crime to murder him, the murderer is not executed by the Court because he has, in the words of the Talmud, 'killed a dead man'. In that case, how can a murderer ever be executed since his victim may have been a *terēfah*? It can only be because the Torah relies on the *rubba* principle and the majority of men are not *terēfah*. But, continues the argument, you might say that the murderer is only executed after we have cut up the body of the victim and conducted a post-mortem examination to determine whether or not he was a *terēfah*. The reply is that it is forbidden to mutilate a human corpse. But, the argument continues further, perhaps the prohibiting of mutilating a corpse is set aside for the purpose of saving the life of the murderer (i.e. so as to give the murderer the possibility, albeit a remote one, of escaping the death penalty, as he will do if the victim is discovered to be a *terēfah*). There would then be no proof from the law that the *rubba* principle is accepted. No murderer would be executed unless the corpse were first examined. To this the reply is given that even if the corpse were to be examined for all the different forms of *terēfah* it would still be necessary to rely on *rubba* for, if we did not, the victim may have been *terēfah*, because the organ penetrated by the sword which killed him was already perforated and because of the sword-cut this would not show up in the examination. R. Kanna's proof stands.

As a point of interest it might be noted that this passage is discussed at length in R. Ezekiel Landau's famous *Responsum* on autopsies, *Responsa Noda' Bi-Yhudah, Tinyana*, no. 210, and has become the *locus classicus* for the whole question. The implication of the Talmudic argument at this stage seems to be that a corpse may be mutilated if the purpose is to save life, even, in this case, the life of a murderer and again even, as here, where there is only a very remote chance of the mutilation resulting in the saving of a life.

Ravina's proof is from the law of false witnesses. Of a false witness in a capital charge Scripture says: 'shall ye do unto him, as he had thought to have done unto his brother' (Deuteronomy 19: 19). But by an *a fortiori* argument a false witness against a *terēfah* is not executed since even if a man actually murders a *terēfah* he is not executed. Moreover, the false witness in a charge against a *terēfah* cannot be executed because the law is that the *terēfah*, as a man 'already dead', would not be executed by the Court even if found guilty, so that the false witness cannot have imposed on him the penalty he intended to have imposed on his victim. In the case of a *terēfah* there cannot have been any such intention. It follows from all this that a false witness against a *terēfah* is never executed. In that case, how can the law of false witnesses ever be applied since the victim may have been a *terēfah*? It can only be because the *rubba* principle is accepted and the majority of men are not *terēfah*. To this it might be objected, observes the Talmud, that the corpse of the victim is examined to see whether or not he was a *terēfah*, but this cannot be. The teacher Beribbi is quoted as saying; 'If they [the false witnesses] did not kill him [the victim, i.e. they were discovered to be false before the man they testified against had been executed] they are killed but if they did kill him [i.e. if they were not found to be false until the Court, acting on their testimony, had executed the man on charge] they are not killed.' That is to say, a false witness is only executed when he only *proposed* to commit his offence, when his offence was discovered while his potential victim was still alive. If the false witness had not merely *proposed* to do it but had actually committed the crime, i.e. his crime had not been discovered until the Court had executed the victim, then the false witness is not executed. Thus the law that a false witness is executed only applies if the victim is still alive. A living person cannot be examined to determine whether or not he is a *terēfah* so how can the law of false witnesses ever be applied? It can only be because we rely on the *rubba* principle and Ravina's proof stands.

This law of false witnesses, that they are executed if their evil designs have not been realised but are not executed if they have, is obviously puzzling. It should have been the other way round if a distinction is to be drawn at all. If they are executed for only *proposing* to do it why should they not be executed if they actually did it? See Mishnah and Gemara *Makkot* 5b where the matter is said to have been debated by the Sadducees and Pharisees and where Beribbi's statement is quoted. The post-Talmudic teachers seek to provide a rationale for this strange law. Among the solutions suggested are: God has allowed the victim to be executed so it is his fate and he is probably guilty even though the witnesses are false; or if the witnesses have carried out their evil designs they do not deserve the atonement that would be theirs if they were executed; or if the man has been executed the likelihood is that the witnesses are not, in fact, false despite the evidence to the contrary. See e.g. *Meíri* to *Makkot* ad loc. and David Hoffman, *Responsa Melammed le-Hoíl*, part III, no. 101.

The final proof is R. Ashi's. R. Ashi argues that the *rubba* principle can be derived from the act of *sheḥitah* itself. *Sheḥitah* is performed by cutting through, with a sharp knife, the animal's food-pipe and wind-pipe. Now the rule is that the slightest perforation of the food-pipe renders the animal *terēfah*. Consequently, unless we are to rely on the *rubba* principle, that the majority of animals are not *terēfah*, *sheḥitah* could never be effective to permit the meat of the animal to be eaten since the animal might have had a perforated food-pipe, through which the knife has cut, so that any subsequent examination would be impossible. R. Ashi's proof stands.

Halevy, *Dorot ha-Rishonim*, vol. II, chapter 68 end, pp. 561–2, gives a novel interpretation of R. Ashi's 'from *sheḥitah itself*'. What is the significance of 'itself'? Why does R. Ashi not simply say: 'It is derived from *sheḥitah*'? *Rashi* understands it as : '*sheḥitah*, the very subject we have been discussing up to now', i.e. in this tractate *Ḥullin*, the preceding discussions of which are all connected with the laws of *sheḥitah*. According to Halevy this demonstrates conclusively that when R. Ashi presented his proof he must have already had before him some, at least, of the material now in tractate *Ḥullin*, arranged more or less in the order we now have it. He must have had this *rubba* discussion, which, after all, is a general discussion not a *sheḥitah* one, in its present position, i.e. coming after material already arranged as part of tractate *Ḥullin*. Hence R. Ashi states: 'We derive it from *sheḥitah* itself', i.e. from this very topic being considered in this part of tractate *Ḥullin*. Two things require to be said. First, it is possible that the meaning of 'itself' is not as *Rashi* has it but that the principle of *rubba* can be derived from the impossibility of examining the animal to see whether or not it is *terēfah* – not, as in some of the earlier proofs, from circumstances which obtain *after* the animal has had *sheḥitah* but from *sheḥitah* itself! Secondly, even if we do understand the passage as *Rashi* does, this affords no proof that R. Ashi already had before him a rudimentary form of our present tractate *Ḥullin*, as Halevy suggests, since the words '*sheḥitah* itself' may not have been R. Ashi's own but those placed into R. Ashi's mouth by the editors when they presented the series of proofs (cf. Neusner, *Formation of the Babylonian Talmud*, p. 34), which, as we shall see, are, in any event, contrived.

At this stage the matter has been proved by R. Ashi and some of the previous Amoraím. But the Talmud now states that R. Ashi repeated his argument to R. Kahana; in another version, it is said, R. Kahana repeated it (the argument of R. Ashi? or, perhaps, his own argument, as above) to R. Shimi, who objected that the arguments presented only proved that the *rubba* principle was relied on where there was no alternative, where otherwise the law would be impossible of application. It by no means follows that *rubba* may be relied on even when one can have certainty. For instance, in the case of *sheḥitah* it is perfectly true that we must rely on *rubba* that the food-pipe has not been perforated, but why should this prevent our examining the rest of the animal to determine whether or not it is *terēfah* due to some defect in another of its organs? Or, in the case of the boy or girl, why should we rely on *rubba* if we can wait until they are no longer minors when it can be determined for certain whether or not they are sterile? And, the Talmud continues, unless this distinction is made, how could R. Meir, who, as above, in the case of the boy or girl, does not rely on *rubba*, eat meat? And even if it be argued that, in fact, he did not, what of the Paschal lamb and the meat of other sacrifices it is a religious obligation to eat? We must perforce make the distinction between where there is and is not an alternative and by the same token how can *rubba* be derived from the Scriptural proofs adduced, since in these there is no alternative but to rely on *rubba*?

Here the *sugya* reaches its conclusion, leaving us somewhat in the air. Despite all the attempted proofs there is none for relying on *rubba* where there is an alternative. Even the successful proofs only prove reliance on *rubba* where there is no alternative. *Rashi* suggests that according to the conclusion of the *sugya* we do rely on *rubba*, as the Talmud does everywhere, except according to R. Meir, but it is not derived, as was thought throughout until the conclusion, from any Scriptural verse. *Rashi* states that, according to the conclusion, it is a 'law given to Moses on Sinai', i.e. it is an established law with full divine authority and can be relied on even where certainty can be had; but there is, in fact, no *Scriptural* warrant for this. Thus the whole series of attempted proofs has no practical application and is a purely academic exercise. It is even possible that it was a kind of challenge in the days of the Amoraím to seek to prove the *rubba* principle from Scripture, each Amora trying his hand, the results being collected by the editors to be presented in the form we now have them as part of a *rubba sugya*.

Our *sugya* provides us with an excellent illustration of how the Talmud was put together. First, let us note the order in which the proofs are presented:

	Name	*Date*	*Proof*
(1)	R. Eleazar	d. 279	head of burnt-offering
(2)	Mar son of Ravina	fourth century	head of Paschal lamb
(3)	R. Nahman b. Isaac	d. *c.* 356	fat tail
(4)	R. Sheshet son of R. Idi	end of fourth century	beheaded heifer
(5)	Rabbah b. Shila	third to fourth century	red heifer
(6)	R. Aha bar Jacob	fourth century	scapegoat
(7)	R. Mari	beginning of fourth century	smiting father
(8)	R. Kahana	uncertain which	murderer
(9)	Ravina	fifth century	false witnesses
(10)	R. Ashi	fifth century	*sheḥitah*

The Amoraím mentioned could not have presented their proofs together in the same time and place. Some two hundred years divide the earliest from the latest. Nor, as can be seen from the table, are the proofs presented in chronological order. The only way to understand the series is that each Amora offered his proof independently of the others and these were later put together in this order by the editors. Why did they choose this particular order?

A careful examination of the proofs and the discussion on them uncovers the pattern. Thus: (1) is refuted because the head of the burnt-offering can be split open, as the Talmud observes, and this does not offend against the prohibition of cutting the pieces into further pieces. Very well, it is implied, you have refuted proof (1) but we now adduce proof (2), to which your refutation will not apply. Here the term is 'breaking' and would presumably include splitting. The refutation is that the burning of the bone does not constitute 'breaking'. Very well, we adduce proof (3). Here the tail must be whole and this would presumably exclude any type of severance. No, it would not include partial cutting. Very well, we adduce (4). Here the heifer must be as intact afterwards as it was at the time it was beheaded and this presumably excludes any interference with it. This stands, though not without us having to face the difficulty of proof that the heifer has to be *kasher*. (5) is now adduced, which also stands but which has to face the same difficulty of proof. (6) is now adduced. Again this stands but only after difficulties have been raised. All these are proofs from kindred matters, sacrifices and animals that are treated as sacrifices. We now adduce (7), dealing with a law other than sacrifice, but to do with execution. This stands, but has to face objections. We now adduce another proof having to do with execution, (8), as if to say, even if in (7) circumstances can be found where it is certain that the man is his father, what of (8) where there can be no certainty, only probability. (According to the reading which omits the conclusion of (7), as above, (7) is, in fact, refuted, hence the need for further proof.) This stands, but has to face the objection that possibly an examination can be made after death. We now adduce (9), where the victim must be alive and so cannot possibly be examined. We now adduce (10) to which, unlike *all* the others, even those that stand, no objection whatsoever can be raised. This clinches the argument.

Thus the sequence of thought is completely logical, but can only be understood as an artificial arrangement of earlier material to produce this literary pattern. The Amoraím themselves obviously did not present their proofs in response to the difficulties they found in each other's statements. Even if they all lived at the same time and in the same place, which they did not, this would have involved the preposterous notion that each presented his proof in such neat order that (2) was able to take the matter up where (1) left off; (3) where (2) left off; and so on in neat sequence. It must be as clear as can be that the editors have re-shaped the material they had so as to provide a dramatic sequence of thought. In other words, we have here a contrived literary unit constructed out of the raw materials. It is tempting, but would be hypercritical, to suggest that the editors made it all up out of their own heads, attaching names at random to the series of proofs. There is too much circumstantial evidence for that, though the fact that there is a round number of proofs, ten, a number of significance in Jewish thought, may not be entirely coincidental. In any event, the basic statements of the Amoraím have been elaborated on and a framework of a literary nature provided to produce a literary unit, the proofs being presented *as if* each Amora took up the matter where the previous one has left off.

It remains only to be noted that the mnemonic at the beginning of the *sugya*, in brackets, for the whole series of proofs, is undoubtedly post-Talmudic and must have been composed some time after the *sugya* was complete in its present form.

6

Davar she-lo ba le-'olam: conveyance of a thing not yet in existence

The *sugya* described here is *Kiddushin* 62a–63a. The *sugya* is appended to the Mishnah which rules as follows. If a man betroths a woman and one of them is a Gentile but he declares that he wishes the betrothal to take effect after his or her conversion to Judaism, the betrothal is invalid. Similarly, if he is a slave but he declares that he wishes the betrothal to take effect after he or she has been freed, it is invalid. Two further cases are: a man betroths a married woman, the betrothal to take effect when her husband dies; or a man betroths his wife's sister, the betrothal to take effect when his wife dies. Finally, there is the case of a man who declares to his neighbour: 'If your wife will give birth to a girl she is betrothed to me.' In all these cases the betrothal is invalid on the following principle: that which cannot take effect now because of some major legal objection does not take effect even when that obstacle is no more.

Davar she-lo ba le-'olam, the term used in our *sugya*, means literally 'a thing that has not yet come into the world'. The question is whether the conveyancing or transfer of something or of something being effected is valid if the thing is not yet in existence. This is formulated by the Amoraím as: 'a man can transfer [lit. 'make another acquire'] a thing not yet in existence [*adam makneh davar she-lo ba le-'olam*]' or 'a man cannot transfer a thing not yet in existence [*eyn adam makneh davar she-lo ba le-'olam*].' The Amoraím examine various Tannaitic statements from which the conclusion is drawn that some Tannaím hold that a man can transfer something not yet in existence while others hold that he cannot. The reasons for the debate are not state explicitly in the Talmud but the later commentators are in all probability correct when they see it as depending on whether or not there is sufficient consent and intention where the transfer is of a thing that is not yet in existence. For an effect to be recognised as valid in law, when that effect requires the intention and consent of a person, this intention and consent must be given without equivocation. In normal instances of transfer it can be assumed that it is being done with the full degree of consent required. But where the thing to be transferred or brought into effect is not yet in existence there may be sufficient mental reservations, precisely because the thing is not in existence, to interfere with the degree of consent and intention required. Instances of this debate cover every type of acquisition, *kinyan*. Thus, is the cases dealt with in the Mishnah, the concern is with the 'acquisition' of a wife, i.e. the valid betrothal of a woman so that she becomes a married woman in the eyes of the law and cannot marry another without the bill of divorce, the *get*. Since the Mishnah rules, in the cases recorded there, that the betrothal is invalid, it is said that the Mishnah follows the opinion: *eyn adam makneh davar she-lo ba le-'olam*, 'a man cannot cause a thing not yet in the world to be acquired'. For instance, where the man is at present a Gentile, who cannot effect a valid betrothal, the woman he wishes to 'acquire', that is to betroth, the woman he can legitimately betroth in Jewish law, does not exist at the time of the betrothal. He wishes, therefore, his present act to take effect with regard to something not yet in existence. Since the reason why the betrothal is ineffective in the Mishnah and the transfer is ineffective in other cases of *davar she-lo ba le-'olam* is because the requisite degree of consent and intention is lacking, it follows that in all such cases where circumstances can easily be brought about for the thing to come into existence, there is good reason to suppose that intention and consent are not lacking. This helps us to appreciate why the whole of our *sugya* implies that even according to those authorities who hold that the transaction is invalid, there are circumstances (where the effect can easily be produced), where it will be valid. Conversely, it is implied, even those authorities who hold that normally the transaction is valid, even if the thing is not yet in existence, may agree if the circumstances are such that there are difficulties of one kind or another which prevent the thing not yet in existence from coming easily into existence.

The *sugya* opens with a discussion on a Mishnah (*Terumot* 1:5) dealing with *terumah*, the tithe given to the priest. Untithed produce (*tevel*) must not be eaten. The effect of the separation of the *terumah* and the other tithes is thus to permit the rest of the produce to be eaten. Any produce separated as *terumah* may only be eaten by a priest. A further rule is that *terumah* is only to be separated when the produce has been harvested, detached from the soil. If a farmer declares that a portion of his crops growing in the field should be *terumah* his declaration is ineffective. The field remains in its untithed state and, when it is harvested, the tithes will have to be given. The Mishnah rules: '*Terumah* from unattached produce cannot be separated for attached produce and if it has been separated it is not *terumah*.' The meaning is, if the farmer took some of his unattached produce, produce that had been harvested, and declared it to be *terumah* for the produce still attached to the soil (i.e. to exempt him from giving further *terumah* from the attached produce), this is invalid since there is no obligation to separate *terumah* while the produce is still attached to the soil. Consequently, the act of separation has no validity. The attached produce will still require to be tithed when it is eventually harvested and the amount of unattached produce that has been separated as *terumah* does not, in fact, become *terumah* and even the priest may not eat it, since it is still *tevel*.

A problem, arising out of the Mishnaic rule, is set by the third-century Palestinian Amora, R. Assi, to his teacher, R. Johanan. We have noted that *terumah* from unattached produce cannot be separated for attached produce and the same would apply if *terumah* is separated from attached produce for unattached. But suppose the farmer declared at the time of separation that his intention is not for the *terumah* to become such immediately but rather when the produce will be detached from the soil. At present it cannot be *terumah* since there is no tithing for produce attached to the soil. Equally obvious is the fact that he can, of course, separate the *terumah* later when it does become detached. R. Assi's problem is whether or not the present separation, with the express intention of its taking effect when the produce will become detached, makes the produce separated become *terumah* retrospectively, when eventually the produce does become detached. The detached produce is not yet in existence in its detached *terumah*-liable stage so that the question would seem to depend on whether or not we follow the opinion of those who hold that an effect can be brought about even though its object is not yet in existence – *adam makneh davar she-lo ba le-'olam.* R. Johanan replies that it would be effective even according to the authorities who hold that there can be no transfer of a thing not yet in existence – *eyn adam makneh davar she-lo ba le-'olam.* R. Johanan's reason is that 'it is in his hand', i.e. it lies in the power of the farmer to detach the produce from the soil. Consequently, although the detached produce is not yet in existence it can easily come into existence, depending as it does solely on the act of the person concerned, the farmer. R. Johanan's formulation is: 'Whatever is now in his hand [in his power to do] is not treated as something which requires an act [to bring it into being].' R. Assi seeks to refute R. Johanan's argument from our Mishnah. The Mishnah rules in all the cases it considers that the betrothal is invalid because all the cases are those of *davar she-lo ba le-'olam.* But one of the cases is that of the Gentile who wishes the betrothal to take effect when he becomes converted to Judaism. Surely, objects R. Assi, this lies entirely in his own power and according to R. Johanan the betrothal ought to be valid. The reply given on R. Johanan's behalf is that R. Hiyya bar Abba has stated in the name of R. Johanan himself that a Court composed of three Jews is required for a conversion to be valid. Hence it does not lie in the power of the Gentile to become converted. He requires the cooperation of the three who will constitute the Court to accept him and their cooperation does not depend on him but on their own choice.

The comment (Soncino, p. 313, note 3) that 'the answer given here shews that one encountered real difficulties before he could be converted, and was often denied it altogether' is way off the mark. The Talmud says nothing at all here about the difficulties of conversion to Judaism. All the Talmud means is that since a Court has first to be constituted it does not lie in the power of the Gentile alone to become converted to Judaism and hence the case in the Mishnah is not analogous to that of separating *terumah*, where it depends solely on the farmer and on no other to detach the produce from the soil.

An objection is now raised by the Palestinian Amora, R. Abba bar Memel (third to fourth century). R. Johanan has stated that the act is effective, even where the thing is not yet in existence, if it lies in the power of the person concerned to bring the thing into existence and so produce the effect. In that case it should follow that if the owner of a slave-girl betroths her, the betrothal to take effect after he has granted her her manumission, the betrothal should be valid (i.e. and it is notorious that it is, in fact, invalid). In other words, if R. Johanan is correct, the rule in the Mishnah would only apply to the man who betrothed a slave-girl owned by another. Where he himself was the owner the betrothal ought to be effective since it depends entirely on him to grant her her freedom and so change her status to one in which she can be betrothed. To this the Talmud replies: 'In that case there is an animal whereas now there is another's consent.' The meaning of this is, the slave-girl's status, while she is still a slave is, *vis-à-vis* the owner, that of an 'animal', i.e. she has no powers of consent, she is owned by her master, whereas after her manumission she becomes in law a fully fledged human being with independent powers of consent. Consequently, although it does lie in the power of her owner to free her, it is still considered to be a case of *davar she-lo ba le-'olam*, since her new status will be so entirely different from her present status (i.e. unlike the status of the produce which lacks only detachment from the soil and which, apart from this, has the same status now as later).

A saying of the third-century Palestinian Amora, R. Oshea, is now quoted. R. Oshea said that if a man betroths his own wife, the betrothal to take effect after he has divorced her, the betrothal is invalid. But according to R. Johanan's reasoning it ought to be effective since the husband does have the power to divorce his wife (i.e. and it is different from the case of the slave-girl in that the wife *now* has the same powers of consent that she will have later so that no violent change of status is involved as it is in the case of the slave-girl). To this the reply is given that although the husband does have it in his power to divorce his wife, he does not have it in his power to make her consent to the betrothal once he has divorced her. No woman can be betrothed without her consent. Here it is a case of *davar she-lo ba le-'olam*, since the desired effect cannot be produced by the husband alone, unlike the case of the produce where it depends entirely on the farmer himself. (The Talmud could have given this reply to the earlier question regarding the slave-girl. It is not in his power to make her consent to the subsequent betrothal. Evidently, at first the Talmud thought that, since the act of manumission depends solely on the owner, the need for her subsequent consent to the betrothal does not matter since the non-existence of the thing has, as it were, been weakened. Now that the Talmud does introduce this idea that the woman's consent is required, the same reply can be given in the case of the slave-girl; see the *Tosafists* s.v. *nehi de-veyado.*) In that case, the Talmud continues, we can solve a problem set by the same R. Oshea. He set the following problem. The smallest coin to effect a betrothal, i.e. given as a token for the act of betrothal, is a *perutah.* Suppose a man gives two *perutot* to a single woman, declaring that he betroths her now with one of these and with the other after he will have divorced her. Is the second betrothal valid? But we have just explained that R. Johanan agrees that where the effect depends on the woman's consent it is a case of *davar she-lo ba le-'olam.* Why, then, is it treated by R. Oshea as problematical? The Talmud replies that the reason why R. Oshea sees the matter as problematical is that where a husband wishes to betroth his own wife, the betrothal to take effect after her divorce, he is seeking to bring about now an effect that is meaningless in law. He is seeking to have a betrothal, albeit a subsequent one, take effect for a woman who is already married to him and that is impossible. Here the wife's later status is certainly a *davar she-lo ba le-'olam.* But in R. Oshea's case the woman is single at the time of the betrothal and here it can possibly be argued that, since she can be validly betrothed now, a betrothal at this time, to take effect after the first betrothal and her divorce from it, can be valid. We thus have three cases of *davar she-lo ba le-'olam*:

(1) R. Johanan: *terumah*: certainly valid, because it lies solely in his power
(2) Betrothal of the man's own wife: certainly invalid, because she may not consent later and cannot now be betrothed
(3) Betrothal of single woman: R. Oshea uncertain, because he can betroth her *now*

A *Baraita* is now quoted in support of R. Johanan. This *Baraita* reads: '*Terumah* must not be separated from produce detached from the soil for produce attached to the soil and if it had been separated it is not *terumah*. How so? If he declared: "Let the detached produce of this furrow be *terumah* for the attached produce of that furrow", or if he declares: "Let the attached produce of this furrow be *terumah* for the detached produce of that furrow", he has said nothing at all. But if he declares: [let it take effect] "When it will be detached" and it was later detached, his declaration stands. R. Eliezer b. Jacob went even further. Even if he declares: "Let the detached produce of this furrow be *terumah* for the attached produce of that furrow" or: "Let the attached produce of this furrow be *terumah* for the detached produce of that furrow [adding in both instances] when the produce will have grown to a third of its full height" and it did grow to a third and was then detached, his declaration stands.' The first part of the *Baraita* thus supports R. Johanan, stating quite explicitly that if the farmer declares that it should be *terumah* when it is detached it is *terumah*, i.e. because it is in his power, as R. Johanan says, to detach it. The second part of the *Baraita*, the ruling of R. Eliezer b. Jacob, goes further. Produce is only liable to tithing when it has grown to at least a third of its full maturity and then detached from the soil. Now while the farmer does have it in his power to detach the produce from the soil, it does not lie in his power to make it grow to the requisite height. Why, then, does R. Eliezer b. Jacob rule that even here it is *terumah*? It can only be because R. Eliezer b. Jacob holds, as *Rashi* observes and as can be seen from the discussion later on in our *sugya*, that a transfer can be effected even if the thing is not yet in existence – *adam makneh davar she-lo ba le-'olam*. Thus the first opinion in the *Baraita* is that a man cannot transfer a *davar she-lo ba le-'olam* except where, as in the case of the *Baraita* and as R. Johanan explains it, it lies in his power to produce the required effect. But R. Eliezer holds that in all circumstances *adam makneh davar she-lo ba le-'olam*.

The puzzling phenomenon that R. Assi's and R. Johanan's formulation is in virtually the same words as the *Baraita* has, in fact, numerous parallels in the Babylonian Talmud, where an Amora makes a statement and it is then said that the same rule is found in a *Baraita* and, so it generally appears, with exactly the same wording. I. H. Weiss, *Dor*, vol. II, pp. 242–4, goes so far as to suggest that these *Baraitot* are not authentic and have been invented or, if they are, the Amoraím have plagiarised them. Abraham Weiss, *le-Ḥeker ha-Talmud*, pp. 35–63, takes strong issue with I. H. Weiss, arguing that the phenomenon is best explained on the grounds of literary transmission and its methods. Sayings of earlier teachers were repeated so often that when the later Amoraím came to render their decisions they would naturally do so in the form in which they had become accustomed to hearing these teachings. See my article 'Are there fictitious Baraitot in the Babylonian Talmud?' in *HUCA*, 42 (1971), 185–96. If this is correct, R. Assi is not here presenting for R. Johanan's consideration an entirely new problem he had made up out of his own head. His use of the expressions found in the *Baraita* shows that R. Assi is really asking R. Johanan whether he, R. Johanan, is aware of an *earlier* distinction that can be made and R. Johanan replies that he is and gives the reason as 'because it lies in his power'. This does not rule out the possibility that the formulation is not R. Assi's own but has been put into his mouth by the editors on the basis of the *Baraita*.

There now follows a debate between the early-fourth-century Babylonian teachers Rabbah and R. Joseph. There are two stages in the growth of produce before it reaches the third-of-its-growth stage. The first of these is called *agam* (interpreted as 'bending'), that is, the first sprouting of the crops when there is sufficient length in the blade to bend it towards its root. The *agam* stage is merely that of the earliest sprouting. The second stage is called *shaḥat*, 'fodder'. The blades are sufficiently long to be suitable when removed for cattle, but are not yet at the stage of a third-of-its-growth. Rabbah argues that even R. Eliezer b. Jacob, who holds that the *terumah* separation is valid, only does so when it has reached the *shaḥat* stage at least. Where it has only reached the *agam* stage even R. Eliezer b. Jacob will agree that it is not *terumah*. But R. Joseph argues that R. Eliezer b. Jacob holds that the *terumah* is valid even at the *agam* stage. The point of this debate is that even those authorities, such as R. Eliezer b. Jacob, who hold that *adam makneh davar she-lo ba le-'olam*, only do so where the thing is, at least, partially in existence. No one holds that something can take effect on a totally non-existent thing. If, for instance, a farmer declared that he wishes his *terumah* to be for produce he will not even have, let alone harvest, until much later, it is obvious that the separation has no validity. Thus there must be some stage of partial existence even according to R. Eliezer b. Jacob and the debate between Rabbah and R. Joseph is whether or not the *agam* stage is to be considered partially existent for the purpose of the law, or totally non-existent.

Now the Mishnah states that when a man declares to his neighbour: 'If your wife will give birth to a girl let her be betrothed unto me' the betrothal is invalid, since if the neighbour's wife is not even pregnant the girl who was later born did not enjoy even partial existence at the time of the declaration. The second-century Palestinian Amora, R. Hanina, explains that if the neighbour's wife was pregnant at the time, the betrothal is valid (because this clause of the Mishnah follows the opinion of R. Eliezer b. Jacob so that where there is partial existence now it is valid). The Talmud comments that according to Rabbah, R. Hanina's comment refers only to where the neighbour's wife's pregnancy was discernible at the time (just as only the *shaḥat* stage suffices in the case of *terumah*) whereas according to R. Joseph the betrothal is valid, if the wife is pregnant, even if her pregnancy was not discernible (which corresponds to the *agam* stage).

A different version of the debate between Rabbah and R. Joseph is now quoted. According to this version all agree that the separation of the *terumah* is only valid, even according to R. Eliezer b. Jacob, if the produce has reached the *shaḥat*, not the *agam*, stage. The debate between Rabbah and R. Joseph concerns another matter. Rabbah holds that even if it has reached the *shaḥat* stage it is only valid if the field is one watered by the rain and requiring no artificial irrigation. The crops of such a field do not generally fail and here, at the *shaḥat* stage, the produce can be said to enjoy partial existence. But the crops of a field requiring artificial irrigation do frequently fail and here it would be invalid even at the *shaḥat* stage. R. Joseph disagrees, holding that no distinction must be made between the two kinds of field. Consequently, the Talmud concludes, R. Hanina's explanation of the Mishnah must refer to where the wife's pregnancy is discernible (since both Rabbah and R. Joseph are now said to require the *shaḥat* stage and reject the *agam* stage), but then the betrothal is valid according to both Rabbah and R. Joseph since a pregnancy takes its course by normal means and is analogous to the field watered by the rain and requiring no artificial methods of irrigation for its growth.

The *sugya* concludes with a statement of Abbaye and a discussion on this. Abbaye observes that there are three Tannaim who hold that a man can effect a transfer of something not yet in existence (*adam makneh davar she-lo ba le-ʻolam*). The three Tannaim are: R. Eliezer b. Jacob (as above); Rabbi (the name given to R. Judah the Prince); and R. Meir. Rabbi's statement occurs in the following context. The verse states: 'Thou shalt not deliver unto his master the servant' (Deuteronomy 23: 15; *The Torah*: Deuteronomy 23: 16). Rabbi applies this verse to a man who buys a slave from his master on the condition that he will set him free and R. Nahman b. Isaac explains this to mean that the buyer states, at the time of the purchase, 'When I buy you, you belong to yourself from now.' Thus it follows that Rabbi holds *adam makneh davar she-lo ba le-ʻolam*, since when the man buys the slave he is still a slave and yet his manumission becomes effective from that time. As for R. Meir, a *Baraita* is quoted in which it is said that R. Meir holds, in all the cases referred to in our Mishnah (betrothal to take place after conversion, after manumission, after the death of the husband, after the death of the wife's sister), that the betrothal is valid. Thus

R. Meir, too, holds that *adam makneh davar she-lo ba le-'olam*. In the same *Baraita* it is stated that R. Judah the Prince holds that in all these cases the betrothal is valid according to Biblical law but that in the case of the husband and wife's sister the Sages refused to countenance the betrothal since to do so would lead to 'enmity', i.e. the husband would become aware that his wife is looking forward to his death and the sister that her husband wishes her to die. The Talmud asks: In that case why does Abbaye refer only to R. Meir in this *Baraita* and not to R. Judah the Prince? The obvious answer is given, Abbaye has already referred to Rabbi, in the other case, and he *is* R. Judah the Prince.

The Talmud now asks why Abbaye does not list the opinion of R. Akiba, who also appears to hold the same opinion as the other three in his list. R. Akiba's statement is found in a Mishnah (*Nedarim* 11: 4). A husband can annul the vows of his wife (Numbers 30). But, the Mishnah rules, if she vows that the work of her hands is forbidden to him there is no need for him to annul the vow since it is invalid in any event. She has no power to impose a vow on the work of her hands since she is obliged to work for her husband by the terms of her marriage contract. She cannot impose a prohibition on something that is not hers. R. Akiba holds that annulment is required since, otherwise, she may provide him by her work with more than that to which he is entitled by law and on this the vow can take effect. Hence, we see that according to R. Akiba a vow can take effect on the work still to be done and this is *davar she-lo ba le-'olam*. The reply is given in the name of R. Huna son of R. Joshua that the Mishnah deals with a wife who declares that her hands be dedicated to their Maker, i.e. it is not the work still to be done upon which she imposes her vow but on the hands themselves. Hence it is not at all a case of *davar she-lo ba le-'olam* and this is why R. Akiba is not mentioned in Abbaye's list of authorities.

Rashi, s.v.*ke-man*, holds that the ruling follows R. Eliezer b. Jacob that *adam makneh davar she-lo ba le-'olam* but the *Tosafists*, s.v. *ve-amar R. Hanina*, hold that the ruling is the opposite. In the case discussed in the Middle Ages and later of a man selling his portion in Paradise, the sale is declared to be invalid in law because, among other reasons, it is a sale of *davar she-lo ba le-'olam*, see *Responsa Meshiv Davar* by N.Z.J. Berlin, part III, no. 14. The relevant material on *davar she-lo ba le-'olam* is given in *ET*, vol. VII, pp. 30–67 and in *Kesef Nivḥar*, no. 37, pp. 58a–63b. *Kesef Nivḥar* observes that the Talmud in general, when dealing with this subject, speaks of three cases: (1) Where the object to be transferred is not yet in existence; (2) Where the one to whom it is to be transferred is not yet in existence; (3) Where a condition is made to depend on something not yet in existence. The main Talmudic passages, in addition to ours, are: *Yevamot* 92b–93b; *Ketubot* 58b–59b; *Nedarim* 85a–86b; *Gittin* 13b; 42b–43a; *Kiddushin* 78b; *Bava Metiz'a* 16b; 66b; *Bava Batra* 63ab; 79a–b; 141b–143a; 157a–b.

7

Kol she-eyno be-zeh aḥar zeu afilu be-vat aḥat eyno: whatever cannot be established in a consecutive sequence cannot be established even in a simultaneous sequence

This is a comparatively brief *sugya*, *Kiddushin* 50b–51a. The meaning of the central term is: where the law is insistent that a certain effect – B – cannot follow another effect – A – then it implies that A and B cannot take effect even when they occur simultaneously. Since the taking effect of A frustrates the taking effect of B and the taking effect of B frustrates the taking effect of A, this frustration operates not only when one follows the others but even when both occur together, even though if each were to occur on its own it would take effect.

The *sugya* is here appended to a Mishnah which reads: 'If a man betroths a woman and her daughter or a woman and her sister simultaneously, they are not betrothed' (i.e. the betrothal is invalid and no *get*, 'bill of divorce', is required before either can marry another). A man cannot betroth his wife's daughter, mother or sister and if he did the act of betrothal is invalid (Leviticus 18: 17–18). This is stated explicitly in the Torah. But the Mishnah goes further to rule that if he betroths a woman and her daughter or two sisters, the betrothal to take effect simultaneously, it is still invalid. The Talmud asks how do we know this law, to which the fourth-century Babylonian Amora, Rmai bar Hama, replies, it is because Scripture states: 'Neither shalt thou take a wife to her sister, to vex her' (Leviticus 18: 18). Rami bar Hama understands this to mean that if a man *takes* (i.e. betroths) a woman and her sister simultaneously (the case in the Mishnah) it is invalid – 'neither shalt thou take'. As Rami bar Hama puts it: 'The Torah said: When they become rivals to one another [i.e. in a simultaneous betrothal] he can have no *taking* of any one of them.' The rule of the Mishnah has thus Scriptural authority according to Rami bar

Hama. Rava objects that the verse cannot possibly mean what Rami bar Hama says it means. The verse does not refer at all to a simultaneous betrothal but to a man who *takes* (i.e. has intercourse with) the sister of a woman he had *previously* married. That this must be correct Rava proves from the verse which occurs at the end of the Levitical list of prohibitions: 'the souls that commit them shall be cut off from among their people' (Leviticus 18: 29). This shows that we are dealing with a man who has intercourse with his wife's sister. For if we are dealing, as Rami bar Hama holds, with a simultaneous betrothal, which the Torah declares to be invalid, there would be no penalty at all if he cohabited with either or, for that matter, with both, since neither is his wife's sister.

Rava, thus dissatisfied with Rami bar Hama's proof, proceeds to advance a different reason for the rule in the Mishnah. Rava argues that the Mishnah is best understood on the basis of his master's principle, that is of Rabbah, who lays down the rule: *kol she-eyno be-zeh aḥar zeh afilu be-vat aḥat eyno*, 'Whatever cannot be established in a consecutive sequence cannot be established even in a simultaneous sequence.' This is a general legal principle laid down by Rabbah and is to be applied to the case in the Mishnah. Since, according to the Biblical law, there is no validity to the betrothal of a wife's sister, it must follow, on Rabbah's principle, that, as the Mishnah states, there is no validity to the simultaneous betrothal of two sisters. If a man first betroths sister A and *subsequently* betroths sister B, the betrothal of sister B is invalid. Consequently, on Rabbah's principle, the betrothal of A and B at the same time has no validity.

The *sugya* now proceeds to examine Rabbah's principle on its own. This is prefaced with the term *gufa*, 'the main statement', used in the Talmud whenever a statement referred to incidentally in the course of a discussion is then examined on its own. Abbaye raises an objection from a *Baraita* (*Tosefta, Demai* 8: 13). This *Baraita* deals with the laws of tithing produce. The tithes are: *terumah*, a 40th, 50th or 60th, given to the priest; *ma'aser rishon*, 'the first tithe', a tenth of the remainder of the produce, given to a Levite; *ma'aser sheni*, 'the second tithe', a tenth of the remainder, it or its value, to be taken to Jerusalem and consumed there. Any produce from which the tithes have not been separated is known as *tevel*, 'untithed produce', and is forbidden to be eaten. It is the *separation* of the tithes which removes the prohibition from *tevel*, not the actual giving to the priest or Levite. *Terumah* may only be eaten by a priest but *ma'aser rishon*, though it must be given to the Levite, may be eaten by a non-Levite. Once *ma'aser rishon* has been separated it is no longer *tevel*, i.e. the Levite is not obliged to separate from it *ma'aser sheni*, though he is obliged to separate a tenth for the priest, known as *terumat ma'aser*, 'the terumah given from *ma'ser*'. The *Baraita* deals with the case of a farmer who separated more than a tenth for *ma'aser rishon* and the *Baraita* rules that if he did this the remainder of the produce is considered to be tithed, and may be eaten once *ma'aser sheni* has been separated, but the amount separated as *ma'aser rishon* is not treated as *ma'aser rishon*. The Levite may not eat of it, even after he has separated *terumat ma'aser*, since there is more than a tenth of the farmer's produce and this surplus is *tevel*. The Levite has now in his possession an admixture of *ma'aser rishon*, which he may eat, and *tevel*, which he may not eat. The farmer (or, possibly, the Levite) must now separate as *ma'aser sheni* an amount proportionate to the surplus in the hands of the Levite, in addition to the amount he separates as *ma'aser sheni* to free his own produce from the prohibition of *tevel*. The same rule would apply if the farmer separated more than a tenth for *ma'aser sheni*, there would be an admixture of *ma'aser sheni* and ordinary food but here there would be no practical difference since ordinary food may, of course, be eaten in Jerusalem and, once *ma'aser sheni* has been separated, there is no longer any prohibition of *tevel*.

See *Meíri* for a further discussion of what the Levite is to do with the admixture and that some hold that there is no remedy at all for the admixture, not as we have explained it here.

In any event, we see from the *Baraita* that the tithing is effective so far as the remainder of the produce is concerned. But, Abbaye objects, if Rabbah is correct, the tithing should be null and void. If a man separates an exact tenth as *ma'aser rishon* and then separates some more of the produce for the same *ma'aser* it is obvious that the second separation has no validity. Once the *ma'aser* has been separated there is no meaning to the separation of a further quantity for the same purpose. Consequently, tithing is an effect that cannot take place consecutively and, according to Rabbah, it cannot therefore take place simultaneously. Since this is so why is the amount separated, too large for *ma'aser*, treated as *ma'aser* at all? To this the reply is given that *ma'aser* is in a totally different category. A man can separate his *ma'aser* by giving half of the grains. Consequently, when the *ma'aser* has been separated together with a surplus it is incorrect to see this as the simultaneous separation of *two* amounts of *ma'aser* so that Rabbah's principle would come into operation. All that is, in fact, separated is a single tithe cutting across the grains, as it were, the remainder being the surplus. But where a man betroths two sisters it is absurd to say that there is only a single betrothal of two halves of the sisters. Here, indeed, there is the simultaneous betrothal of two and here Rabbah's principle comes into operation.

The Talmud objects that this reply seems to be contradicted by Rabbah himself in a ruling of his regarding the tithing of cattle. Cattle is tithed in the following way. Tha animals are passed one by one through a narrow gate, the farmer counting from one to ten. Each tenth animal to pass through the gate is marked and is later offered as a sacrifice. If the farmer counted, in error, the tenth animal as the ninth and the eleventh as the tenth, the law is that the eleventh animal is not *ma'aser* ('animal tithe'), since it is not, in fact, the tenth, but is still sacred and has to be offered as *shelamin*, 'a peace-offering'. Rabbah's ruling concerns two animals that came through the gate together, after the farmer had counted nine, and he declared them both to be *ma'aser*. One of these, rules Rabbah, is *ma'aser* and the other *shelamin*. Since they both came out together after the ninth, we cannot, in fact, determine which is *ma'aser* and which *shelamin*, so the following procedure is adopted. The animals are left alone until they become blemished and as such no longer fit for sacrifice. A sum of money is then taken and the sanctity of the blemished *shelamin* is redeemed with this sum, the money being used to buy another animal to be offered as *shelamin*. As for the *ma'aser*, no redemption is required, the rule being that a blemished *ma'aser* animal loses its sanctity and may be eaten without redemption. From Rabbah's ruling here we see that when two animals both come through the gate after the farmer has counted nine and where he declared both to be *ma'aser*, one of them does become *ma'aser*. But since *ma'aser* cannot be effected consecutively (i.e. if ten had been counted and the tenth animal became *ma'aser* there would obviously be no significance to the act if the farmer declares the eleventh one, too, to be *ma'aser*), it should not take effect simultaneously (i.e. and here the previous reply is inapplicable, since half animals cannot be brought as sacrifices).

The reply to this is given by quoting a Mishnah (*Bekhorot* 9: 8) in which the rule is stated that if the farmer, in error, counted the tenth animal as the ninth (i.e. imagining it to be the ninth when in reality it was the tenth) it becomes *ma'aser*. We see from this that *ma'aser* can take effect even in error and hence it can take effect simultaneously. The meaning here would seem to be, since *ma'aser* can so easily be effected (even in error), that Rabbah's principle does not apply. Here even though it cannot take effect consecutively it can still take effect simultaneously. Rabbah's principle does not mean that *because* the effect cannot take place consecutively *therefore* it cannot take place even simultaneously. Rabbah's principle only means that since it cannot take place consecutively this is an *indication* that it does not take place even simultaneously. Thus there can be exceptions to Rabbah's principle and *ma'aser*, which can take effect so readily, even in error, is such an exception. But betrothal cannot be effected in error and hence, in the case of the two sisters, Rabbah's principle does apply.

So far we have managed to cope with two objections to Rabbah's principle. The principle does not operate, the Talmud has suggested in reply, in the case of *ma'aser* of produce, because half-grains can become *ma'aser* and in the case of animal *ma'aser* because it can become effective even in error. It follows that if it can be shown that there is a case in which the effect cannot come about either in error or by halves and there is, none the less, a ruling in such a case that it can take place simultaneously, even though it cannot take place consecutively, Rabbah will have been refuted. The Talmud now proceeds to demonstrate that there is such a case.

The case is that of a thanksgiving offering. Together with the animal sacrifice 40 loaves have to be brought. As soon as the animal is slaughtered in the Temple the loaves become automatically sanctified as thanksgiving loaves and can then only be eaten by the priests. The sanctification of the loaves cannot take effect by halves, i.e. 80 half-loaves cannot be sanctified, nor can it be in error, i.e. if at the time of the sacrifice the intention was for 40 dark loaves to be sanctified and the loaves there were, in fact, light coloured, these loaves have no sanctity. There is a debate between the early third-century Palestinian Amoraím, Hezekiah and R. Johanan, regarding a thanksgiving offering that was sacrificed together with 80 loaves. Hezekiah holds that 40 of these do become sanctified but R. Johanan holds that none of the loaves become sanctified. Now it is obvious that if 40 loaves had first been sanctified and it was then declared that another 40 be sanctified, the second 40 have no sanctification. How can they have any sanctity, since there is no longer any thanksgiving offering to sanctify them? Since this is so, Rabbah's principle ought to operate. Since the second 40 cannot become sanctified *after* the first 40, there ought to be no sanctification of any of the loaves where all 80 are brought together. In other words it would appear from the debate between Hezekiah and R. Johanan that only the latter agrees with Rabbah's principle and this is unlikely. (*Rashi* adds that since Hezekiah is the teacher of R. Johanan it is unlikely, if he rejects Rabbah's principle, that Rabbah would still maintain it merely because of the opinion of the disciple, R. Johanan.)

To this the reply is given that the debate between Hezekiah and R. Johanan is not at all what it appears to be on the surface. The third-century Palestinian Amora, R. Zera, has, in fact, explained, in any event, that if the man intended only 40 of the 80 loaves to be sanctified they are sanctified and on this there can be no disagreement. Conversely, if the man's intention was to sanctify all 80 loaves there can be no disagreement that, as Rabbah's principle states, there is no sanctification whatsoever, not even of 40 of the loaves. The debate is only where the man brought 80 loaves but did not reveal his intention in bringing 80 instead of 40. Hezekiah holds in this case that the man's intention was to bring only 40 loaves to be sanctified; the reason why he brought, in fact, 80 was solely in order to have 40 loaves to fall back on if the first 40 were lost or destroyed. R. Johanan, on the other hand, holds that, since the man brought 80 loaves, we are justified in assuming that his intention was for all 80 to be sanctified and this is ineffective because of Rabbah's principle.

The *sugya* now reverts to the original attempts at explaining the Mishnah. Rava, disagreeing with Rami bar Hama's attempt, explains the Mishnaic rule on the basis of Rabbah's principle. Now in the following *sugya* (*Kiddushin* 51a) there is a debate between Abbaye and Rava regarding the case of a man who betroths one of two sisters, that is to say, he declares: 'One of you be betrothed to me' without specifying any particular one. Abbaye holds that in this case the betrothal is valid in the sense that neither of the sisters can marry another without a *get* from the man who betrothed one of them. Rava disagrees, holding the betrothal to be invalid because it is: 'a betrothal that cannot lead to intercourse' (*kiddushin she-eyn mesurin le-viah*). The purpose of betrothal is to lead eventually to intercourse so that, according to Rava, it is reasonable to conclude that any betrothal which by its very nature precludes intercourse (as here, where, if the betrothal is valid, he will not be allowed to have intercourse with either since she may be his wife's sister) is bound to be invalid. Since this is Rava's view, the Talmud asks, why does he have to explain the ruling in the Mishnah on the basis of Rabbah's principle? The Mishnah is perfectly intelligible on the basis of Rava's own principle. If, as Rava holds, the betrothal of even one of two sisters is invalid, the betrothal of both is invalid *a fortiori*. The reply given is that, indeed, Rava can explain the Mishnah perfectly well on his own premiss. He only invokes Rabbah's principle for the benefit of Rami bar Hama who, by seeking a Scriptural verse for the Mishnaic rule, evidently does not agree with Rava's principle. Rava is saying, in so many words, 'I personally have no difficulty in explaining the Mishnah but you evidently do not agree with me and do have a difficulty. The only way out of the difficulty for you is not to rely on the verse you quote, which you fail to understand, but to rely on Rabbah's principle.'

Rabbah's principle is referred to in only two other Talmudic passages: '*Eruvin* 49a–50a and *Nedarim* 69b. The '*Eruvin* passage contains, with only very minor variants, the whole discussion, as in our passage, from *gufa* to the debate between Hezekiah and R. Johanan inclusive. This section is also prefaced by *gufa*. This is important for the literary analysis of the Talmud in that it clearly demonstrates that the editors had before them this whole section as a complete unit, which they then inserted in *Kiddushin* and '*Eruvin*, in both instances after there had been an incidental reference to Rabbah's principle. The *Nedarim* is very brief and deals with a husband's annulment of his wife's vow (Numbers 30). The annulment by a husband of his wife's vow is effective if he performs the annulment within 24 hours of hearing of the vow. This is known as *hafarah*, 'annulment'. If, however, when he hears of the vow, the husband declares that he wishes the vow to stand, he no longer has the power of annulment. This is known as *hakamah*, 'establishment (of the vow)'. A problem set by Rabbah in *Nedarim* is: what is the law if a husband declared that his intention was for the vow both to be annulled and stand, i.e. he declared: 'Let there be *hakamah* and *hafarah* simultaneously'? The Talmud states that the problem can be solved on the basis of Rabbah's own principle of *kol she-eyno be-zeh aḥar zeh afilu be-vat aḥat eyno*. There can be no *hakamah* after *hafarah* (since the *hafarah* has cancelled out the vow, there is no longer any vow to be established) and there can be no *hafarah* after *hakamah* (since that is precisely what *hakamah* means, that the vow stands and can no longer be annulled). Consequently, Rabbah's principle applies. Since the two cannot take effect consecutively they cannot take effect simultaneously. On the face of it, and as the *Ran* ad loc. holds, this means that *neither* is effective and it is as if the husband had said nothing at all. The vow has not been annulled but neither has it been established and the husband, within 24 hours, has the right either to establish it or to annul it. But Maimonides (*Yad*, *Nedarim* 13: 22) rules that the *hakamah* stands but not the *hafarah*. The *Ran* and other commentators find Maimonides' ruling very puzzling. Since neither *hakamah* nor *hafarah* can take effect after the other has taken effect, then, on Rabbah's principle which the Talmud applies to the case, *neither* should take effect when they occur simultaneously. R. Hayyim Soloveitchik, *Ḥiddushey Rabbenu Ḥayyim ha-Levi*, *Nedarim*, pp. 37 a–b, very ingeniously suggests that, in Maimonides' understanding, the Talmudic application of Rabbah's principle only refers to *hafarah* not to *hakamah*. The argument is as follows. The reason why there can be no *hafarah* after *hakamah* is because that is precisely what *hakamah* signifies, the rejection of any further possibility of *hafarah*. Hence Rabbah's principle applies. Since *hafarah* cannot take effect after *hakamah* it cannot take effect together with *hakamah*. The reason why there can be *hakamah* after *hafarah*, on the other hand, is not because in essence *hafarah* prevents *hakamah* from taking effect but simply because once *hafarah* has taken effect there is no longer any vow. Consequently, here Rabbah's principle does not operate since, in essence, there can be *hakamah* after *hafarah*, i.e. there is no basic principle that *hafarah* itself frustrates *hakamah*. Therefore, according to Maimonides, the *hakamah* does stand since with regard to *hakamah* Rabbah's principle does not apply. Rabbi A. I. Karelitz, in his notes to *Ḥiddushey Rabbenu Ḥayyim ha-Levi*, entitled *Ḥazon Ish* (end of volume, pp. 8–9), finds R. Hayyim's distinction contradicted by our *sugya*. In the case of *ma'aser* the reason the second separation of the same *ma'aser* is ineffective is not because of the first separation in itself but simply because once *ma'aser* has been separated the produce is no longer subject to tithes! It is possible that Maimonides is making a rather different distinction. In all the cases considered in our *sugya* of A followed by B there is no difference whatsoever between A and B, except that A happens to be first. For instance, in the case of the two sisters, the betrothal of sister B cannot take place after the betrothal of sister A but if the betrothal of sister B had taken place first exactly the same obstacle would have been provided to the betrothal of sister A. Similarly, in the case of *ma'aser* the first tenth prevents the second from taking effect, but only because the first tenth is the *first* tenth and similarly with regard to the animal tithe and the 40 loaves. Hence here B frustrates A as much as A frustrates B and hence Rabbah's principle applies. The two frustrate one another and so cannot take effect simultaneously. But in the *Nedarim* case the difference between *hakamah* and *hafarah* is not only which came first. The function of the two is different. The function of *hakamah* is to frustrate *hafarah* whereas the function of *hafarah* is, as R. Hayyim notes, simply to remove the vow. It follows that it is the *hakamah* that frustrates the *hafarah*, not the other way round. Consequently, Rabbah's principle does apply to *hafarah* but not to *hakamah* as Maimonides rules.

8

Yesh ḥoresh telem eḥad: a single act of ploughing can result in a number of penalties

The main *sugya* is *Makkot* 21b–22a, though there is a reference also in *Pesaḥim* 47a–b. The general principle is that an offence against a Biblical, negative precept renders the offender liable to a flogging. Even if a single act is performed but the act offends against a number of negative precepts, there is a separate penalty of flogging for each offence.

In the Mishnah, to which the *sugya* is appended, it is stated that it is possible for a man to plough a single furrow (*yesh ḥoresh telem eḥad*) and yet be liable (to a flogging) for offending against eight separate, negative precepts. The man ploughs with an ox and an ass yoked together (Deuteronomy 22: 10) and they are sacred animals dedicated to the Temple (Deuteronomy 15: 19). At the time of ploughing he sows seeds in a vineyard (Deuteronomy 22: 9), i.e. as the Talmud explains, while ploughing he covers the seeds with the earth the plough throws up, which falls under the definition of 'sowing'. It is, moreover, the Sabbatical year in which it is forbidden to sow (Leviticus 25: 4) and it is a Festival on which work is forbidden (Leviticus 23). The plougher is in a field in which corpses are buried and he thus contaminates himself through contact with a grave and he is a priest (Leviticus 21: 1–3) and a Nazirite (Numbers 6) to whom such contact is forbidden. The eight prohibitions are thus: (1) ploughing with an ox and an ass; (2) ploughing with a sacred ox; (3) ploughing with a sacred ass; (4) sowing mixed seeds in a vineyard; (5) sowing on the Sabbatical year; (6) sowing on the Festival; (7) a priest contaminating himself; (8) a Nazirite contaminating himself. R. Hanania b. Hakhinai adds a ninth prohibition: the plougher is wearing at the time a garment of wool and linen (Deuteronomy 22: 11). The Sages refuse to count this since it is an offence totally unconnected with the ploughing. But H. Hanania retorts that neither have the offences of the priest and Nazirite anything to do with ploughing. The distinction made, none the less, by the Sages is obvious. The prohibition of wearing the garment has nothing whatsoever to do with the act of ploughing. Even if the man wore no garment at all his ploughing would be unaffected. But although the prohibition of contamination in itself has nothing to do with his ploughing, yet were it not for the ploughing he would not have entered the place in which he suffers contamination. The *sugya* opens with a report by the late-second, early-third-century Palestinian Amora, R. Jannai, that a group of Sages had met and decided that there is a penalty of flogging for one who covers mixed seeds in a vineyard with earth, as this constitutes 'sowing'. R. Johanan objects that there is no need for R. Jannai's statement in the name of the group. The ruling can be inferred from the Mishnah, one of whose prohibitions is that of ploughing in a vineyard, which can only be on the grounds of 'sowing', as above. R. Jannai replies that, indeed, this ruling can be inferred from the Mishnah but he claims that it is his report that has provided R. Johanan with the clue. As R. Jannai is said to have put it: 'If I had not raised the shard for you, you would not have discovered the pearl beneath it.' Resh Lakish demurs, that, were it not for the fact that 'a great man', R. Jannai, had praised R. Johanan's perspicacity in inferring it from the Mishnah, it could have been argued that there is no proof to the ruling from the Mishnah. A *Baraita* is quoted in which R. Akiba holds that even to preserve mixed seeds in a vineyard, e.g. by weeding the vineyard so that the seeds can grow there, renders the perpetrator liable to a flogging. Consequently, the Mishnah might follow the opinion of R. Akiba and the offence is not because of 'sowing' but because of 'preserving'. If this is correct, it can be argued, the Sages, who disagree with R. Akiba and do not admit that there is any prohibition of 'preserving', may hold that neither is any prohibition of 'sowing' incurred merely by covering the seeds with earth. Hence, R. Jannai's report is required, that even according to the Sages, who admit no prohibition of 'preserving', there is a prohibition on the grounds of 'sowing'. The Talmud rounds off this section by quoting a *Baraita* in which R. Akiba supports his view by referring to a Biblical text.

See *Tosafists Bava Metzi'a* 17b s.v. *i lav*, that one does not normally find pearls under a shard. The *Tosafists* suggest that the reference is to a shard-like stone at the bottom of the sea under which pearls are sometimes found and refers to *Bava Kama* 91a: 'You have dived into deep waters and have only succeeded in bringing up a shard.' Possibly, however, the 'shard' is the oyster shell and the meaning in *Bava Kama* is: 'You have dived into deep waters to no avail because all you have brought up is a shell containing no pearl' and the meaning here would, then, be: 'If I had not brought up the shell you would not have discovered the pearl it contains.'

At this stage a discussion is introduced among fourth- and fifth-century Amoraím. We have established that the act of covering the seeds is considered to be 'sowing'. Now if it constitutes 'sowing' with regard to seeds in a vineyard, it must also constitute 'sowing' with regard to a Festival. In that case, Ulla asks R. Nahman, there are nine prohibitions, not eight, since in addition to the offence of ploughing on the Festival there is the offence of sowing on the Festival. To this R. Nahman replies that the Tanna of the Mishnah does not exhaust all the instances and could have included the instance of sowing on the Festival but chose instead to omit this. Ulla refuses to accept R. Nahman's reply. The Tanna in the Mishnah states explicitly that there are *eight* prohibitions; *eight*, surely, means eight, and not nine.

Rava (variant reading Rabbah) gives a different reply to the question why the Mishnah does not count sowing on the Festival. Rava argues that although with regard to the Sabbath there is a separate penalty for each type of work, even when several of these were carried out together, yet with regard to a Festival 'there is no division of work', i.e. although two separate offences, that of ploughing and of sowing have been committed, since these were carried out at the same time, there is only one penalty, for working on the Festival. To this Abbaye raises an objection from a *Baraita*. The *Baraita* states that if a man on a Festival day boils the sciatic sinew in milk and then eats it, he incurs five penalties of flogging: for eating the sciatic sinew (Genesis 32:32; *The Torah*: Genesis 32:33); for cooking food unnecessarily on the Festival (i.e. only food that can be eaten on the Festival may be cooked and the sinew may not be eaten at all); for boiling meat and milk together (Exodus 23:19; 34:26; Deuteronomy 14:21 are interpreted by the Rabbis as prohibiting the boiling of any meat and milk together and the eating of the result); for eating meat boiled in milk (as above); and for kindling a fire on the Festival. From this *Baraita* we see that there is a separate penalty for cooking on the Festival and for kindling a fire, which refutes Rava. To this the reply is given that the *Baraita* must be emended. The fifth prohibition is not for kindling a fire on the Festival but the *Baraita* should read instead that we are dealing with one who cooks a sciatic sinew of carrion and the offence is an additional one of eating, not of cooking, that of eating carrion (Deuteronomy 14: 21). To this it is objected that R. Hiyya has taught in a *Baraita*, commenting on the previous *Baraita*, that, of the five prohibitions, three are for cooking and two for eating. But if the *Baraita* is emended as suggested it emerges that there are only two prohibitions for cooking and three for eating. In reply a different emendation is suggested. Instead of kindling fire on a Festival the *Baraita* should be emended to include kindling with wood from an *asherah* (a tree sacred to idolatrous worship) of which Scripture states: 'And there shall cleave nought of the cursed thing to thine hand' (Deuteronomy 13: 17; *The Torah*: Deuteronomy 13: 18). There are now, as R. Hiyya taught, three prohibitions for cooking and only two for eating.

The Talmud continues with an objection raised by R. Aha son of Rava to R. Ashi. Since at this stage of the argument we have emended the *Baraita* so as to include the wood of an *asherah*, there ought to be another penalty, that of 'Neither shalt thou bring an abomination into thine house' (Deuteronomy 7: 26) which makes a total of six, not five. Hence still another emendation is suggested. Instead of kindling fire on the Festival the *Baraita* deals with a fire kindled with wood belonging to the Sanctuary, which it is forbidden to destroy, since Scripture states: 'And burn their groves with fire [but] Ye shall not do so unto the Lord your God' (Deuteronomy 12: 3–4).

It is perhaps worth noting that although the Amoraím mentioned flourished over a very long period of time and must have presented their arguments over this period, yet the whole passage hangs together as if it had been compiled as a literary unit. First there is the objection, arising out of the previous discussion regarding 'covering' as 'sowing', that there ought, in that case, to be a further Festival prohibition. To this the reply is given that the Tanna omits one. To which it is objected, if the Tanna states that there are *eight* he must mean eight and no more than eight. To which the reply is given, the Mishnah does not count Festival prohibitions as two because there is no division of work on the Festivals. To this the objection is raised, what of the *Baraita* of the sciatic sinew? (This is raised by Abbaye but only makes sense in response to Rava's interpretation which, in turn, only makes sense in response to the earlier discussion.) To this the reply is given, emend the *Baraita* to omit kindling fire on the Festival and to include a further 'eating' prohibition, of carrion. To which it is objected that R. Hiyya states that there are three prohibitions of cooking not of eating. To this the reply is given, kindling is reinstated, but not kindling fire on the Festival but kindling with wood of an *asherah*. At a later date R. Aha son of Rava produces a fatal objection to this reply, in that case there would be six, not five, prohibitions. To which the final reply is given, that kindling is, indeed, reinstated, but not the kindling of fire on the Festival nor the kindling of *asherah* wood but the kindling of wood belonging to the Temple. It is possible, of course, that all this did occur fortuitously over the generations but surely it is far more plausible to see it all as an artificial, contrived re-working of earlier material by the editors so that a clear pattern of argumentation is presented.

The *sugya* now continues with a list of seven Amoraím, each of whom objects that since our Mishnah evidently intends to include every possible case of a prohibition that can be incurred with this single act of ploughing, at least one further prohibition can be found, and why does the Mishnah fail to record this? First, R. Oshia protests that the Mishnah might have included the prohibition of one who sows in a 'rough valley', prohibited by 'which is neither eared nor sown' (Deuteronomy 21: 4). Secondly, R. Hanania protests that there could have been included one who erases a divine name as he ploughs. This merits a flogging because, as above, Scripture states: 'And burn their groves with fire [but] Ye shall not do so unto the Lord your God' (Deuteronomy 12: 3–4). R. Abbahu's objection is that the Mishnah could have included one who cuts away a leprous sore as he ploughs. The prohibition is found in the verse: 'Take heed in the plague of leprosy' (Deuteronomy 24: 8), understood as meaning that the sore must be taken care of i.e. preserved and not cut away. Abbaye finds two further prohibitions the Mishnah could have included. These are: removing, as he ploughs, the breastplate of the High Priest from the ephod, of which Scripture says: 'And ... the breastplate be not loosed' (Exodus 28: 28) and removing, as he ploughs, the staves of the ark from their rings, of which Scripture says: 'they shall not be taken from it' (Exodus 25: 15). R. Ashi's objection is that the Mishnah could have included one who ploughs with a plough made of *asherah* wood, the prohibition being, as above, 'And there shall cleave nought of the cursed thing to thine hand' (Deuteronomy 13: 17; *The Torah*: Deuteronomy 13: 18). Ravina objects that the

Mishnah could have included one who cuts down goodly fruit trees as he ploughs, the prohibition being: 'for thou mayest eat of them, and thou shalt not cut them down' (Deuteronomy 20: 19).

Finally, the objection put by R. Zeira to R. Mani is recorded: let the Mishnah include one who has taken an oath not to plough on a Festival. When he does plough he incurs the further penalty for breaking his oath. The reply is that such an oath has no validity since no oath is binding when it is for the purpose of placing a prohibition on something already forbidden by the Torah. Such an oath is akin to taking an oath to refrain from some act and then taking another oath to refrain from the same act. The second oath has no effect and there is only a penalty for breaking the first oath. Here, too, the man is already besworn not to plough on the Festival since all Isreal has been besworn at Sinai to keep the precepts. But, it is objected, the Mishnah could have included the man who takes a general oath not to plough at all, neither on the Festival nor on week-days. Here, since the oath does take effect so far as the week-days are concerned, it takes effect, too, so far as the Festivals are concerned. The analogy would be with a man who first took an oath not to eat a particular loaf of bread and then took a second oath not to eat any bread. Since the second oath is more embracing than the first it embraces, as it were, that particular loaf of bread as well. A new reply is attempted. The reason the Mishnah does not refer to the case of the oath is because an oath, or, for that matter, any verbal declaration, can be annulled by a Court of three persons if there are good grounds for the annulment. The Mishnah only lists prohibitions which remain permanently, not those that can possibly be annulled. But, in that case, what of the sacred animals mentioned in the Mishnah? The vow by means of which these had been dedicated can be annulled and yet the Mishnah does refer to this type of prohibition. The reply is that the Mishnah deals with an ox that is a first born and is thus dedicated to the Temple automatically. There is no possibility of annulment here since the animal's dedication is not by means of a verbal declaration.

The difficulty here is that the Mishnah mentioned both an ox and an ass. The ox can be a first-born but what of the ass? *Riban*'s commentary 21a s.v. *ve-hen mukdashin*, understands the reference to the ass to be in accordance with the view that there is a Biblical prohibition on working with the first-born of an ass. This is very uncertain, see *Tosafists* s.v. *ha-ḥoresh*, that the Mishnah only refers in fact to an ox that has been dedicated and the total of eight prohibitions is arrived at not by counting the ox and ass as two but by counting mixed seeds in a vineyard as two, one for sowing mixed seeds on their own in any field and one for sowing seeds in a vineyard. Cf. Albeck's *Mishnah*, *Nezikin*, to this Mishnah, *Supplements*, p. 467.

But, it is objected, what of the Nazirite prohibition which the Mishnah mentions. As a verbal declaration, the Nazirite vow can be annulled. To this the reply is given, the Mishnah refers to a Samson type of Nazirite, i.e. a Nazirite who was ordered to become one in a dream, like Samson. Such a Nazirite must observe the rules and cannot hope for annulment since it is not the result of any verbal declaration. But, it is objected, this cannot be, for a Samson Nazirite is not prohibited from becoming contaminated through contact with a corpse, just as we find that Samson himself did allow himself to be contaminated. The final reply is that the reason the Mishnah does not include the case of the man who took an oath is because the Tanna of the Mishnah holds that such an oath is not binding even where the week-days as well as the Festivals were embraced by it. The oath would only take effect for the week-days not for the Festivals. In the analogy mentioned above, if a man took an oath not to eat a particular loaf of bread and then took another vow not to eat any bread, his second oath would only take effect on all other bread, not on that particular loaf which he may not eat in any event because of his first oath. In the words of the Talmud: Our Tanna does not accept the principle of a more-embracing prohibition, i.e. the rule that a prohibition cannot take effect where there is already a prohibition applies even where the second prohibition is more embracing in scope than the first.

This list of objections is obviously late, featuring as it does those of R. Ashi and Ravina. (The mnemonic at the beginning of this section, listing the names of the Amoraím, is post-Talmudic and does not occur at all in some texts, see *DS*.) It would appear that various Amoraím tried their hands at discovering new possibilities to be included in the Mishnah. They are all very remote and it would therefore seem that all this is a purely academic exercise, not really to be taken seriously, which is why no reply is given to the first six objections, see *Tosafists* s.v. *matkif lah*. R. Zeira's is less remote and to this a reply is, in fact, eventually given. The order in which the Amoraím are listed is more or less chronological, except for R. Zeira. This was put last because there is a discussion on it, unlike the others, and a reply is eventually given. It is possible that R. Zeira's objection and the discussion on it were originally quite independent of the rest of the list. It would seem, too, that the whole of this section was originally an independent *sugya*, appended after the other by the editors, though it does seem somewhat strange that two of the prohibitions, erasing the divine name and ploughing with *asherah* wood, are virtually the same prohibitions derived from the same proof-texts as those in the previous section.

9

Simanim de-oraita o de-rabbanan: whether reliance on distinguishing marks for the purpose of identification is Biblical or Rabbinic

The main *sugya* is *Bava Metzi'a* 27a (last line on page)–28a, though there is a cross reference to it earlier, on page 27a.

In the whole of the second chapter of *Bava Metzi'a* (cf. *supra*, p. 34) it is accepted as the rule that a lost article must be returned by the finder to the one who claims that he lost it, if the latter substantiates his claim either by producing two witnesses that it is his or by declaring the distinguishing marks of the article. These are known as *simanin* (or, in the Hebrew form, *simanim*, sing. *siman*). *Simanin* are thus treated as a reliable means of identification. But it is not clear whether reliance on *simanin* has Biblical warrant – *simanin de-oraita* – or whether such reliance is by Rabbinic enactment only – *simanin de-rabbanan.*

The *sugya* begins with the stock formula when a problem is set: *ibbaye le-hu*, 'they [the anonymous scholars] set a problem'. The problem is: 'Are *simanin de-oraita* or *de-rabbanan*?' The practical difference, the Talmud continues, is whether or not a bill of divorce (*get*) can be returned when its *simanin* have been stated. A husband sends a *get*, which has to be written specifically for that husband and wife (see *supra* p. 24), through his agent, to deliver it to the wife and the *agent* loses the *get* but a *get* is later found. The agent describes the *simanin* of the *get* he has lost and these coincide with the *simanin* of the *get* that has been found. Can *simanin* be relied on sufficiently to enable the agent to take the *get* and deliver it to the wife? Is it the same *get* or is it another with, fortuitously, the same names of the husband and wife, and therefore invalid? Now if *simanin* are relied on by Biblical warrant, this reliance will not only apply to monetary matters such as a lost article but also with regard to religious law, e.g. so that the wife will be released from the marriage bond by that *get*. But if reliance on *simanin* in the case of the lost article is only the result of a special Rabbinic enactment, such an enactment is only effective in monetary matters, where the Rabbis enjoy authority to change the law if the good of society demands it, but it cannot be effective in religious law since if, in Biblical law, the *get* is possibly invalid the Rabbis have no authority to render it valid through reliance on *simanin*, and thus contradict a Biblical law.

The Talmud, having stated the problem, now proceeds with attempts to solve it one way or the other. The first attempted proof is from the Mishnah (*Bava Metzi'a* 2: 5, 27a) to which the *sugya* is appended. The Mishnah comments on the verse dealing with the restoration of a lost article to the loser: And so shalt thou do with his garment; and so shalt thou do with every lost thing of thy brother's' (Deuteronomy 22: 3). Since the verse speaks of 'every lost thing of thy brother's' why does it specify, in addition, his 'garment'? The Mishnah states: 'The garment was included in all these, why, then, was it mentioned separately? To compare all other articles to the garment. Just as a *garment* has *simanin* and has someone who lays claim to it so, too, every lost article [cannot be kept by the finder] if it has *simanin* and someone who claims it.' That is to say, two conditions are required for the law of the return of the lost article to apply. The first of these is that the article must have distinguishing marks by means of which it can be identified. The second condition is that the owner must claim it, i.e. he must have retained his ownership. But if there is evidence that the owner had abandoned the article, before the finder possessed it, the finder may keep it. These two conditions are derived from the fact that Scripture singles out the 'garment'. The 'garment' is thus singled out so that it should act as a prototype of lost articles that have to be returned. Generally speaking, a garment satisfies both these conditions; it has distinguishing marks and the owner persists in retaining his ownership. Now on the face of it, the Mishnah derives the law of *simanin* from the Scriptural verse in which the 'garment' is mentioned and this surely means that, according to the Mishnah, *simanin* have Biblical warrant – *simanin de-oraita*. No, the reply is given, there is no proof from the Mishnah. It is possible that the Mishnah holds that *simanin* are *de-rabbanan*. The Biblical text quoted in the Mishnah is not to teach us that *simanin* are to be relied on but to teach us the other condition stated in the Mishnah, that the owner must retain his ownership. In that case why does the Mishnah refer to *simanin*, which are Rabbinic and are not derived from 'garment'? It is simply because, since the Mishnah is quoting the verse and since by Rabbinic law, at least, *simanin* are relied on, the Mishnah sees no harm in referring to the *simanin* condition as well as the other condition, though, in fact, only the latter has Biblical warrant.

A further attempt to prove it is now made. The Mishnah has explained why 'garment' is mentioned on its own in the verse. But in the verse the word 'ass' also occurs. Why is the ass mentioned on its own? The reply given in the previous *sugya* (*Bava Metzi'a* 27a) is: we might have supposed that, if the claim is made that the ass is his by a man who cannot describe the *simanin* of the ass itself but only those of its saddle, this is insufficient means of identification. That is why the Torah refers specifically to the ass. For the return of the ass where this is itself identified no verse is required. It can be derived from the general rule. So the verse intends to teach us that the ass must be returned even to the one who only identifies the saddle. In any event, we surely see from this that *simanin* are relied on by Biblical law since the law regarding the *simanin* of the saddle is derived from a word in Scripture, the word 'ass'. No, the reply is given, there is no proof from the verse and the interpretation of it as referring to the saddle. True the verse does teach us that secondary identification, i.e. not of the article itself but of something normally attached to it, like the saddle to the ass, is sufficient. But this secondary identification might mean identification by the man who makes the claim producing witnesses, i.e. he produces not the *simanin* of the saddle but witnesses that he owns the saddle.

A third attempt is now made to prove it from the verse: 'and it shall be with thee until thy brother seek after it' (Deuteronomy 22: 2). On this the Rabbis comment: 'Would you imagine that you have to give it to him before he seeks it? But the verse means: Seek *him* to see whether or not he is a fraud.' The Rabbinic homily is to understand *derosh oto*, 'seek it', as 'seek *him*', i.e. make inquiries of him in order to establish whether or not he is telling the truth when he claims that the article is his. Now, it is here suggested, how can this inquiry be carried out if not by demanding of him that he states the *simanin* and since this is based on a Biblical verse it proves that *simanin* are *de-oraita*. To this the reply is given that the inquiry can be conducted not by demanding *simanin* but by demanding that he produce witnesses who will testify that it is his.

The Rabbinic homily quoted here resembles that found in a later Mishnah (*Bava Metzi'a* 2: 10) but the quote here cannot be from this Mishnah since according to the Mishnah the verse means that a man suspected of fraud must produce witnesses, i.e. the verse deals, according to the Mishnah, with a man known previously to engage in fraud. In all probability (see *Tosafists* s.v. *deráshehu*) this is an independent *Baraita* and the attempted proof is from 'seek *him*', and this would seem to mean by asking him to produce *simanin*, since if he is required to produce witnesses it would be *they* (and not *he*) who establish the claim. The progress of thought in this section is clear. The weakest of the attempted proofs is from 'garment'. This is easily refuted since the Mishnah derives two conditions from the verse (*simanin* and retention of ownership) and it is possible, as the Talmud replies, that the verse only refers to the second condition not to *simanin*. But then the interpretation of 'ass' is quoted. This is a much stronger proof since only one derivation is mentioned. For all that, the reply is given, there is no proof since the reference might be not to *simanin* but to witnesses. Finally, the strongest proof of all is attempted; as if to say, but surely here where the verse speaks of seeking *him* it must mean by demanding *simanin*. The reply is, no, even here the reference is to witnesses.

The Talmud now attempts a proof from a Mishnah (*Yevamot* 16: 3) dealing with a completely different topic. A corpse is found, the identity of which is unknown but which resembles a missing husband. How is the corpse to be identified so as to enable the wife to remarry? The Mishnah states that the face must be recognisable and that, consequently, a headless corpse cannot be identified as that of the missing husband even if there are *simanin* on the body or the garments of the corpse which coincide with those of the missing husband. But if *simanin* are *de-oraita* they would be relied on to permit the woman to remarry. The statement in the Mishnah seems to prove that the Mishnah holds that *simanin* are *de-rabbanan*.

The reply is given that the Mishnah may only mean that no reliance is to be placed on vague *simanin* of the body, e.g. that it is of a tall or short man. Since there are numerous men who are tall and numerous men who are short, these are not really adequate means of identification at all and would be unacceptable even if *simanin* are *de-oraita*. As for the reference in the Mishnah to *simanin* of the garments, these may, indeed, be adequate *simanin* and they do establish that the garments are those of the missing husband, yet the Mishnah still rules that the woman may not remarry because the husband may have lent his garments to another man whose corpse this is. In that case, the Talmud asks, why do we allow a man to claim an ass through his identification of the saddle; he may have lent his saddle to another whose ass this is? To this the reply is given that people do not normally borrow saddles, because these do not fit animals for which they were not made and would make the animal sore. Or, the Talmud continues, 'If you want I can say' that the reference to the garments is, like that to the corpse, not to proper *simanin* but to vague ones such as, the garments are white and red. These are not *simanin* at all.

In the discussion the question has been raised whether or not borrowing is to be taken into account. In that case, the Talmud continues, why have we learnt in a *Baraita* that if an agent bearing a *get* lost it and then found it, after a long period, tied to his money-bag or purse or signet ring, this is sufficient means of identification and the *get* can be used to divorce therewith the wife? But if we take borrowing into account he may have lent these objects to someone else and has forgotten that he has done so in the long period that has elapsed. To this the reply is that people do not lend these objects: money-bags and purses because it was held to bring bad luck and signet rings because of the fear that they may be used to forge documents.

There is considerable confusion in our texts. Once the 'if you want I can say' reply has been given, what is the significance of the question regarding the *get*, since at this stage of the argument it is held that we do not take borrowing into account? The reply: 'If you want I can say' has obviously been misplaced and should come at the end of the section (as in the Munich codex, see *DS*, and in the parallel passage in *Yevamot* 120b) *after* the question whether or not one takes borrowing into account has been exhausted.

The Talmud now puts forward the suggestion that this question, whether or not *simanin* are *de-oraita*, is debated by Tannaím. A *Baraita* is quoted dealing with the previous question of identifying a corpse. The Sages hold that a mole on the corpse on the same part of the body on which the missing husband had a mole is insufficient evidence that the corpse is that of the missing husband, but R. Eleazar b. Mahabai holds that it is sufficient and that the woman may remarry on the strength of the identification. Thus it would appear that the Sages hold that *simanin* are *de-rabbanan* and R. Eleazar b. Mahabai holds that *simanin* are *de-oraita*. No, suggests Rava, it may be that the Sages, too, hold that *simanin* are *de-oraita* and they would rely on other *simanin* to allow the woman to remarry. They only refuse to do so in the case of a mole because they hold that it is likely for such a mole to be found on the body of one born under the same star and at the same time as the missing husband (*ben gilo*, 'his double'). This corpse may be that of the husband's double. R. Eleazar holds that it is unlikely for a mole to be on the same spot, even in a double. 'If you want I can say', continues the Talmud, both authorities, the Sages and R. Eleazar b. Mahabai, hold that *simanin* are *de-oraita* and both hold that it is unlikely for a mole to be found on the husband's double and therefore a mole is an adequate *simanin*. But the Sages hold that *simanin* tend to change their colour after death, so that the mole found on the corpse is not an adequate *siman* at all. 'If you want I can say', the Talmud continues, all authorities hold that *simanin* do not tend to change after death so that if *simanin* were *de-oraita* all would agree that the women may remarry but, in fact, both hold that *simanin* are *de-rabbanan*. In that case why does R. Eleazar b. Mahabai allow the woman to remarry? It is because he holds that a mole is a far better *siman* than any other since it is extremely unlikely that the corpse is of another man who happened to have a mole on exactly the same place. This is known as a *siman muvhak*, 'a perfect *siman*'. This is effective even if *simanin* are *de-rabbanan*. But the Sages hold that a mole is not a *siman muvhak*. It has the same standing as other *simanin* and since *simanin* are *de-rabbanan* the woman may not remarry.

See *Maggid Mishneh* to *Gezelah Va-Avedah* 13: 3 that from our *sugya* it emerges that there are three types of *simanin*: (1) *siman muvhak*. This is so conclusive as evidence that it is relied upon even if *simanin* are *de-rabbanan*, and even to permit a woman to remarry. This is really far more than a *siman*. It amounts to positive identification as if by witnesses. (2) A very weak *siman*, e.g. that the garment is white or red. This is not relied upon even if *simanin* are *de-oraita* and not even for the purpose of restoring a lost article. It is not a *siman* at all. (3) Average *simanin*, i.e. a man states the weight of the article he has lost or, say, the hands of the corpse have an unusual shape. These *simanin* are definitely relied upon to restore a lost article and it is in connection with these that there is the debate whether they are *de-oraita* or *de-rabbanan* and so whether they can be relied upon even to permit a woman to remarry. When it is said in our *sugya* that the testimony of witnesses is accepted even if there are no *simanin* it means that the witnesses identify the corpse by direct perception. They *know* that it is so. The other Talmudic pasages dealing with reliance on *simanin* are: *Yevamot* 120a–b; *Gittin* 27b; *Ḥullin* 79a–b; 95b–96a. The *Yevamot sugya* is virtually a duplicate of ours. But a close examination of the way the material has been arranged in the two *sugyot* shows that the editors have arranged the *Yevamot* material so as to accord with the main theme of corpse identification mentioned in the *Yevamot* Mishnah, to which that *sugya* has been appended, whereas in our *sugya* the material has been arranged so as to fit in with the more general question discussed here of reliability on *simanin* and matters arising out of this. The *Yevamot* arrangement is: (1) The Mishnah dealing with the *simanin* of the corpse and its garments, from which it appears that *simanin* are not *de-oraita*. (2) But this contradicts the *Baraita* regarding the *get*. (3) Abbaye replies: this question, whether *simanin* are *de-oraita* or *de-rabbanan*, depends on the debate between the Sages and R. Eleazar b. Mahabai, the Mishnah following the view of the Sages, the *Baraita* the view of R. Eleazar b. Mahabai. (4) Rava disagrees: the debate is rather whether a mole is likely to be found on the husband's double. (5) 'Others say' the debate is about whether there is change after death. (6) 'Others say' that Rava says: all hold that *simanin* are *de-rabbanan* and the debate is whether a mole is a *siman muvhak*. (7) According to the opinion that both authorities hold that *simanin* are *de-oraita*, the Mishnah deals with 'tall' or 'short' and as for 'garments' we take borrowing into account. (8) Continues, as in our *sugya* at the beginning, with this question of whether borrowing is taken into account. Our *sugya* embraces the material found in the *Yevamot sugya* but contains much more material, i.e. that which precedes the discussion around the question of the corpse and that which follows it. It is not possible to determine whether or not the *Yevamot sugya* depends on ours or whether the two *sugyot* are independent of one another but use the same 'raw material' in their different constructions. Cf. Abraham Weiss, *The Babylonian Talmud as a Literary Unit* (New York, 1943), p. 208, note 152.

There now follows a saying of Rava: If you would say that *simanin* are not *de-oraita*, why do we return a lost article on the strength of *simanin*? That is to say, if Biblical law refuses to place any reliance on *simanin*, what social purpose is served by Rabbinic law accepting *simanin*? The reply is that the finder is quite willing to give up the article he has found on the strength of the *simanin* produced by the man who claims it, since he knows that if he loses an article it will be returned to him when he produces *simanin*. Strictly speaking, since *simanin* are not *de-oraita* he should be entitled to keep the article. Yet he will be quite content to obey the new Rabbinic enactment and surrender the article because he appreciates that the new enactment is for the benefit of all losers and he may himself be a loser one day. A kind of social contract can here safely be assumed. But R. Safra demurs to the explanation attributed to Rava: 'Can a man benefit himself with his neighbour's goods?' To be sure the finder may be content to surrender the article, but it really belongs to the rightful owner and the man who lays claim to it by producing the *simanin* may not be the rightful owner since *simanin* are not *de-oraita*. Any benefit that comes as a result of the new Rabbinic legislation must be for the rightful owners, for the losers not the finders, if it is to be acceptable. Therefore, we should rather explain (Rava would rather say, *Rashi*) that all losers are prepared to take the risk that if *simanin* are relied on, their article may be surrendered to someone to whom it does not belong. They are quite content to take the risk because the alternative would be that they have always to produce witnesses and these may not be forthcoming, whereas *simanin* are generally present.

If that is the case, the Talmud now asks, how do we explain the rule in the Mishnah (*Bava Metzi'a* 1: 8): 'Rabban Simeon b. Gamaliel said: If one finds three bills of indebtedness on the same debtor by three different creditors they are to be returned to the debtor but if one finds bills of three different debtors but for the same creditor they are to be returned to the creditor.' We have argued that the effectiveness of the new legislation is because the loser is prepared to take the risk since otherwise he might never recover his property. In the case of the three bills made out against three different debtors the reason, presumably, why they are returned to the creditor is because he declares the *siman*, namely, that there are three, otherwise how would he know how many bonds there were? But here the reasoning that the loser is prepared to take the risk in order to have the goods returned to him does not apply. The debtors would be quite content for the bonds to remain with the finder. All the debtor wants is that the bill should not be given to the creditor. To this the reply is given that in the case of the bonds a logical principle is at work. If the three bonds are made out against the same debtor they are returned to him because he must have lost them, otherwise how does it come about that bonds made out against him by three different creditors are found together? Consequently, the bills must have been paid and he had had them returned to him and then lost them. Conversely, if the three bonds are on three different debtors for the same creditor it can safely be assumed that he lost them, otherwise why would the three be found together? (And this is far more than an ordinary *siman*; it is a *siman muvhak*, which, as above, is effective even if *simanin* are *de-rabbanan* in the case of re-marriage and, consequently, there is no need here for the special Rabbinic enactment.)

But, the Talmud asks, another clause in the same Mishnah states that if one finds a bundle of bills wrapped together, they are to be returned to the creditor if he states as a *siman* that they are wrapped together, even if all the bills are against the same debtor. This can only be because of the Rabbinic enactment and here why should the debtor, if they are really his, take the risk? Consequently, the Talmud concludes, it is hard to defend the view that *simanin* are *de-rabbanan* since the reason for the Rabbinic enactment if there were such would not apply in all cases in which objects are returned on the strength of *simanin*. Therefore, what Rava really said was that *simanin* must be *de-oraita* and this is proven from the verse of 'seek *him*' and the earlier rejection of the proof (that it might mean 'seek him' by demanding witnesses) is itself rejected.

There now follows a series of problems set by Rava on the assumption that *simanin* are *de-oraita*. The Talmud interjects, what do you mean by 'on the assumption'? Rava has just stated that *simanin* are quite definitely *de-oraita*! To this the reply is given that the expression 'on the assumption' is not entirely out of place since the proof from 'seek him' can, as above, be refuted 'as we have explained it'.

This seems to show that this whole section has been added later, after the previous *sugya* had been completed. 'As we have explained it' can only refer to the discussion in the previous section of the *sugya*.

Rava's series of problems is set if it is held that *simanin* are *de-oraita* and hence enjoy full Biblical authority. Supposing two men lay claim to the lost article and each states its *simanin* accurately. To which of them should it be surrendered? It should be surrendered to neither but must be left in the Court (until Elijah comes, *Rashi*). Since each has as powerful a claim to the article as the other and one of them is obviously a fraud, there is no valid reason for giving it to either one. If A states the *simanin* but B has witnesses that it belongs to him, it is given to B. Even though *simanin* are *de-oraita* the testimony provided by witnesses is more reliable. If both A and B have *simanin* but one of them has, in addition, a single witness to support his claim, then since a single witness is not trusted to testify in monetary matters the witness's testimony is disregarded and the article has to be left in the Court as if it were simply a case of both producing *simanin* alone. If A has witnesses that he had woven the garment but B has witnesses that he lost it, it is given to B since even if A had woven it this does not prove that he did not sell it and it was purchased by B. If A states the garment's length and B its width, it is given to A. The width of the garment can be arrived at by seeing it on its owner but it is impossible to guess the length of the garment since, in those days, the garment was wound around the owner's person lengthwise and a fraud would have no means of knowing how many times it had been wound. If A states the length and width separately but B states the total of the length and width only, it is given to A. His information is more precise. If A states the length and breadth and B the weight, it is given to B, since it is harder to guess the weight than the length and width. The husband states the *simanin* of a *get* and the wife does the same; it is given to her (i.e. it is assumed that she is telling the truth that it had been delivered to her and she lost it so that the *get* was effective and she may now remarry). To this the Talmud objects, what kind of *siman*? If the meaning is the *siman* of the *get's* size, this is no indication since the wife may have seen the *get* in her husband's possession. The reply is that the *siman* is that of a hole at the side of this or that letter. This is a *siman muvhak*, for how would she know that the *get* has this peculiarity. If the husband states a *siman* of the cord (to which the *get* is attached) and the wife does the same, it is returned to her. To this the Talmud again asks, what kind of *siman*? If it is a *siman* of colour, red or white, she may have seen the cord while the *get* was in her husband's possession. The reply is, it refers to the length of the cord, which she could not guess. If the husband states, as a *siman*, that it was found in a valise and the wife does the same, it is given to him. Since she knows that he always keeps his documents in a valise she may simply be guessing. With this the *sugya* is concluded.

To be noted in this last section is the logical order in which the problems are presented, one leading more or less naturally from the other.

10

Devarim she-be-lev eynam devarim: mental reservations in contracts are disregarded

The sugya is *Kiddushin* 49b–50a. *Devarim she-be-lev eynam devarim* literally translated is: 'words in the heart (= the mind) are not words'. As a technical, legal term the meaning is: if, in any contractual arrangement, there are mental reservations contrary to its verbal or practical implications, these reservations are disregarded.

The *sugya* is appended to a Mishnah which reads: 'If a man betroths a woman, stating as a condition "that I am a priest" [i.e. he assures her that she is being betrothed by a member of a priestly family, the aristocracy] and he is found to be [only] a Levite [belonging to a lower social class] or [he states that] he is a Levite and he is found to be a priest [she may not wish to marry into the higher social class]; a Nathin [a Gibeonite, a bastard according to Rabbinic law] and he is found to be a *mamzer* [a bastard according to Biblical law] or a *mamzer* and he is found to be [only] a Nathin; a resident in a small town and he is found to be a resident of a large town or a large town and he is found to be of a small town; "on the condition that my house is near to the bath-house" and it is found to be distant, or distant and it is found to be near [and she may not want to live too near to the bath-house]; on the condition that he has a daughter or an adult slave-girl and he has none, or that he has none and is found to have; on the condition that he has no children and he has; or on the condition that he has children and he has none; in all these cases the betrothal is invalid even if she [subsequently] stated: "It was my intention [lit. 'in my heart'] to be betrothed unto him" [regardless of his status or condition]. The same law applies where she misled him.'

The *sugya* opens with an actual case in which the fourth-century

Babylonian Amora, Rava, gave a ruling. A man sold all his property with the clear intention of emigrating from Babylon to the Land of Israel but said nothing of this at the time of the sale. Neither in the bill of sale nor in any verbal statement was any condition attached to the sale, yet all the circumstances are such that the man's intention was for the sale only to be valid if, in fact, he did emigrate, otherwise he wished to retain his property. Now if the man had stated explicitly at the time of the sale that it was conditional on his emigrating, if eventually he remained in Babylon the sale would be null and void, the condition being unfulfilled. In the case under consideration, however, there was no explicit condition, only an assumed one, although the assumption was perfectly clear. Rava ruled that the sale was valid even if the man did not eventually emigrate. 'It is a case of words', declares Rava, 'that are in the heart and words that are in the heart are not words.' The mental reservation that would invalidate the sale was disregarded by Rava. The point here is not that the man is disbelieved about his true intention. All the circumstances go to show that it was. Yet since he made no condition at the time of the sale, the act of sale itself is without reservation and the man's mental qualification is insufficiently strong to upset the categorical nature of the sale. The reason for Rava's ruling would appear to be that unless the condition has been verbalized it remains vague and inchoate, without sufficient power to upset the sale. The man's determination to sell only conditionally is weak, otherwise he would have stated this explicitly. His mental reservation consists only of 'words in the heart' and these are not treated as 'words'.

The Talmud asks: 'How does Rava know this?', i.e. what is his authority for the ruling. It is suggested that, possibly, Rava derives his ruling from a Mishnah ('*Arakhin* 5: 6). (Actually, although *di-tenan*, 'for we have learnt in a Mishnah', is used, and the reference is to this Mishnah in '*Arakhin*, the full quote is, in fact, an elaboration on the Mishnaic rule and is found in *Sifra*, *va-yikra*, 3, end.) Here there is a comment on the verse: 'he shall offer it of his own voluntary will' (Leviticus 1: 3). The Hebrew is: *yakriv oto li-retzono*, which is rendered as: 'he *shall* offer it' but 'of his own voluntary will', i.e. he *must* offer the animal he had set aside as a burnt-offering, he is *compelled* to offer it, yet it is offered 'of his own voluntary will'. How can this be, since if he is compelled to offer it it cannot be of his own voluntary will? The reply is that he must, indeed, be coerced but the coercion must take the form of compelling him to say: 'I assent'. From this it follows that assent given under coercion is treated in law as a valid assent. But even though the man declares eventually that he gives his assent, since it is only obtained through coercion, presumably he has strong mental reservations and does not consent 'in his heart'. This shows that the 'words in his heart' are disregarded, that *devarim she-be-lev eynam devarim*. But, the Talmud continues, there is no support from this for Rava's decision because 'we are witnesses that he wishes to have atonement', i.e. the reason the assent is valid is not because the mental reservation is disregarded but rather because there is no mental reservation. Everyone knows ('we are witnesses') that a man who sets an animal aside as a burnt-offering really wishes the animal to be brought as such; he wishes to have the atonement the sacrifice affords him, which is why, after all, he set it aside in the first place. His reluctance actually to bring it has to be overcome by coercion, but once the coercion has been exerted he can be assumed really to mean it when he declares his assent. The assent *is* given 'in the heart' so that there is no support from this for Rava's ruling.

Possibly, the Talmud continues, Rava derives his ruling from the second clause in the '*Arakhin* Mishnah. After the statement that assent given under coercion is valid in the case of sacrifices, the Mishnah adds: 'And so, too, do you find it in connection with bills of divorce and manumission of slaves: He is compelled until he declares: "I assent." There are instances when a wife is entitled to petition for a divorce and a slave to be free of his master. But the assent of the husband and master is required. This can be obtained by the Court exercising coercion until there is assent. This shows that assent given under duress is valid and here the reply given in the case of sacrifices, that the man wants to find atonement, does not apply. Here, then, is a clear case of mental reservations being disregarded and a support for Rava's ruling. No, the Talmud continues, there is no proof since the principle obtains: 'it is meritorious to obey the words of the Sages', i.e. the Sages who order the husband to divorce his wife or the master to free his slave. Consequently, here, too, it can be argued, the reason it is effective is not because the mental reservation is disregarded but rather because, as in the case of sacrifices, there is no mental reservation. True it is under duress at first but when eventually the man gives his assent he gives it unreservedly because he knows 'deep down' that it is right to obey the Sages and he does so wholeheartedly.

Having attempted two proofs for Rava's ruling and having refuted both of these, the Talmud now quotes R. Joseph, who sought to prove the case from a Mishnah (*Kiddushin* 3: 5). The Mishnah reads: 'If a man betroths a woman and he [subsequently] said: "I thought that she belonged to a priestly family" but she belongs, in fact, to a [lesser] Levite family or [he thought] she belonged to a Levite family and she belongs to a priestly family; that she was poor and she is really rich, or that she was rich and is really poor; she is betrothed because she did not mislead him.' But should she be betrothed since, according to the man's testimony, which we have no reason to doubt, he did not, in fact, intend to betroth that woman? It can only be because it was a mental reservation (he did not state explicitly that he only betroths her on the understanding that she really is what he imagines her to be) and this is disregarded. Abbaye objects that the Mishnah might merely be stating a strict view, i.e. when the Mishnah rules that 'she is betrothed' it might only mean that just to be on the safe side she should not marry another without first receiving a *get*, as if the betrothal had been valid. There is only proof that a mental reservation is not taken into account when to disregard it results in strictness. There is no proof that it is totally disregarded, e.g. if someone else betrothed her afterwards, before she had received the *get*, she might well require a *get* from the second man, too, since, possibly, the mental reservation is taken into account so that, the first betrothal being invalid, the second betrothal is valid.

Thus far we have advanced a little further on the road to proof. We have, at least, established that where strictness is the result the mental reservation is disregarded. Abbaye now proceeds to demonstrate that it is disregarded totally, even when to do so results in leniency. Abbaye's proof is from our Mishnah, the Mishnah to which the *sugya* is appended. Here the rule is stated that where the man betrothed the woman on the condition that he is a priest or Levite etc. and it is later discovered that he is not what he had claimed to be, she is not betrothed, even if she declares that she was willing to be betrothed to him whatever his status. Now here the Mishnah states 'she is not betrothed' and this expression can only mean that there is no validity whatsoever to the betrothal and she can marry another without first receiving a *get*. This demonstrates that a mental reservation is totally disregarded, even when this results in leniency.

The Talmud objects that there is still no proof. True, in the case of the Mishnah the mental reservation is totally disregarded but that might be because there has been an *explicit condition* that he only betroths her if he really is what he says he is. Here if the mental reservation is to be effective it has to cancel out the explicit condition and this, the Mishnah holds, it cannot do. But where the mental reservation does not have to cancel out an explicit condition (as in the case of the property sale where, if the mental reservation is to be accepted, all this had to do is to *explain* the conditions of the sale) it may well be effective.

Thus far we have been unsuccessful in finding support for Rava's ruling. At the most we have been able to establish that mental reservations are not taken into account when to disregard these results in strictness. We have not succeeded in proving, as Abbaye sought to do, that they are disregarded totally, even where it results in leniency. In other words, the matter is in doubt and, consequently, where the prospective emigrant sold his real estate the question is whether or not the sale is valid (in view of his mental reservation) and since he has possession doubt cannot disturb it. The Talmud now quotes R. Hiyya bar Avin who reported that a case of this kind came before the Court of R. Hisda, which presented it for consideration to the Court of R. Huna (first half of third century) and this Court did succeed in proving conclusively that mental reservations are totally disregarded.

Unlike those in many other Talmudic passages, the case considered is a severely practical one. The reports are that an actual case came before the Court of R. Hisda and R. Huna, before Rava, at a much later period and, as at the end of the *sugya*, before R. Ashi at a later period still. No doubt sales of property with the intention of emigrating from Babylon to the Land of Israel were not infrequent in view of the highly meritorious act of settling in the Land of Israel.

The proof is from a Mishnah (*Me'ilah* 6: 1) dealing with the trespass-offering that has to be brought if profane use has been made, inadvertently, of Temple property. A man instructs his agent to bring him a money-bag that lies on a window ledge and the money in the bag belongs to the Temple, the man overlooking this fact. The Mishnah rules that as soon as the agent, acting on the man's behalf, takes up the money-bag, profane use has been made of Temple property and the man issuing the instructions is liable to a trespass-offering. This rule applies, the Mishnah continues, even if the man later declared that his intention was for his agent to bring him a different money-bag, one that did not belong to the Temple. Thus it can be seen that the man's mental reservation is disregarded. Now since a sacrifice can only be brought where there is a certain obligation, not a doubtful one (for to bring a doubtful sacrifice is to risk offering an unconsecrated animal, which is forbidden), it must follow that the mental reservation is totally disregarded as a certain ruling, not a doubtful one, proving the case conclusively.

The Talmud is still dissatisfied. The ruling of the Mishnah may apply not because mental reservations are disregarded but rather because there is no mental reservation. The man's intention may have been for the money-bag the agent actually took and he only declares later that it was not because he wishes to spare himself the expense of bringing a sacrifice. To this the reply is given that if he simply wished to avoid bringing a sacrifice he could easily have achieved this aim by later declaring that he knew the money-bag contained Temple money. The rule is that a trespass-offering can only be brought where there has been unintentional transgression. No 'atonement' is available for one who intentionally makes profane use of Temple property. No, the Talmud objects, this option was not open to him since to choose it would mean that he declares to all and sundry that he was a sinner in wishing intentionally to use Temple property and 'people do not declare themselves to be wicked'. Finally, the Talmud states that if his intention had been simply to avoid bringing a sacrifice he could have achieved his aim by later declaring that he had remembered that the money belonged to the Temple before the agent took it on his behalf. A *Baraita* is quoted in which it is stated that where this happens it is the agent, not the man himself, who is liable to the trespass-offering. Consequently, the man has the option of avoiding the expense of the sacrifice by declaring that he remembered. Since he did not avail himself of this option, it is clear that he is an honest man and is telling the truth when he says that he had the mental reservation. In that case, why is the mental reservation disregarded? It can only be because mental reservations are disregarded – and this proof is conclusive.

It is now implied, though not stated explicitly, that Rava's ruling was not, in fact, original to him. A similar case had been brought for consideration to the Court of R. Hisda and eventually to the Court of R. Huna, long before Rava's day. There the decision that *devarim she-be-lev eynam devarim* found its conclusive proof in the Mishnah from *Me'ilah.* This decision was handed down and Rava evidently knew of it so that when the case came before Rava he was able to decide it on the basis of his tradition. He had ample precedence for his ruling. The final reply to the original question: 'How does Rava know this?' is thus that he knows it from R. Huna's decision which, in turn, is based on the correct understanding of the Mishnah in *Me'ilah.* (It is not possible to determine whether or not R. Huna actually used the formula: *devarim she-be-lev eynam devarim.* He may simply have rendered the decision and the actual formula is Rava's.) In any event this formula is a further instance of Amoraic abstraction, a legal formulation of teachings found in earlier, Tannaitic, sources.

The stages in the *sugya* are:

(1)	Rava's ruling	
(2)	First attempted proof:	case of sacrifice
	refuted:	wishes to have atonement
(3)	Second attempted proof:	case of divorce and manumission
	refuted:	wishes to obey the Sages
(4)	R. Joseph's proof:	case of betrothal
	Abbaye:	refuted: there it is strictness
(5)	Abbaye's own proof:	our Mishnah
	refuted:	there it is a *condition*, which is stronger
(6)	R. Huna's proof:	Mishnah *Me'ilah*
	refuted:	wishes to avoid sacrifice
(7)	Proof stands:	could have said that it was intentional
	refuted:	people do not declare themselves wicked
(8)	Proof finally stands:	could have said that he remembered

A careful examination of this *sugya* demonstrates its completely neat and logical progression of thought. The refutation offered to (2) does not apply to (3); that offered to (3) does not apply to (4); that offered to (4) does not apply to (5); that offered to (5) does not apply to (6); (7) and (8) are elaborations of the final proof (6). Clearly such an order is artificial though dramatically effective. R. Huna gave his decision long before Rava. (The discussion on R. Huna is probably the work of the later editors.) R. Joseph and Abbaye are similarly independent of Rava. And even in the discussion on Rava the material is not presented in the order we might have expected; note, especially, how our Mishnah, to which the *sugya* is appended, is not produced immediately but only when the other attempted proofs and their refutation have led up to it. The only possible way of understanding all this is that the final editors have used earlier material and have presented this with their own framework so that a literary unit is the result.

The theme of *devarim she-be-lev eynam devarim* is discussed at length in *Kesef Nivḥar*, no. 45, pp. 78a–79a and in *ET*, vol. 7, pp. 170–86. The actual formula occurs in only two other Talmudic passages: *Nedarim* 28a and *Me'ilah* 21a. In the *Nedarim* passages it is stated: 'Even though we have established the rule that *devarim she-be-lev eynam devarim* yet....' The *Me'ilah* passage is a comment on the Mishnah in *Me'ilah* quoted in our *sugya* and reads: 'What does this Mishnah teach us? It teaches that *devarim she-be-lev eynam devarim*.' This would suggest that both the *Nedarim* and the *Me'ilah* passages are later than our *sugya*, the conclusion of which they accept.

The *sugya* finally discusses further cases of sale of property with the intention of emigrating from Babylon to the Land of Israel. Basically these cases have nothing to do with the theme of *devarim she-be-lev* because in them the seller states explicitly that he sells his property on the condition that he emigrates and if he does not he cancels the sale. The cases are only recorded here because of the association provided by the theme of selling property when the intention is to emigrate.

A man sells his property, stating that he only does so because he intends to emigrate to the Land of Israel. If he does not emigrate and remains in Babylon the sale is null and void. The man did go to live in the Land of Israel but, failing to find adequate accommodation there, he returned to Babylon. Is the sale null and void? Do we say that since he did, in fact, emigrate to the Land of Israel his condition has been satisfied and the sale is valid; or do we rather say that the meaning of his condition was for him actually to reside in the Land of Israel? In other words, does the clause in the contract: 'On condition that I go up to the Land of Israel' mean literally 'to go up' or does it mean 'to settle there'. Two versions of Rava's ruling in this case are given. According to one version, Rava ruled that to 'go up' means to settle there and the sale is null and void but according to the other version, Rava ruled that to 'go up' means simply to go there and the sale stands.

Finally, a case is recorded that came before R. Ashi, of a man who sold his property, stating explicitly that he only did so on the condition that he emigrated to the Land of Israel, but eventually he did not actually go there and then wished to cancel the sale. Two versions of R. Ashi's ruling are given. According to the first version, R. Ashi said: 'If he wants he can still go up', and the sale is valid. According to the other version, R. Ashi also ruled that the sale was valid but he put it in this form: 'Can he not go up if he wants to?' The Talmud asks, what is the difference between the two versions, since according to both the sale stands? The practical difference is where it became known after the sale that it was dangerous to journey to the Land of Israel because of robbers and the like. If R. Ashi simply said: 'If he wishes he can still go up', the sale is valid, since though it is dangerous it is still possible. But according to the second version: 'Can he not go up if he wants to?', the sale is invalid. This formulation suggests that there is nothing at all preventing the man from realising his ambition to emigrate, but where there is, the condition has not been fulfilled and the sale is null and void.

Note the two versions of R. Ashi's ruling and the statement of the practical differences between these, all of which must have been recorded by the final editors some time later than the time of R. Ashi.

11

Ḥazakah: presumptive state

The principle of *ḥazakah* is found in numerous Talmudic passages. It is probably the most ubiquitous of all Talmudic themes. The term is from a root meaning 'to be strong', 'to persist in', 'to grasp', hence *ḥazakah* means 'to follow the presumptive state', 'that which has been seized hold of'. Where there is a doubt in law or in the circumstances of a given case, the matter under consideration is not treated as a mere doubt but as if it were a certainty. It remains in that presumptive state which obtained when the doubt arose. If, for instance, there is a doubt whether a given piece of meat is *kasher*, it is forbidden but only as a doubtful prohibition. But if the doubt arose whether an animal had been properly slaughtered it is treated as forbidden as if it were a certainty, because here there is a presumptive state, the animal while alive being forbidden. Similarly, if a husband delivered to his wife a doubtful *get* she is treated as a married woman not by doubt but by certainty, since before the *get* had been delivered she had the presumptive status of a married woman and she remains in this state until she has definitely emerged from it. Thus *ḥazakah* determines the law in all cases of doubt so that the matter is no longer treated as doubtful. Naturally, *ḥazakah* does not tell us anything about the actuality of the law or the circumstances. It does not tell us, for instance, that where there are doubts regarding the slaughtering of the animal the animal has not really been slaughtered correctly. How could *ḥazakah* possibly do this? *Ḥazakah* is rather a matter of *procedure*. Where the case is in doubt, the *ḥazakah* principle informs us, the correct procedure to be adopted is to leave it in the state which previously obtained. It is as if the law were saying, prove that the circumstances have changed the status of the thing and if no proof is forthcoming leave it as it is. The procedure is not to demand proof that it has not changed but to demand proof that it has. Our *sugya*, *Ḥullin* 10b, seeks to discover Scriptural authority for the principle of *ḥazakah*.

We consider here only the *sugya*, this one, dealing with the question of the authority for the *ḥazakah* principle. The Talmudic passages in which the theme occurs are far too numerous to record. Moreover, the term *ḥazakah*, in addition to its most frequent use, that of presumptive status, means, in many passages, other quite different legal principles, e.g. sometimes the term is used of a mode of acquisition and sometimes in the sense of *rubba* where *ḥazakah* then means: 'It has been established as extremely likely.' *Kesef Nivḥar*, no. 60, part II, pp. 6a–19a, gives a useful survey of the various type. J. L. Kroch's *Ḥazakah Rabbah* (Leipzig–Jerusalem, 1927–63), is a massive work of many volumes on the theme in all its ramifications. *ET* devotes a large part of two whole volumes to the theme: vol. XIII, pp. 453–753; vol. XIX, pp. 1–423. Cf. the fine introduction to the theme in vol. XIII, pp. 453–65 and the bibliography, p. 465.

The *sugya* opens with: 'How do we know that which the Rabbis say: A thing is retained in its presumptive state (*ḥazakah*)?' The reply is given by R. Samuel b. Nahmani in the name of the third-century Palestinian Amora, R. Jonathan, who quotes a Scriptural verse: 'Then the priest shall go out of the house to the door of the house, and shut up the house seven days' (Leviticus 14: 38). The verse deals with a 'leprous house', a house in which a plague-spot of discoloration had appeared on one of its walls. The minimum size of the spot for the house to be unclean when it is shut up is a *geris*, a bean. At the end of the seven days the priest has to open the house to see whether or not the spot has increased in size. During the seven days that the house is shut up anyone who enters there becomes unclean (verse 48). If the house is in error shut up for a spot that is less than a bean in size, the 'shutting up' is invalid and the house does not contaminate. Now from the whole tenor of these verses it appears that plague-spots were subject to considerable fluctuations, increasing and decreasing in such a way as to render it doubtful at any given moment whether the spot had changed its size. Since the spot is on the walls of the house inside and the priest is obliged to 'go out' of the house before he shuts it up, then it is always possible that at the moment of his shutting up of the house (the moment from which the house contaminates) the spot has decreased and is no longer the size of a bean. And yet the Torah states that whoever enters the house during the seven days after it had been shut up is unclean, and as of certainty not as of doubt. This can only be because of the *ḥazakah* principle. When the priest first observed the spot it did have the minimum size, at least, of a bean and we, therefore, assume that it has remained in that state. Even if at the end of the seven days, when the house is opened up, it is seen that the spot has diminished to less than the requisite size, or has even vanished entirely, the house is seen, none the less, as having been unclean during the seven days. This can only mean that until we know for certain that a thing has emerged from its presumptive status it retains that status. Thus R. Jonathan proves that the *ḥazakah* principle enjoys Scriptural authority.

The formulation in Soncino, p. 46, note 6: 'And as the house has acquired the status of being unclean, it is presumed to remain so, and requires to be "shut up" is very imprecise. The house does not acquire the status of being unclean *until* it is 'shut up'. The *ḥazakah* is not of the house but of the plague-spot. Since the spot did have the size of a bean when the priest saw it, we assume, through application of the *ḥazakah* principle, that it had remained of this size at the moment of 'shutting up'.

The Talmud states that the fourth-century Babylonian Amora, R. Aha b. Jacob, raised an objection to R. Jonathan's proof. It is possible that the Torah refers to the priest going out of the house backwards so that he can observe the spot all the time and, at the moment he shuts the door, can see that it has not decreased in size to less than that of a bean. Thus there is no proof that the Torah relies on *ḥazakah*.

Abbaye remarks to R. Aha b. Jacob: 'There are two replies to your objection.' First, the Torah cannot refer to the priest going out backwards since Scripture would not call such an abnormal manner of exit 'going out'. Secondly, the Torah does not specify where the spot is found and this is as if the Torah had stated that the house is unclean wherever the spot is found, even if it is found on the inside of the door itself. But if the spot is on the inside of the door how can the priest see it, even if he does go out backwards? And if you will argue, continues Abbaye, that the priest can open up a window in the door through which he can look to see if the spot has retained the requisite size, this will not do. For there is a law stated in the Mishnah (*Nega'im* 2: 3) and derived from Scripture that for the house to be unclean the priest must be able to see the spot by the ordinary light of the house. The house is not unclean if he can only see the spot by opening a window. Thus, Abbaye argues, R. Aha's attempted refutation is itself refuted and R. Jonathan's proof stands.

Rava now seeks to defend R. Aha b. Jacob against Abbaye's strictures. Rava argues that there is no proof from Scripture that the *ḥazakah* principle is accepted since, as R. Aha b. Jacob has said, Scripture may be speaking of the priest going out backwards. That going out in this fashion is still referred to by Scripture as 'going out', contrary to Abbaye, can be seen from the verse 'Then the priest shall go out' (Leviticus 14: 38) referring to the High Priest's exit from the Holy of Holies on the Day of Atonement. The Mishnah (*Yoma* 5: 1) informs us that he used to go out backwards in order not to have his back to the sacred ark and yet the Torah refers to this as 'going out'. As for Abbaye's second objection regarding opening a window, this can easily be met. The objection is only where the spot cannot be seen at all unless the window is opened. In our case the priest has already seen the spot by the ordinary light of the house. The sole purpose of opening the window is to see whether or not the spot behind the door has decreased from the requisite size and for this purpose a window may be opened. That is to say, even if we do not rely on the *ḥazakah* principle, as we do not at this stage of the argument, the principle can at least be followed for the purpose of permitting the opening of the window. For here, once the window has been opened, the house is declared definitely unclean not through the operation of the *ḥazakah* principle but through direct observation.

Rava has now defended R. Aha b. Jacob against Abbaye's strictures. But the Talmud quotes a *Baraita* (*Sifra*, *metzora*', 6: 6) from the Scriptural interpretation of which we can see that R. Aha b. Jacob's interpretation is untenable. The *Baraita* states that from the words 'Then the priest shall go out of the house' we might have held that it is in order for the priest to go to his own house before shutting up the affected house, i.e. by means of a long rope. But since the verse continues 'to the door of the house' this shows that the priest must be adjacent to the door when he shuts up the house. On the other hand, we might have held that the priest may shut up the house while standing underneath the lintel of the affected house, therefore Scripture states 'shall go out of the house', i.e. he must leave the house entirely. Consequently, he must leave the house entirely and yet be adjacent to it, which means that he must stand *beside* the lintel. Now from this *Baraita* we learn that there is a special Scriptural injunction – 'to the door of the house' – that the priest must not shut the door by means of a long rope at a distance. But on R. Aha b. Jacob's interpretation this would be invalid in any event, since how could the priest then see the spot on the inside of the door even if the window had been opened? R. Aha b. Jacob is thus refuted.

The Talmud replies that R. Aha b. Jacob will hold that it is still possible for the priest to know that the spot has not decreased since there may be a row of men who call out that the spot has retained its size.

Thus at the conclusion of the *sugya* there is still a possibility that R. Jonathan's proof is refuted, as R. Aha b. Jacob refutes it. According to this, one would have to say that there is, in fact, no Scriptural proof for the *ḥazakah* principle and this is derived, see *Maharsha*, from 'a law given to Moses at Sinai'. Cf. *Rashi*, *Ḥullin* 12a, s.v. *pesaḥ*, that the same conclusion is arrived at with regard to *rubba* in the *sugya* which follows ours, see *supra* p. 60.

The stages in the *sugya* are:

(1) Where is the *ḥazakah* principle found?
(2) R. Jonathan: plague-spot; may have decreased
(3) R. Aha b. Jacob: perhaps priest goes out backwards
(4) Abbaye: (a) backwards not called 'going out'
(b) what if behind door
(5) Rava: (a) it is called 'going out' – High Priest
(b) it can be behind door and window opened
(6) Refutation of R. Aha b. Jacob: verse dealing with 'long rope'
(7) Defence of R. Aha b. Jacob: row of men

Note how the *Baraita* in (6) has been left to the end. It is only produced *after* Rava has defended R. Aha b. Jacob. Note, too, that the whole discussion is purely theoretical and academic, since no one really disputes that the principle of *ḥazakah* is accepted.

12

Gadol kevod ha-beriot: the law and regard for human dignity

The *sugya* is *Berakhot* 19b–20a. The term *gadol kevod ha-beriot*, lit. 'great is the dignity of human beings', occurs in the *sugya* and is the central point of the whole discussion. The problem considered is, under which circumstances can there be a relaxation of the law where the purpose is to safeguard human dignity?

The *sugya* opens with a statement by the early-third-century Babylonian Amora, R. Judah, in the name of his master, Rav: 'If one finds *kilayim* (a mixture of wool and flax, Leviticus 19: 19) in his garment, it must be stripped off even in the market place.' The reason is: because Scripture says: 'there is no wisdom nor understanding nor counsel against the Lord' (Proverbs 21: 30), which means: 'Wherever there is a profanation of God's name no respect is to be paid to a teacher', i.e. where regard for the dignity of a teacher, and *a fortiori* an ordinary person, is in conflict with the requirements of the law, it is the former that must yield.

An objection is raised from a *Baraita* dealing with a mourner and the congregation which accompanies him on the return from a funeral. If the mourner decides to return by way of an unclean path, i.e. a path that crosses a field in which there are graves, the congregation should follow him in that path out of respect for him (i.e. even if some of them are priests who are forbidden to become contaminated by a corpse or a grave (Leviticus 21: 1)). Thus we see that a prohibition is set aside out of regard for human dignity and thus contradicts Rav's ruling.

This follows the reading in our editions. Some texts (see *SM* and *DS*) have a different reading, namely, if the congregation returns by way of the unclean path, the mourner, even if he is a priest, should follow in that path out of respect for *them*. The point, however, is the same. We see that a prohibition is set aside out of regard for human dignity.

To this the reply is given that R. Abba (see Hyman, *Toledot*, s.v. *Abba*, that there were a number of Amoraím of this name) interpreted (*tirgemah*) the *Baraita* as referring to a *bet ha-peras*, the prohibition of which is only Rabbinic. A *bet ha-peras* is a field containing graves that has been ploughed up so that the bones are scattered and are no longer in one place as in the Biblical law of contamination through contact with a corpse. According to Biblical law, such a field does not contaminate so that a priest may enter there; but the Rabbis ruled that it does contaminate and the priest may not enter there. That is why the prohibition is set aside, because there is only a Rabbinic prohibition in any event and a Rabbinic prohibition is set aside for the sake of human dignity. R. Judah in the name of Samuel is quoted as saying that a man can walk through a *bet ha-peras* by blowing in front of him, so that any bones that may be there will be blown out of his path and he does not then suffer contamination at all, even by Rabbinic law. And R. Judah bar Ashi is quoted as saying that if a *bet ha-peras* has been thoroughly trodden under it no longer contaminates. All this demonstrates that the rule of *bet ha-peras* is a lenient one because the contamination and hence the prohibition is only by Rabbinic law. There is no proof that a Biblical law, as in the case of *kilayim*, is set aside for the sake of human dignity.

A further proof is now attempted, introduced with the usual formula: *ta shema*', 'come and hear'. The early Tanna R. Eleazar bar Zadok is quoted as saying: 'We used to leap upon the coffins in order to go out to meet Jewish kings and the Sages did not only permit it in order to meet Jewish kings but also to meet Gentile kings so that if one has merit [to see the Messiah] he will notice the difference between [the majesty of] the Jewish king and the Gentile kings.' Now R. Eleazar bar Zadok was a priest and the meaning of his testimony is that a priest may contaminate himself through contact with a corpse for the sake of human dignity, i.e. to pay respect to royalty. To this the reply is given that the matter can be understood on the basis of a statement by the fourth-century Babylonian Amora, Rava. Rava interprets the Biblical law of the 'tent': that if a corpse lies in a tent, or under any other cover, it is forbidden for a priest to go over that tent or cover since to do so makes him subject to contamination. Rava observes, however, that since the majority of coffins have a space of at least one hand's-breadth between the corpse and the coffin lid, this space acts as a barrier and the contamination is, as it were, contained. According to Biblical law, then, it was permitted in any event for R. Eleazar bar Zadok to leap on the coffins. The only prohibition is Rabbinic, the Rabbis ruling that all coffins contaminate because of the minority which do not have the space of a hand's-breadth between the corpse and the lid. Since the prohibition is only Rabbinic it was set aside for the sake of human dignity, but there is still no proof that a Biblical prohibition is set aside.

A further proof is now attempted. A *Baraita* is quoted which states: 'Great is human dignity (*gadol kevod ha-beriot*) for it pushes aside a negative precept of the Torah', which shows that even a Biblical prohibition is set aside and thus refutes Rav. To this the reply is given that Rav bar Sheva has interpreted (*tirgemah*) the *Baraita* in the presence of R. Kahana (Babylonian Amora, early fourth century) that the negative precept referred to is that of 'thou shalt not turn aside' (Deuteronomy 17: 11), i.e. the command not to disobey the teachers of Israel. But, continues the Talmud, 'they laughed at him' since this, too, is a Biblical, not a Rabbinic, prohibition. To this R. Kahana retorted: 'If a great man says something do not laugh at him. All Rabbinic laws are based on "thou shalt not turn aside" and out of respect for human dignity the Rabbis permitted it.' Thus, again, there is only proof that a Rabbinic prohibition is set aside for the sake of human dignity and there is no refutation of Rav's ruling.

Rashi seems to understand the discussion as follows. Those who laughed at Rav bar Sheva understood him to mean by 'thou shalt not turn aside' cases where the teachers of Israel explain the meaning of a Biblical law. Consequently, they laughed at him since it is a Biblical law that is being set aside. But R. Kahana explained to them that Rav bar Sheva only meant to say that all *Rabbinic* laws are based on 'thou shalt not turn aside' but are none the less Rabbinic. A somewhat different understanding of the passage is possible. Those who laughed at Rav bar Sheva did so because since 'thou shalt not turn aside' is a Biblical injunction to obey Rabbinic law it is a Biblical law that is being set aside. R. Kahana replies: true though it is that the Torah enjoins us to obey Rabbinic law yet it is *Rabbinic*, not Biblical, law that is being obeyed. This passage is the *locus classicus* for the status of Rabbinic law; see Maimonides, *Sefer ha-Mitzvot*, *shoresh rishon* and commentaries. Maimonides holds that there is a Biblical injunction to obey Rabbinic law whereas Nahmanides disagrees, holding that the meaning of our passage is that the Rabbis 'pegged on' their teachings to the verse 'thou shalt not turn aside'. Nahmanides argues that if Rabbinic law really enjoys Biblical authority, why does the law make numerous distinctions between matters of Biblical law and matters of Rabbinic law, e.g. in cases of doubt and the like? Cf. the subtle analysis of the whole question by R. Meir Simhah Kagan, *Meshekh Ḥokhmah* to Deuteronomy 17: 11, pp. 281–2, that, according to Maimonides, the command 'thou shalt not turn aside' is only a *general* command to obey the Rabbis, not a command to obey the *details* of Rabbinic law. These latter only enjoy Rabbinic authority. Cf. Rabbi J. L. Bloch, *She'urey Halakhah* (Tel-Aviv, 1958), no. 10, pp. 52–6, that, according to Maimonides, Biblical law is to be compared to a father instructing his son to do this or that. Each thing the father orders is his direct command. Rabbinic law is to be compared to a father instructing a son to obey the son's teacher. Here the command is general.

A *Baraita* is now quoted dealing with the law of finding a lost animal. From the word *ve-hit'alamata*, 'hide thyself' (Deuteronomy 22: 1 and 4), a Rabbinic understanding is that there are three cases where it is permitted to refrain from returning the lost animal. The *Baraita* lists these as: where the finder is a priest and the animal is in the cemetery; where the finder is an elder and it is beneath his dignity to lead an animal; where the loss to the finder in expenses is greater than the loss to the owner if the animal is not returned. In all three cases the Torah declares: 'hide thyself', i.e. do not bother to return the animal to its owner. From this we see that the elder is not obliged to return the lost animal because it is beneath his dignity; from which we see that even a Biblical prohibition – not to refrain from restoring a lost animal – is set aside for the sake of human dignity. To this the reply is given that there is a special verse – *ve-hit'alamta* – to permit it. But why not take this, asks the Talmud, as a paradigm for all prohibitions to be set aside where human dignity is at stake? To this the reply is given: 'Religious law cannot be derived from monetary matters', i.e. it by no means follows that because the Torah allows a man to place his own dignity before his neighbour's monetary interests, the loss of his animal, that the Torah will allow a religious prohibition to be set aside.

Another *Baraita* is now quoted. Here there is a comment on the verse 'Or for his sister' (Numbers 6:7) in which it is specified that a Nazirite (and even if he is also a priest) may not contaminate himself for his dead *sister* but may contaminate himself for a *met mitzvah*, a corpse there is no other person to bury. And by an elaborate process (see *Rashi*) this is extended even to the Nazirite and priest who is on his way to offer his Pachal lamb or to circumcise his son. He, too, must contaminate himself for a *met mitzvah*. From this we see that the Biblical precepts of offering the Paschal lamb and of circumcision are set aside for the *met mitzvah* (an example of regard for human dignity) and this shows that, contrary to Rav, human dignity does take precedence even over a Biblical command. To this the reply is given that there is a special verse – 'Or for his sister' – which makes it an exception. But why not derive other cases from this, i.e. since here it is a religious law that is being set aside? To this the reply is given: 'there it is, sit down and do not do', i.e. it is indirect. The offence of failing to offer the Paschal lamb or circumcise the child is only an indirect one, whereas the offence of *kilayim* is a direct one, the garment being worn to avoid loss of dignity. It by no means follows from the permission of the Torah to have an indirect offence set aside for the sake of human dignity that it permits the setting aside of a direct offence for the sake of human dignity. Thus according to the conclusion of the *sugya* there are three instances: (1) A positive direct Biblical offence – *kilayim*. This may not be set aside for the sake of human dignity, hence Rav's ruling. (2) A direct but Rabbinic offence – *bet ha-peras* and skipping over the tombstones. (3) A Biblical but indirect offence – the Paschal lamb and circumcision. This can be set aside. In other words two conditions must obtain for Rav's principle to come into operation. These are: (1) it must be a Biblical offence; (2) it must be direct. An indirect offence, even if it is Biblical, and a Rabbinic offence, even if it is direct, may be set aside in order to safeguard human dignity.

See *Rashi* for the difficulty that when the Nazirite and priest contaminates himself it *is* direct and Biblical. *Rashi* observed that the law of contamination is not simply *set aside* for the Nazirite and priest. The law of contamination does not apply here at all. Just as the Torah permits a priest, for instance, to contaminate himself for his relatives it permits him to contaminate himself for a *met mitzvah*. The man going to offer the Paschal lamb or to circumcise his son, on the other hand, does not enjoy any special *status*. His going for the purpose just happens to coincide with his discovery of the *met mitzvah*. Here it is a case of a law being *set aside* for the sake of human dignity and is only permitted because it is indirect, as the Talmud says. From our *sugya* it would follow that if A saw B wearing *kilayim* there is no need for A to do anything about it, since the offence he commits by doing nothing is an indirect one. However, Maimonides (*Yad*, *Kilayim* 10: 29) evidently did not have the reading 'in his garment' but simply: 'One who finds *kilayim*' and he understands our *sugya* as referring not to the wearer but to the one who observes it. This is called 'direct' because the wearer commits a direct offence. Maimonides also adds 'even if he [the wearer] is his teacher', i.e. Maimonides understands this to be the reference to 'no regard is to be paid to a teacher'. Cf. the famous *Responsum* of Ezekiel Landau, *Noda' Bi-Yhudah*, *Kama*, *Orah Hayyim*, no. 35, who discusses the question whether a husband should be informed of his wife's infidelity where to do so would offend human dignity. The *Baraita*: '*Gadol kevod ha-beriot*' is quoted in *Shabbat* 81b; 94b; '*Eruvin* 41b; *Megillah* 3b; *Menaḥot* 37b but our *sugya* is the only discussion on the whole theme of human dignity. The saying: 'Whenever there is a profanation of God's name no regard is paid to the dignity of a teacher' does not appear to be Rav's but is an addition by the editors and is, in fact, a quote from elsewhere. In fact, in the other instances where this occurs in the Talmud ('*Eruvin* 63a; *Sanhedrin* 82a; *Shevu'ot* 30b) it appears on its own and in connection with the dignity of scholars not in connection with the general theme of human dignity. As above, this is no doubt why Maimonides adds: 'even if he is his teacher'. On our reading it is difficult to know why a teacher should be mentioned here at all unless, as we have suggested, this is really a quote from an independent saying and has simply been tagged on to the verse because it is a familiar comment on the verse. The real point of the *sugya* is the concern with '*human* dignity' (*kevod ha-beriot*) not with 'the dignity of scholars' (*kevod ha-rav*). It should also be noted that in the instances given in the three passages the question is with regard to the special dignity reserved for scholars, e.g. whether or not a scholar should demean himself in order to testify in a Court of Law; whereas in all three instances in our *sugya* the question concerns general human dignity, e.g. the burial of a corpse; being unclothed in public; respect for royalty. (The case of the elder and the animal is not because of respect for scholarship but because since he is the kind of person who does not lead animals in the street to expect him to do so is an affront to general human dignity.) Thus the best way of understanding the saying is to see it as a quote, not strictly germane to our theme, that has become so closely associated with the verse in Proverbs that it is quoted as if it were part of that verse. The pattern of the *sugya* is:

(1) R. Judah in the name of Rav: *Kilayim*, must strip off
(2) Reason: verse in Proverbs and 'wherever...'
(3) Objection: mourner
(4) Reply: R. Abba; *bet ha-peras*; only Rabbinic
(5) Objection: R. Eleazar bar Zadok: Biblical
(6) Reply: no, also Rabbinic: Rava, space
(7) Objection: 'negative precept *of the Torah*', Biblical
(8) Reply: 'thou shalt not turn aside'
(9) Objection: 'They laughed'; Biblical
(10) Reply: R. Kahana; also Rabbinic
(11) Objection: elder; Biblical
(12) Reply: special verse
(13) Objection: derive from it other Biblical offences
(14) Reply: religious law different

(15) Objection: Paschal lamb
(16) Reply: special verse
(17) Objection: derive then other Biblical, religious offences
(18) Reply: indirect

One can see, even at a cursory glance, that the series of proofs has been presented in a neat, artificial sequence. The reply in (4) is not relevant to (5) since here the offence is Biblical, hence (6), here, too, Rabbinic. But what of (7) where 'of the Torah' is mentioned? Reply, as in (8) to (10). But what of (11) where it is clearly Biblical? Replies (12) to (14), yes, but there it is a monetary offence here a religious one. But, (15) to (17), religious offence and Biblical? Reply, (18), indirect. It is obvious that the editors have presented the material they had so as to provide this neat pattern of proof, refutation and counter-refutation. Each item is only put forward when its time has come, as it were, when it implies a further refutation to which the previous reply is inoperative.

13

Hazmanah milta: whether the designation of an object for a particular use is effective

The *sugya* is *Sanhedrin* 47b–48b. *Hazmanah* means 'to set aside', 'to designate'. The basic question considered is whether an object that acquires a certain status in law when used for a particular purpose acquires that status even when it has only been designated for that purpose. The example given is the weaving of a garment (a shroud) for a corpse. It is forbidden to enjoy any benefit from a corpse, its grave or its shroud. Abbaye holds that the mere designation for the purpose suffices to render the garment forbidden – *hazmanah milta hi*, lit. '*hazmanah* is a thing', i.e. it has substance so that the garment is forbidden as if it had actually been used. Rava holds that mere designation is insufficient to render the garment forbidden – *hazmanah lav milta hi*, lit. '*hazmanah* is not a thing', i.e. has no substance, is ineffective, and the garment is not forbidden until it has actually been used as a shroud.

The *sugya* begins with the debate between Abbaye and Rava: 'It has been stated: If one weaves a garment for a corpse: Abbaye said: It is forbidden. But Rava said: It is permitted. Abbaye said it is forbidden; *hazmanah* is effective. But Rava said it is permitted; *hazmanah* is ineffective.'

The term *itmar*, 'It has been stated', the usual Talmudic term to introduce a debate between Amoraím is obviously an editorial device. From the fact that 'Abbaye said... But Rava said' is repeated, it would seem to be equally certain that the explanation of Abbaye and Rava's views on whether *hazmanah* is effective or ineffective is not Abbaye and Rava's own but it similarly editorial. Thus the paragraph should be paraphrased as: 'Abbaye said: It is forbidden. But Rava said: It is permitted. The reason why Abbaye said that it is forbidden is because Abbaye holds that *hazmanah* is effective while the reason Rava said that it is permitted is because Rava holds that *hazmanah* is ineffective.' When the Talmud continues with:

'What is the reason?' it introduces a new feature, namely, the support the Amoraím find for their views in Scripture and why they disagree with each other's derivation from Scripture. It is impossible to know how much of all this is Abbaye's or Rava's own and how much the work of the editors, but the actual *wording* appears to be that of the editors with the exception of: 'It is forbidden' and 'It is permitted.' On this kind of analysis into the original statements of the Amoraím and the editorial elaborations, see H. Klein, articles on 'Gemara' and 'Sebara', *JQR*, new series, 38 (1947), 67–91; 43 (1953), 341–63; *JSS*, 3 (1958), 363–72.

The Talmud proceeds to ask: 'What is Abbaye's reason?' i.e. on what authority does he base his ruling. The reply is that the word *sham*, 'there', occurs in a verse which speaks of the dead: 'And Miriam died *there*, and *there* was she buried' (Numbers 20: 1; my italics) as well as in the verse which speaks of the heifer whose neck was broken: 'and shall break *there* the heifer's neck' (Deuteronomy 21: 4, my italics). Now the rule is that the heifer becomes forbidden for any use from the moment it is brought down *there*, i.e. to the valley and so it follows, according to Abbaye, that the garment woven for the corpse is forbidden by the mere act of designation just as the heifer becomes forbidden even before it has actually been beheaded. Rava relies on another verse in which there is a reference to 'there'. This verse speaks of idolatry: 'Ye shall surely destroy all the places where the nations ye are to dispossess serve *there* their gods' (Deuteronomy 12: 2; my italics). Now if an object or an animal is set aside to be offered to an idol, it does not become forbidden until it has actually been used for the purpose. Consequently, Rava derives from this his rule that the garment does not become forbidden merely because of designation. We thus have two Scriptural verses. In one – that of the heifer – the object does become forbidden merely by designation. In the other – that of idolatry – the object does not become forbidden merely by designation. The question, then, is whether the law of the garment is to be derived from that of the heifer or from that of idolatry.

The Talmud now asks further why Rava fails to agree with Abbaye, why, in other words, does Rava prefer to derive the law from idolatry and not from the heifer. The reply is given, Rava prefers to derive accessaries from accessaries (i.e. the garment is *for* the corpse and the object *for* the idol) whereas the heifer is itself a forbidden object and can, therefore, the more readily become forbidden merely by designation. Abbaye, on the other hand, prefers to derive the 'normal' from the 'normal' (i.e. laws to be observed as they come about in the normal course of human life) whereas idolatry is 'abnormal' (forbidden even to Gentiles, *Rashi*). Here mere designation is insufficient since the man so designating for an 'abnormal' purpose may change his mind and does not really mean it until he actually does it. Thus according to Abbaye all cases are derived from the law of the heifer that mere designation is forbidden and the law of idolatry is the sole exception, since in that case there is no real designation (because it is 'abnormal' and he may change his mind). But according to Rava, all cases of accessaries are derived from the law of idolatry and there are no exceptions. The heifer is no exception since it is not an accessary but the forbidden thing itself.

An attempt is now made to refute Rava from a Mishnah (*Kelim* 28: 5) dealing with the law of *midras*, 'resting'. If a person with an issue (see Leviticus 15) sits or rests on any object that is sometimes used for this purpose that object becomes unclean. But if the object is used for other purposes, and not for sitting, the law of *midras* does not apply, e.g. scales or axes because these 'say' to the man sitting, as it were: 'Stand up and we will do our work.' The Mishnah states that if a veil has been sat on it does become subject to *midras*, because people sometimes fold their veils and sit on them. But once the veil has been designated (lit. 'given') to be used as a mantle to wrap around a book it loses its *midras* character, becoming an object that is used entirely for a purpose other than sitting. (The point here is that normally a veil is used for *both* purposes, as an item of dress and as something on which to sit, when it is folded. But a mantle wherewith a book is covered is never taken from it to be used for sitting on.) From this we see that mere designation is effective and this refutes Rava. Say rather, the Talmud replies, the veil has not only been designated but actually used as a wrapper for the book, i.e., the Mishnah refers to both designation and subsequent use. In that case, asks the Talmud, since the veil has actually been used why refer to designation at all? To this the reply is given that use on its own, without prior designation for the purpose, does not suffice, just as designation on its own, according to Rava, does not suffice. A rule of R. Hisda to this effect is quoted. R. Hisda ruled that if a cloth had been designated as a wrapper for *tefillin* and had then actually been used as a wrapper for *tefillin* it is forbidden to wrap money therein. But if it had been designated but not actually used, or used without prior designation, it is permitted to wrap money therein. But, continues the Talmud, according to Abbaye, if it had been designated it would be forbidden even if not actually used, whereas even if it had been used it is permitted if there had been no prior designation.

A *Baraita* is now quoted. Here it is said that if a tomb had been built for a living person (i.e. for a man now alive, to be used for his burial when he dies) it is permitted to have use of it (since it is not, in fact, for a corpse, the man being still alive). But if even a single row of stones had been added for a corpse (i.e. the row was added after the man had died) it is forbidden. This refutes Rava since the addition of a row of stones is no more than a designation. The reply is given that the *Baraita* means: it is forbidden if the corpse is already there in the tomb. To this the Talmud objects: if the corpse is already there in the tomb, the tomb would be forbidden even if no further stones were added since it is now a tomb that contains a corpse. The Talmud replies that the corpse was subsequently removed from the tomb. Hence, when a row of stones has been added there is both designation and use, but where no stones have been added there is only use but no designation and this is analogous to R. Hisda's case of the *tefillin*. The Talmud now adds a ruling of Rafram bar Pappa in the name of R. Hisda, to the effect that if the row that has been added can still be identified that row can be removed and the rest of the tomb is then permitted (once the corpse has been removed). The point here is, since, according to R. Hisda, there has to be both use and designation for it to be forbidden, then although the whole of the tomb has been used it is only the row that has been added that has been designated, so that once the row has been removed the rest of the tomb is permitted, on the grounds that there has been use but no designation. That row of stones, however, is forbidden even after its removal since so far as that row is concerned there has been both use and designation.,

A *Baraita* is now quoted: 'If a man hews out a grave for his father but then buries his father in another place he must never use that grave to bury therein', i.e. it is forbidden to use that grave to bury someone else therein since to do so would be to have benefit from a grave. This refutes Rava, since the grave has only been designated for the father's corpse and has not actually been used. The reply is given that the prohibition is not because of 'benefit' from a corpse and if the grave had been designated for another corpse, not the father, it would, indeed, be permitted. The reason it is forbidden is out of respect for the father, i.e. once the son had set the grave aside for his father it is disrespectful to his father's memory to use it to bury therein someone else. And, the Talmud continues, this explanation is in any event preferable since the *Baraita* continues: 'Rabban Simeon b. Gamaliel says: Even if a man merely hews out stones for his father's grave and then buries his father in another grave, he must never used that grave (into which the stones will be placed) for burial.' Now if the reason is because of respect for the father we can understand why Simeon b. Gamaliel forbids even the stones to be used. He evidently holds that it is disrespectful for the son to use even the stones. But if the reason is because of *hazmanah*, 'designation', it would then follow that R. Simeon b. Gamaliel forbids even the stones on the same grounds of *hazmanah* and this is impossible since even Abbaye only forbids a *garment* that has been woven for a corpse. Abbaye would not forbid the yarn spun to be woven into the shroud. Abbaye only holds designation to be effective where the object designated can be used for the purpose that renders it forbidden. He does not forbid that which is designated to be designated, namely, the yarn for the shroud for the corpse and the stones for the tomb for the corpse.

Soncino translates: 'If one hews a grave for his father and buries him elsewhere, he [himself] may never be buried therein.' This would seem to be the interpretation of the *Tur*, *Yoreh De'ah* 364. But the difficulty about this interpretation is that it seems to place a prohibition on the son when the son is dead, which seems absurd, unless the meaning is that the son must never be buried there so as not to have the satisfaction *while alive* of knowing that he will be buried there. Maimonides (*Yad*, *Evel* 14: 20) formulates it as: 'he should never bury another corpse there', i.e. the son must not use the tomb to bury therein another corpse because he would then be benefiting from the tomb.

A further *Baraita* is then quoted, this time to refute Abbaye. The Baraita reads: 'It is permitted to have benefit from a new grave but if an abortion has been cast therein it is forbidden.' This shows that *hazmanah* is ineffective. The new grave is not forbidden until the abortion has been cast there. The reply is that a new grave is in any event forbidden because it has been designated as a grave. When the *Baraita* speaks of a new grave it means a grave not set aside at all for a corpse but simply to be used in the future when required. If it had been set aside for a corpse it is forbidden, as

Abbaye states. In that case why does the abortion have to be cast therein? Why does not the mere designation for the abortion suffice to render it forbidden? It is because we might have argued that, as Rabban Simeon b. Gamaliel, who is quoted, actually holds, an abortion does not render a grave forbidden. According to Rabban Simeon b. Gamaliel a grave containing an abortion is only forbidden while the abortion is there and not because of the grave but because of the abortion itself. Once the abortion has been removed from the grave the grave is permitted. That is why the first Tanna speaks of the abortion being cast there. He personally holds that the grave is forbidden even if there is only the designation of the grave for the abortion. But he speaks of it being cast there to show that Rabban Simeon b. Gamaliel holds that even if it has been cast there the grave is permitted once it has been removed.

A Mishnah (*Shekalim* 2: 5) is now quoted to refute Abbaye. The Mishnah rules that if money was collected for the purpose of burying the dead poor any surplus must also be used for burying the dead and for no other purpose. But if the money had been collected to bury a particular person then any surplus belongs to his heirs, it being assumed that the donors do not wish to have this returned to them but are content that it be enjoyed by the dead man's family. But if Abbaye is correct, all the money had been designated for the dead so why is the surplus permitted? The reply is, at first, given that the Mishnah refers to money collected while the man was still alive. But this cannot be, the Talmud observes, since there is a *Baraita* in which it is stated explicitly that the reference in the Mishnah is to money collected after the man had died.

Yes, the Talmud now implies, the Mishnah does seem to contradict Abbaye's ruling. But it has to be appreciated that the Mishnah states in its conclusion that R. Meir and R. Nathan disagree with the ruling of the first Tanna of the Mishnah. R. Meir holds that the surplus must not be touched 'until Elijah comes' and R. Nathan holds that the surplus must be used only for the dead man, i.e. to build a monument over his grave or sprinkle aromatic spices over it. Thus while it is true that the first Tanna seems to contradict Abbaye, R. Nathan appears to contradict Rava. Consequently, both Abbaye and Rava will be obliged to explain the Mishnah, each according to his view. This is how Abbaye will explain it. All three Tannaím hold, as Abbaye does, that *hazmanah* is effective. The question at issue is whether the original *hazmanah* of the donors was of all the money or only of the actual expenses, not of the surplus. The first Tanna holds that only the actual expenses were designated but the surplus was never designated for the corpse and hence the heirs may have it. R. Nathan holds that, on the contrary, the whole of the money, including the surplus, is designated, hence the surplus may only be used for a monument and so forth. R. Meir is uncertain whether the surplus is designated, in which case the heirs may not have it, or whether it was not designated, in which case they may. Consequently, R. Meir holds that we have to wait until Elijah comes and he will be able to inform us whether or not the surplus was designated.

Rava, on the other hand, will hold that all three Tannaím will agree with him that *hazmanah* is ineffective. In that case why does R. Nathan hold that the surplus is forbidden to the heirs? It is not because of *hazmanah* but for an entirely different reason. The man has been humiliated by having to be the object of charity and while he is prepared, while alive, to have the money collected for his actual burial he does not wish to suffer this humiliation for the sake of the surplus if that goes to his heirs. This is R. Nathan's view, i.e. the man does not, in fact, bequeath this surplus to his heirs. The first Tanna disagrees and holds that he does. R. Meir is uncertain whether he does not and so he rules that it must await the coming of Elijah who will be able to tell us whether he does or does not.

It appears from this passage that money designated for the dead, according to Abbaye, is treated like the woven garment not the spun yarn. The reason is probably because the designation of the money is more immediate in that the money can *now* be used for the dead, unlike the yarn, see *Tosafists*, s.v. *motar ha-met*.

A *Baraita* is now quoted which seems to refute Abbaye. The *Baraita* states that if a father and mother cast garments on to the bier of their son (as if to say, nothing is worth anything to us now that we have lost our son) it is meritorious for others to rescue these garments and return them to the parents when their grief will have subsided. This refutes Abbaye. To this the reply is given, the parents only do it out of 'bitterness', i.e. to express their grief but do not really mean to designate the garments for the corpse. But, the Talmud objects, the *Baraita* continues: 'Rabban Simeon b. Gamaliel says: When is this [that the garments should be rescued], only when the garments have not touched the bier? If they have touched the bier they are forbidden.' But if the parents only do it out of grief and do not really mean the garments to be designated for the corpse they should be permitted even if they have touched the bier. To this the reply is given, that, indeed, strictly speaking they are permitted but the Sages placed a prohibition on them when they have actually touched the bier because the reference is to the bier which will be buried with the corpse. Here the garments, if they have touched the bier, may be confused with the actual shrouds and if people see that the Sages permit their removal they might mistakenly conclude that even shrouds are permitted.

Another *Baraita* is now quoted dealing with *tefillin*. This reads: 'If a bag had been made to place *tefillin* therein it is forbidden to place money therein. But if *tefillin* had been placed (temporarily) in a bag it is permitted to place money therein.' This shows that *hazmanah* is effective and refutes Rava. The reply is that the *Baraita* means, the bag was not only made for the *tefillin* but the *tefillin* were actually placed there as well. Thus the *Baraita* accords with the view of R. Hisda that both designation and use are required for it to be forbidden.

Another *Baraita* (*Tosefta*, *Megillah* 2) is now quoted. Here it is stated that if a man instructed a craftsman to make him a sheath for a scroll of the Law or a receptacle for *tefillin* it is permitted to use these for secular purposes until they have actually been used for their sacred purpose. This proves conclusively that *hazmanah* is ineffective and Abbaye is refuted. The reply is given that, indeed, the *Baraita* holds that *hazmanah* is ineffective but Abbaye can produce another *Baraita* from which it is clear that the issue is debated by Tannaím. The *Baraita* is then quoted: 'If *tefillin* were overlaid with gold or covered with the hide of an unclean animal they are unfit for use. If they were covered with the hide of a clean animal they are permitted for use even if the hide had not been dressed for the purpose. But Rabban Simeon b. Gamaliel holds that they are unfit for use even if they had been covered with the hide of a clean animal if the hide had not been dressed for that purpose.' We see that according to the first Tanna there is no need for the hide to be dressed specifically for the purpose of *tefillin*, while Rabban Simeon b. Gamaliel holds that it has to be dressed specifically for the purpose. It follows that according to the first Tanna *hazmanah* is ineffective. Since *tefillin* do not require any specific designation, any designation for the purpose of *tefillin* is irrelevant. It has no meaning, so that a receptacle made for *tefillin* is not forbidden even according to Abbaye. But according to Rabban Simeon b. Gamaliel *tefillin* do require designation and according to him, *hazmanah*, being relevant, is effective (agreeing with Abbaye). Thus all agree that where *hazmanah* is relevant it is effective, as Abbaye holds. The only reason why it is ineffective in the case of *tefillin*, according to one authority, is because there *hazmanah* is irrelevant.

This is *Rashi*'s understanding of the passage. *Tosafists*, s.v. *af 'al pi*, understands it differently. The first Tanna who does not require the hide to be dressed for the purpose holds that *hazmanah* is effective, hence the designation of the hide for *tefillin* suffices and there is no need for the hide to be dressed specifically for the purpose. Rabban Simeon b. Gamaliel holds that the hide does have to be dressed specifically for the purpose because mere *hazmanah* for the purpose is ineffective.

The Talmud, having brought the discussion to a successful conclusion reports that Ravina asked Rava: 'Is there any place where the dead lie unburied while the shrouds are being woven?', i.e. the case debated by Abbaye and Rava is extremely unlikely. The shrouds are always ready to hand. Rava replied: 'It can happen in connection with the dead of Harpania' (where the people are so poor that they wait until someone dies before collecting the money to buy shrouds and these, therefore, have sometimes to be woven while the corpse lies there: *Rashi*).

The *sugya* concludes with an exposition of the final ruling. This reads: 'Meremar expounded (*darash*): "The law follows Abbaye." But the Rabbis said: "The law follows Rava." And the law follows Rava.' This small section appears to have been inserted after the completion of the whole *sugya*, i.e. once the full debate between Abbaye and Rava had been recorded, including the arguments for and against, the editors inform us that the late-fifth-century Amora 'expounded' (the usual term for a clear, public pronouncement of the actual ruling) that the ruling is in accordance with the opinion of Abbaye. The other scholars (the Rabbis), however, disagreed and 'said' (not 'expounded', because they, evidently, occupied no official, authoritative position as Meremar did) that the ruling follows the opinion of Rava. The final conclusion 'And the law follows Rava' was almost certainly added even later (it is probably a post-Talmudic addition), i.e. after the debate between Meremar and the Rabbis had been recorded.

The mnemonic at the beginning of the series of proofs is also almost certainly post-Talmudic, having been inserted when the complete *sugya* as we now have it had been fully arranged and put in its present order.

It is somewhat curious that there are no less than four references to Rabban Simeon b. Gamaliel in this comparatively brief *sugya* and they are from diverse sources. The best way of explaining this phenomenon is that all four deal with laws having to do with 'setting aside' and the editors used this material in building up the *sugya* of *hazmanah*, interpreting the various rulings of Rabban Simeon b. Gamaliel accordingly. It is still odd that apart from the law of the abortion the statements of Rabban Simeon b. Gamaliel are not found in any other passage, Tannaitic or otherwise. For all that it would be hypercritical to suggest that the editors have simply invented these statements, using the name of Rabban Simeon b. Gamaliel because of the abortion law in which he features. The most probable explanation is as we have suggested, that Rabban Simeon b. Gamaliel was known to have stated these four laws but not necessarily in the sense in which our *sugya* understands them. The editors simply built on this material to further their own dramatic aim.

The plan of the *sugya*, after the statements about the debate between Abbaye and Rava, is as follows:

(1) Refutation of Rava (a): Mishnah of veil – mere *hazmanah*
(2) Reply: No – actual use
(3) Elaboration: R. Hisda – both *hazmanah* and use required
(4) Refutation of Rava (b): *Baraita* – row of stones – mere *hazmanah*
(5) Reply: corpse there – both *hazmanah* and use
(6) Elaboration: corpse was later removed
(7) Rafram's statement: independent of *sugya* but relevant
(8) Refutation of Rava (c): grave for father – mere *hazmanah*
(9) Reply: reason is out of respect for father
(10) Elaboration: proof that this must be the reason
(11) Refutation of Abbaye (a): new grave and abortion
(12) Reply: because of Rabban Simeon b. Gamaliel
(13) Refutation of Abbaye (b): Mishnah: surplus
(14) Reply: tentative: collected while alive
(15) Objection: contradicts *Baraita*
(16) Reply: in any event R. Meir and R. Nathan
(17) Consequently: both Abbaye and Rava explain it
(18) Refutation of Abbaye (c): father and mother casting garments
(19) Reply: because of 'bitterness'
(20) Objection: then even if they have touched the bier

(21) Reply: because then confused with shrouds
(22) Refutation of Rava (d): *tefillin*
(23) Reply: actually used – R. Hisda
(24) Refutation of Abbaye (d): receptacle of *tefillin*
(25) Reply: debate of Tannaím
(26) Ravina's question: how is the case at all possible?
(27) Rava's reply: dead of Harpania
(28) Final ruling: Meremar, the Rabbis and final ruling

Why has all this material been presented in precisely this way, since the actual proofs have been taken from varied sources? The answer is fairly obvious: because there is here a logical sequence of thought. The reply in (2) does not apply in (4). Yes, it does, because of elaboration in (6). But the reply does not work in (8), where the father is not buried there and hence is *not* used. Turns now to refutation of Abbaye (11). Reply as in (12). But what of (13)? Then (18), further refutation of Abbaye to which none of the earlier replies is cogent. All of these have to do with corpse except (1), which must come first in order to lead up to the others. Now (22), dealing with a new subject, *tefillin*. Reply as in (23). Refutation of Abbaye (24) and the strongest, since the only reply, as in (25), is that the Tannaím debate it.

The theme of *hazmanah* is found, too, in *Berakhot* 23b (the law of R. Hisda and discussion on it as in our *sugya*); *Megillah* 23b (distinction as in our *sugya* between yarn and woven garment); *Menaḥot* 34b. Cf. *Nedarim* 7a. For a full treatment of the post-Talmudic discussions, see *Kesef Nivḥar*, part I, no. 48, pp. 84a–86a and *ET*, vol. VIII, s.v. *hazmanah alef*, pp. 623–45.

14

Mitzvat 'aseh she-ha-zeman geramah: positive precepts dependent on time from which women are exempt

The *sugya* is *Kiddushin* 33b–35a. *Mitzvat 'aseh she-ha-zeman geramah* is literally: 'A positive precept that is caused by time', i.e. that depends for its performance on a given time and is not a precept that can be carried out at any time. The *sugya* is appended to the Mishnah (*Kiddushin* 1: 7): 'And every positive precept dependent on time men are obliged to fulfil but women are exempt. And every positive precept not dependent on time both men and women are obliged to fulfil. And every negative precept, whether dependent on time or not dependent on time, both men and women are obliged to fulfil.'

The *sugya* opens with a *Baraita*: 'Which are positive precepts dependent on time: *sukkah* (Leviticus 23: 42, only to be carried out on Tabernacles); *lulav* ('palm branch, Leviticus 23: 40, only on Tabernacles); *shofar* (ram's horn', Leviticus 23: 24; Numbers 29: 1, only on the New Year Festival); *tzitzit* ('fringes', Numbers 16: 38, only during the day, not at night); and *tefillin* (Deuteronomy 6: 8, only during the days and not the nights of the week and not on Sabbath and Festivals). And which are positive precepts not dependent on time: *mezuzah* (Deuteronomy 6: 9); *ma'akeh* ('battlement', Deuteronomy 22: 8); returning lost property (Exodus 23: 4; Deuteronomy 22: 1–3); and sending away the mother-bird (Deuteronomy 22: 6–7).'

The Talmud objects: but is this a general rule? There are: eating unleavened bread on Passover (Exodus 12: 18, obligatory for women, too, just as they are obliged to abstain from eating leaven); rejoicing on the Festivals (Deuteronomy 16: 14); and assembly (on the Festival of Tabernacles in the seventh year, Deuteronomy 31: 12). These are positive precepts dependent on time and yet women are obliged to fulfil them. Furthermore, there are the study of the Torah, the duty of procreation and the redemption of the first-born. These are positive precepts not dependent on time and yet women are exempt from having to fulfil them. Thus although the *Baraita* purports to give two general rules – one for precepts dependent on time, the other for precepts not dependent on time – neither is completely accurate, since there are exceptions to both. To this the reply is given that R. Johanan says: 'One does not learn from [a statement of a] general principle even when exceptions are stated', i.e. so that it would appear that these are the *only* exceptions. There are, in fact, or can be, other exceptions as well. In support a Mishnah (*'Eruvin* 2: 1) is quoted and R. Johanan's comment applied to it. The Mishnah deals with the law of *'eruv*, the device by means of which it is permitted for people with houses around a common courtyard to carry therein on the Sabbath. Some food, belonging to all the householders, is deposited in one of the houses on the eve of the Sabbath, and, by a legal fiction, this renders the courtyard as if it were a private domain in which it is permitted to carry. The Mishnah states that an *'eruv* can be of any food except water and salt. But, the Talmud observed, there is also the exception of mushrooms and truffles which cannot be used for the *'eruv*. To this R. Johanan is quoted as replying: 'One does not learn from [a statement of a] general principle even when exceptions are stated.' Hence, even though the *Baraita*, quoted at the beginning, lays down general rules, there are exceptions to these rules.

R. Johanan's statement occurs also in *'Eruvin* 27a (on the Mishnah quoted here) and *'Eruvin* 29a, which is a cross-reference: '*As* R. Johanan said'. A comparison of the first *'Eruvin* passsage with ours is revealing. There the *sugya* opens with R. Johanan's statement. The Talmud then observes that R. Johanan cannot have made his statement in the first instance as a comment on the *'Eruvin* Mishnah, since the clause '*even* when exceptions are stated' seems to imply that R. Johanan's original statement was with reference to a Tannaitic formulation of a general rule in which *no* exceptions are recorded and which he then elaborates on by observing that his observation would apply *even* where exceptions *are* stated. This means that he cannot have made his observation on the *'Eruvin* Mishnah in which exceptions *are* stated explicitly. To this the reply is given that R. Johanan's original observation must have been made on our *Baraita*, which is then quoted as here. We now have the full statement of R. Johanan, i.e. that his observation applies even when exceptions are noted. There follows an attempt by Abbaye or R. Jeremiah to prove the correctness of this. Finally, Ravina or R. Nahman prove it from the *'Eruvin* Mishnah. Thus the same material has been used both in our *sugya* and in '*Eruvin*, but this has been arranged differently in two tractates. The fuller discussion is in '*Eruvin*. Cf. Abraham Weiss, *le-Ḥeker ha-Talmud*, pp. 370–2 and Halivni, *Sources and Traditions*, p. 654, note 2.

There now begins a series of comments on the first rule of the Mishnah, that women are exempt from carrying out positive precepts dependent on time. How do we know this? The reply is given: it is derived from *tefillin*. Just as women are exempt from *tefillin*, which is a positive precept dependent on time, so, too, they are exempt from all such precepts. And that women are, in fact, exempt from *tefillin* is derived from the fact that in the *Shema*' *tefillin* are compared to the study of the Torah: 'And thou shalt teach them diligently unto thy sons, and shalt talk of them when thou sittest in thy house... And thou shalt bind them for a sign' (Deuteronomy 6: 7–8). Now of the study of the Torah the verse states: 'unto thy *sons*' and not 'thy *daughters*'. Women are thus exempt from the study of the Torah and since *tefillin* are compared to the study of the Torah (being placed adjacent to this in the verse) they are exempt from *tefillin*. Once we have established in this way that women are exempt from *tefillin* we can go on to derive other precepts from *tefillin*. Just as women are exempt from *tefillin* they are exempt from every positive precept dependent on time. The Talmud goes on to point out, however, that there is a reference to *mezuzah* in the next verse: 'And thou shalt write them upon the posts of thy house, and on thy gates' (Deuteronomy 6: 9). Thus while it is true that *tefillin* are compared to the study of the Torah, mentioned in the verse preceding that of *tefillin*, it is also true that *tefillin* are compared to *mezuzah*, mentioned in the verse following *tefillin*. Why, then, should we not rather compare *tefillin* to *mezuzah* and deduce from it that women are obliged to carry out the duty of *tefillin*? To this the reply is given that there are two separate sections of the *Shema*': Deuteronomy 6: 4–9 and 11: 13–21. In the first section *tefillin* are, as above, placed between the study of the Torah and *mezuzah*, but in the second section *tefillin* are in verse 18, study of the Torah in verse 19, and *mezuzah* in verse 20. Thus *tefillin* are adjacent to the study of the Torah in both sections but only adjacent to *mezuzah* in the first section. Consequently, it is preferable to compare *tefillin* to the study of the Torah and not to *mezuzah*. Then, the Talmud asks, why not compare *mezuzah* to the study of the Torah, to which it is adjacent in the second section, and women should be exempt from *mezuzah*? To this the reply is given that Scripture continues, after stating the law of the *mezuzah*: 'that your days may be multiplied' (Deuteronomy 11: 21). Is it only men who require life and not women? I.e. since the result of carrying out this precept is long life it must obviously apply to both men and women.

We have now established *tefillin* as the key-text. From it we derive the rule of the Mishnah that women are exempt from positive precepts dependent on time. The Talmud now turns to explore this further. Of the *sukkah* Scripture says: 'ye shall dwell in booths [*sukkot*] seven days' (Leviticus 23: 42). Thus *sukkah* is a positive precept dependent on time and, according to the rule, women are exempt from it. They are, indeed, exempt but the exemption is derived from the second half of the verse: 'all that are home-born in Israel shall dwell in booths'. A *Baraita* (*Sukkah* 28a) derives the exemption of women from the word *ha-ezraḥ* ('home-born'). But why should this verse be required to exempt women who are, in any event, exempted by the general rule? To this Abbaye and Rava each supply an answer. Abbaye suggests that *ha-ezraḥ* is required because otherwise we might have said that women are not exempt, i.e. that *sukkah* is an exception to the general rule. This is because Scripture speaks of *dwelling* in *sukkot* and 'dwelling' usually means as one normally 'dwells', husband and wife together. Rava suggests a different reason why *ha-ezraḥ* is required and why, otherwise, we might have supposed that *sukkah* is an exception to the general rule. The same word *fifteenth* occurs both in connection with *sukkah*: 'on the fifteenth day of the seventh month' (Leviticus 23: 34) and in connection with Passover: 'on the fifteenth day of the same month is the feast of unleavened bread' (Leviticus 23: 6). Now, as above, the precept of eating unleavened bread on Passover is binding upon women so that we might have supposed that the use of *fifteenth* in both verses is to teach us that just as women are obliged to eat unleavened bread on Passover they are obliged to dwell in the *sukkah* on Tabernacles. *Sukkah*, too, would, then, have been an exception to the general rule, hence *ha-ezraḥ* is required to teach that women are exempted.

A similar question to that of *sukkah* is now raised. The verse states that on the three Festivals of Passover, Pentecost and Tabernacles there is the duty of pilgrimage to the Temple: 'Three times in the year all thy males shall appear before the Lord God' (Exodus 23: 17). Thus the precept of appearance is one dependent on time and women would have been exempt from it, in any event, because of the general rule. Why, then, does Scripture have to specify 'all thy *males*' to imply 'and not thy *females*', since women would have been exempted by the terms of the general rule? To this the Talmud replies that here, too, there is the phenomenon of the same word in two separate verses. The word *appear* occurs in this verse and it also occurs in the verse dealing with the *assembly* on the Festival of Tabernacles in the seventh year: 'When all Israel is come to appear' (Deuteronomy 31: 11). Now there it is stated explicitly that women are obliged to take part in the *assembly*: 'Gather the people together, men, and women' (Deuteronomy 31: 12). Since the word 'appear' is in both verses we might have supposed that just as *assembly* is an exception to the general rule so, too, *appearance* is an exception. That is why Scripture had to state explicitly 'thy *males*', implying 'and not thy *females*'.

Thus far the following has been established: woman are exempt from *tefillin* and from this we derive that they are exempt from other positive precepts dependent on time. The duty of rejoicing on the Festival is an exception, as above, since here Scripture states explicitly: 'And thou shalt rejoice in thy feast, thou, and thy son, and thy daughter, and thy manservant and thy maidservant, and the Levite, the stranger, and the fatherless, and the widow, that are within thy gates' (Deuteronomy 16: 14). In that case, the Talmud now asks, why derive other positive precepts dependent on time from *tefillin* so as to conclude that women are exempt from them? Let us rather derive from *rejoicing* that women are obliged to carry out even positive precepts dependent on time, just as they have an obligation to rejoice on the Festivals. To this a saying of Abbaye is quoted: a woman is made to rejoice by her husband, i.e. a woman does not, in fact, have an obligation to rejoice. The command is not addressed to the wife but to her husband, who has a duty to make his wife happy. But, the Talmud objects, the verse speaks, too, of the 'widow' and here, since she does not have a husband, the reference can only be to the widow herself, which shows that the obligation is binding upon women. No, the Talmud replies, the verse refers to a widow who is looked after by someone else, i.e. she enjoys hospitality in his home and the command is to him, to make her happy, not to her.

The Talmud now asks, why not derive from the precept of *assembly* that women are obliged to carry out positive precepts dependent on time just as they are obliged to carry out the precept of *assembly*, i.e. and why should we prefer to derive from *tefillin* that they are not so obliged? To this the Talmud replies by referring to the well-known hermeneutical principle: *sheney ketuvim habaím ke-eḥad eyn melammedim*, lit. 'two verses that come together [i.e. for the same purpose] cannot serve as teachers', i.e. if two separate verses both purport to teach the same matter neither of them can serve as a basis of derivation for other similar matters. The logic of the principle is that if Scripture had intended us to derive other matters from one of these verses, Scripture would have recorded only one and the other, too, could have been derived from that one. By giving us two verses, Scripture seems to be warning us, as it were, against deriving other matters from either. Now there are, in fact, two verses, not one, in which it is stated that women are obliged to carry out positive precepts dependent on time. These are: *assembly* and *eating unleavened bread* on Passover. Consequently, we do not use either of these as the basis for our derivation. Instead we use the *single* instance of *tefillin* and so conclude that women are exempt, as they are from *tefillin*.

We thus have two verses stating that women are obliged to carry out precepts dependent on time – *assembly* and *unleavened bread* – and one verse – *tefillin* – stating that they are exempt. Because of the principle of 'two verses' the two cannot serve as the basis of the derivation of other precepts but the single verse can and does.

The Talmud now raises an objection. There are, in fact, *two* verses stating that women are exempt – *tefillin* and *appearance* ('pilgrimage'). If the *two* verses of *unleavened bread* and *assembly* cannot serve to teach that women are not exempt neither can the *two* verses of *tefillin* and *appearance* serve to teach that they are exempt. The reply is that the 'two verses' principle only applies where, as above, one can be derived from the other. In that case the Torah, by recording the other, can be said to be warning us not to use these verses as a basis for derivation. But if one cannot be derived from the other then neither is superfluous and we do not then have *two* verses and then they can serve as a basis for derivation. *Appearance* and *tefillin* cannot be derived one from the other so that here the 'two verses' principle is not invoked. *Appearance* cannot be derived from *tefillin*, for if the Torah had not stated explicitly that women are exempt from *appearance* we would have argued from the *appear–appear* words, as above, that just as women are obliged to carry out the *assembly* precept so, too, they are obliged to carry out the *appearance* precept. Conversely, if the Torah had not stated explicitly that women are exempt from *tefillin* we would have compared *tefillin* to *mezuzah*, as above, and concluded that just as women are obliged to carry out the precept of *mezuzah* so, too, they are obliged to carry out the precept of *tefillin*. Consequently, both *tefillin* and *appearance* require to be stated explicitly. Neither can be derived from the other and hence the 'two verses' principle cannot be here invoked.

In that case, the Talmud continues, *unleavened bread* and *assembly* may both be required so that here, too, the 'two verses' principle cannot be invoked. No, the reply is given. It is true that had the Torah stated that women are obliged to carry out the precept of *assembly* we would not have known that they are obliged to eat *unleavened bread*, for we would have relied on the *fifteenth–fifteenth*, as above, to say that just as they have no obligation to dwell in the *sukkah* they have no obligation to eat *unleavened bread*, i.e., the above comparison in reverse. But the Torah need not have stated that women are obliged to carry out the precept of *assembly* since here the Torah states that even little children had to assemble, *a fortiori* women. Consequently, the *assembly* statement is superfluous so that when it is placed together with that of *unleavened bread* we can invoke the 'two verses' principle.

The Talmud now advances two further difficulties. First, the acceptance of the 'two verses' principle on which we have so far relied is by no means unanimous. There are authorities who reject it and according to them the question remains, why not derive other precepts from *unleavened bread* and *assembly*? The second difficulty is with regard to the second rule in the Mishnah, that women are obliged to carry out positive precepts not dependent on time. This is presumably derived from the law of fearing parents (Leviticus 19:3) which is binding upon women as well as men (*Kiddushin* 29a). But why derive other precepts from *fear*; derive them rather from the *study of the Torah*, from which, as above, women are exempt even though it is a precept not dependent on time. The first difficulty is shelved for the time being. The reply to the second difficulty is that here, too, there is more than one verse. There is the *study of the Torah* and there is procreation, as above. Neither of these is a precept dependent on time and there are thus *two* verses in which it is stated that women are exempt from precepts not dependent on time. There are thus *two* verses to state that they are exempt and only one – *fear* – that they are not exempt. With regard to the two verses, the 'two verses' principle is invoked which leaves the one – *fear* – from which we derive that women are not exempt.

The Talmud now quotes the opinion of R. Johanan b. Berokah who holds that women are obliged to engage in procreation since the command 'Be fruitful, and multiply' (Genesis 1:28) was given to both Adam and Eve. According to R. Johanan b. Berokah we have only one verse – *study* – that women are exempt, so why derive from *fear* that they are not exempt? The reply is that we still have two verses – *study* and *redemption of the first-born*, as above. A woman is not obliged to redeem her son as a father is. But, the Talmud continues, according to R. Johanan b. Berokah we also have two verses saying that they are not exempt – *fear* and *procreation*. We thus have two verses on either side – *study* and *redemption* that they are exempt and *procreation* and *fear* that they are not exempt. The reply is given that *procreation* and *fear* cannot be derived from one another and hence, as above, the 'two verses' principle cannot be here invoked. For if the Torah had only stated that women are obliged to *fear* we would not have concluded that they are obliged to *procreate* since in the *procreation* verse it is stated: 'Be fruitful and multiply, and replenish the earth, and subdue ie' (Genesis 1:28) and women do not engage in conquest. Conversely, if the Torah had stated only *procreation* we would not have derived *fear* from it. Since a married woman cannot always carry out this obligation, because her husband may not allow her to, we would have argued that *no* woman has the duty of *fear*. Consequently, both verses are required and, as above, the 'two verses' principle cannot be here invoked.

Now all this fits in very neatly with the view that 'two verses which come together cannot act as teachers'. But, repeating now the first difficulty, what of those authorities who do not accept this principle at all? Therefore, Rava is reported as saying, the 'scholars of Papunia', identified with R. Aha b. Jacob, resolved the whole problem by quoting a different verse. This verse states: 'And it shall be for a sign unto thee upon thine hand, and for a memorial between thine eyes, that the Torah of the Lord may be in thy mouth' (Exodus 13:9). In this verse 'the whole of the Torah', i.e. all the precepts, is compared to *tefillin* (which, in turn, as above, are compared to the *study of the Torah*). Thus just as women are exempt from *tefillin* they are exempt, too, by the actual comparison in the verse, from every positive precept that, like *tefillin*, is dependent on time. They are not exempt, it follows further, from positive precepts not dependent on time since these are unlike *tefillin*.

The Talmud now observes that all this is correct, on the assumption that *tefillin* are precepts dependent on time. But this itself is disputed (*Shabbat* 61a) and some authorities hold that *tefillin* are not dependent on time, i.e. they have to be worn at night as well as by day and on Sabbaths and festivals. The Talmud neatly replies that the authority who holds this view is R. Meir and it so happens that R. Meir does accept the 'two verses' principle. True, R. Meir cannot use the argument of the Papunians, since according to him *tefillin* are not dependent on time. But then the only reason we had to have recourse to the Papunians was because of those who reject the 'two verses' principle and R. Meir does not, in fact, reject it.

At this stage of the argument, if an authority will be discovered who rejects the 'two verses' principle (and so cannot derive it from *unleavened bread* and *assembly*) and also holds that *tefillin* are not dependent on time (and so cannot derive it by the Papunian derivation) the difficulty will indeed be great. And there is such an authority, R. Judah, who holds that two verses can be used as a basis of derivation (*Sanhedrin* 67b) and also holds that *tefillin* are not precepts dependent on time (*'Eruvin* 96b). The reply is, there are, in reality, *three* verses. These are: *unleavened bread*, *assembly* and *rejoicing* (the Talmud now rejects Abbaye's view, above, that a woman has no obligation to rejoice on the Festivals). Hence there are three instances of a positive precept dependent on time, which women are obliged to carry out. And even R. Judah who rejects the 'two verses' principle, agrees that *three* verses cannot serve as a basis of derivation. The logic of this appears to be that while Scripture might state just one superfluous verse, perhaps for greater emphasis, it would not repeat more than one unless the intention is to emphasise that these three instances are exceptions and, therefore, cannot serve as a basis of derivation.

The principle: *sheney ketuvim habaím ke-aḥad eyn melammedim* is found, too, in: *Pesaḥim* 26a; 45a; *Yoma* 60a; *Gittin* 76a; *Nazir* 37b; *Kiddushin* 24a; our passage; 34b; 35a; 37b; 42b; 43a; 58a; *Sanhedrin* 45b; 67b; 72b; *Shevu'ot* 26b; *'Avodah Zarah* 54b; *Zevaḥim* 24a; 47a; 57a; *Ḥullin* 61a; 113b; *Bekhorot* 49a; *Keritot* 6a; *Me'ilah* 11b; *'Arakhin* 14b. See H. H. Medini, *Sedey Ḥemed*, vol. IV, p. 517 for two different interpretations of this principle: (a) that the two verses cannot serve as a basis of derivation, so the matter is left open; (b) the two verses teach the opposite, which fits in better with the argument in our *sugya*. For other Talmudic passages dealing with *mitzvat 'aseh she-ha-zeman geramah*, see *Berakhot* 20b; *Pesaḥim* 43b; *Sukkah* 28a–b; *Ḥagigah* 4a. The theme is also referred to incidentally in numerous passages. Cf. *ET*, vol. II, pp. 244–7. There is a curious reference in *Ramban*'s list of precepts *not* dependent on time, in which one of the items is *sefirat ha-'omer*, 'counting the *'omer*'. It has been suggested that this is counted as 'not dependent on time' since the time limitation is not in the performance of the precept but belongs to the nature of the precept, i.e. the counting of this particular time, unlike, say, *lulav* which can physically be carried out at any time and is yet limited to Tabernacles. However, I would surmise a guess that *sefirat ha-'omer* is a copyist's error for *sefirat ha-niddah*, 'the counting of the days of separation'. The first section of our *sugya*, concerning R. Johanan's rule, is really independent of the rest of the *sugya* and, as we have seen, is recorded separately in *'Eruvin*. For all that, it has its place here both because of the theme and because it leads up to and prepares the ground for the second section of the *sugya* on the question of derivation.

The pattern of the main *sugya* is:

(1) Rule derived from *tefillin* – which in turn derived from *study*
(2) Question: but let *tefillin* be rather derived from *mezuzah*?
(3) Reply: compared to *study* in both sections of *Shema'*
(4) Question: let *mezuzah* be compared to *study* and women exempt?
(5) Reply: women also need 'life'
(6) Question: why is *ha-ezraḥ* needed for *sukkah*?
(7) Reply: Abbaye: husband and wife *dwelling*
(8) Reply: Rava: *fifteenth–fifteenth*
(9) Question: why 'all *males*' needed for *appearance*?
(10) Reply: *appear–appear* from *assembly*
(11) Question: why not derive from *rejoicing* that women are obligated?
(12) Abbaye's reply: husband's obligation not hers
(13) Question: But what of widow?
(14) Reply: refers to her host
(15) Question: why not derive from *assembly* that obligated?
(16) Reply: *assembly* and *unleavened bread* are 'two verses'
(17) Question: then say *tefillin* and *appearance* are 'two verses'?
(18) Reply: both required, one cannot be derived from the other
(19) Question: then *assembly* and *unleavened bread* both required?
(20) Reply: no, *assembly* not required since even little children
(21) Question: but what of authorities who reject the 'two verses' principle?
(22) Question (b): whence derive precepts not dependent on time?
(23) Reply to (b): derived from *fear*
(24) Question: but why not derive from *study*?

(25) Reply: *study* and *procreation* 'two verses'
(26) Question: but R. Johanan b. Berokah?
(27) Reply: *study* and *redemption* 'two verses'
(28) Question: but then *procreation* and *fear* 'two verses'?
(29) Reply: both required
(30) Question as in (21): but what of those who reject 'two verses'?
(31) Reply: Rava: 'Papunians': verse compared *tefillin* to precepts
(32) Question: but what of authority who holds *tefillin* not dependent on time?
(33) Reply: R. Meir and he does accept the 'two verses...' principle
(34) Question: but what of R. Judah?
(35) Reply: there are three *verses* (12) rejected and (11) reinstated

There is sufficient evidence that the whole passage, complex though it is, follows a carefully worked-out pattern of question and reply, one point leading to another in neat sequence. Note especially how Abbaye in (12) is rejected in (35) but not until the argument has made it inevitable, so that early in the passage the way has been paved for the climax.

15

Heyzek she-eyno-nikar: indiscernible damage to property

The *sugya* is *Gittin* 53a–54b and is appended to the Mishnah (*Gittin* 5: 4) in which the rule is given that there are three instances of damage to property in which the perpetrator is only liable if he did the damage intentionally (*mezid*), not if he did it unintentionally (*shogeg*). The three instances are: (1) contamination of *terumah* (the tithe given to the priest, which cannot be eaten if unclean); (2) mixing *terumah* with ordinary, non-sacred food (*ḥullin*), i.e. mixing some *terumah* in a neighbour's *ḥullin* with the result that the mixture can only be eaten by priests and hence loses a good deal of its market value; (3) 'stirring', i.e. stirring a neighbour's wine as a libation to idols, the wine thus being rendered unfit for use (according to others, see *Gittin* 52b–53a, 'stirring' means mixing wine that has been 'stirred' as a libation with the wine of a neighbour so as to render the whole forbidden). These three are examples of indiscernible damage. The property remains, to the eye of the beholder, as it was before and yet damage has been done to it. The question discussed is whether there is compensation in law for such indiscernible damage, since it is possible to argue that the law only demands compensation for damage that can be discerned as such. The authorities who hold that there is compensation even for indiscernible damage are said to hold that *heyzek she-eyno nikar shemah heyzak*, literally 'damage that is indiscernible has the name of damage', i.e. falls under the heading of damage and requires therefore to be compensated for in law. The authorities who hold that there is no compensation for such damage are said to hold that *heyzek she-eyno nikar lav shemah heyzak*, lit. 'damage that is indiscernible does not have the name of damage'. The debate is between the early-third-century Palestinian Amoraím, Hezekiah and R. Johanan.

As the *sugya* immediately begins to discuss, the Mishnah presents a difficulty according to both views. According to another Mishnah (*Bava Kama* 2: 6) a man is responsible for any damage he does, whether he does it intentionally (*mezid*) or unintentionally (*shogeg*). Why, then, does our Mishnah make a distinction, in the three instances of indiscernible damage, between damage done intentionally and damage done unintentionally? If such damage is held to fall under the general law of damages there ought to be liability even if it was done unintentionally, as in the general law of damages. If, on the other hand, it is not held to fall under the general law of damages, there ought to be no liability even if done intentionally. It is illogical to hold that it falls under the general rule of damages where it was done intentionally and not where it was done unintentionally. Intention has nothing to do with it, as stated explicitly in the Mishnah in *Bava Kama*.

The *sugya* opens with the debate between Hezekiah and R. Johanan. Hezekiah, commenting on the Mishnah, observes that according to the law of the Torah (i.e. the original law before the Rabbis introduced new legislation) the perpetrator of the kinds of damage recorded in the Mishnah is liable whether he did it intentionally or unintentionally. This is because, the Talmud adds, Hezekiah holds that indiscernible damage does fall under the heading of damage. In that case why did the Rabbis introduce the new legislation to exonerate the perpetrator if he did it unintentionally? The reason is, so that he will be encouraged to inform the victim that his property is now forbidden, which he would not do if as a result he were held liable. In that case, why did the Rabbis not exonerate the perpetrator even if he did it intentionally? The reply is that here, since his intention is malicious, he would not inform the victim even if he were exonerated. There is no reason here to exonerate him and here the original law stands and he is liable. R. Johanan, on the other hand, observes that according to the law of Torah he is not liable even if he did it intentionally. The reason is, observes the Talmud, because indiscernible damage does not fall under the heading of damage. In that case why did the Rabbis introduce the new legislation to render him liable where he did it intentionally? The reason is, in order to prevent men contaminating their neighbour's food and drink and getting off scot free. The law cannot tolerate the opportunity of a man doing intentional damage to his neighbour without his having to pay compensation. This would be an open invitation to lawlessness. Thus both according to Hezekiah and R. Johanan one of the two rules in the Mishnah is due to Rabbinic legislation over and above the original law. According to Hezekiah the liability for intentional damage, even where indiscernible, is Biblical and the Rabbinic legislation is for the purpose of exonerating the unintentional act. According to R. Johanan the exoneration for the unintentional act is the Biblical law in its original form. The Rabbinic legislation is to make the perpetrator liable where he did it intentionally.

The next clause of our Mishnah is now quoted in an attempt to refute Hezekiah. The Mishnah states that if priests, while offering up a man's sacrifice in the Temple, do so with an untoward intention (*piggul*, i.e. the intention of eating the meat outside the proper place or after the proper time) they have to compensate the man if they did it intentionally. On this a *Baraita* comments: 'This rule is because of social benefit' (*tikkun ha-'olam*), i.e, it is a Rabbinic enactment. This shows that it is the intentional act that is due to Rabbinic legislation not the unintentional act and this supports R. Johanan and refutes Hezekiah. The reply is that the *Baraita* does not refer to the intentional act referred to explicitly in the Mishnah but to the unintentional act implied by the Mishnah. Since the Mishnah states that the priests are liable for the intentional act, the clear implication, though this is not stated explicitly, is that they are not liable for their unintentional act and it is on this that the *Baraita* makes its comment, namely, that, as Hezekiah states, the exoneration for the unintentional act is due to the new Rabbinic legislation.

R. Eleazar, a contemporary of Hezekiah and R. Johanan, now raises an objection to Hezekiah from a *Baraita*, dealing with the laws of the red heifer and the purifying water into which the ashes of the red heifer were cast (Numbers 19). If any manner of work was done with either it is thereby rendered unfit for the purpose of purification. The *Baraita* states that if a man did such work with the red heifer or purifying water belonging to his neighbour and thereby rendered them unfit he is not liable to compensate his neighbour by the laws of man (i.e. the Courts cannot enforce payment) but he is liable by the laws of Heaven (i.e. he has a moral obligation to pay, though this cannot be enforced). Since there is an obligation by the laws of Heaven this cannot refer to unintentional damage for then there would be total exoneration, as in our Mishnah. It must therefore refer to intentional damage, i.e. the work was done intentionally and maliciously in order to render the neighbour's property unfit. In that case, according to Hezekiah, who holds that indiscernible damage is called damage, the perpetrator ought to be liable by the laws of man.

See *Maharsha*, who raises the obvious difficulty that this *Baraita* is difficult even according to R. Johanan, since even R. Johanan holds that there is compensation, albeit only according to Rabbinic enactment, for intentional damage. Probably the meaning of our passage is that R. Johanan can easily defend his view by postulating that the special Rabbinic legislation was only introduced, as stated, in order to prevent man getting away with malicious damage and this would not apply to the red heifer which was very rare and the case so unusual that no special legislation was required. There is a need to introduce legislation to prevent people contaminating their neighbour's *terumah*, for example, because many people do have *terumah*. There was no need to introduce new legislation to meet the contingency of a man rendering his neighbour's red heifer unfit since it is extremely unlikely that his neighbour will ever have a red heifer. But according to Hezekiah the law of liability for intentional damage is Biblical and with regard to the actual law of damage there is obviously no distinction to be made between rare and less rare forms of damage.

The Talmud states that R. Eleazar, who raised this objection, himself supplied the answer. The *Baraita*, when it speaks of doing work with the heifer and the water, refers to a type of 'work' that only becomes such by intention. For instance, the man brought the heifer into the stall of its mother where it could be suckled, but his intention was for it to thresh corn at the same time and, as for the water, he placed it on the balance of a pair of scales so that all he did in essence was to place it there and it was his intention to use it as a weight in the scales that renders it unfit. Since it is his intention that renders it unfit this is considered to be an indirect form of damage and even Hezekiah will agree that there is no liability by the laws of man.

The distinction between this and the three instances in our Mishnah is clear. There it is the act that does the damage, of contaminating, mixing or stirring. But what of the case of the priests where it is their intention that causes the damage? How does this case differ from the case of the priests? See *Ritba* and other commentaries which raise this difficulty. The distinction appears to be this. Where there has been a *piggul* intention on the part of the priest it is not the intention that invalidates the sacrifice. The *piggul* intention in fact only operates at the time of the actual carrying out of one of the 'services' of the sacrifice, e.g. sprinkling the blood. Thus the intention makes the act a *piggul* act, as it were, and it is this that renders the sacrifice invalid so that it is analogous to the three in the Mishnah. Here, however, the act is innocent and does not render the animal or the water unfit. The fact that there happens to be produce in the stall or an object to be weighed in the balance is external to the act and here, since the act relies entirely on the man's intention to turn it into 'work', it is considered a form of indirect damage so that Hezekiah will agree that there is no liability according to the laws of man.

The Talmud now objects that the fourth-century Babylonian Amora, Rava, has said that if one weighs with the purifying water it is, in fact, fit for use. The *Baraita* cannot, therefore, be speaking of such a case for then the water would still be fit and there would be no need for any compensation since there had been no damage. To this the reply is given that Rava, when he declares the water to be fit, refers to water used as a weight in a balance of scales; but the *Baraita* does not, in fact, refer to this but to a different kind of weighing, namely with the water itself, e.g., the water is placed in a marked vessel with grooves, and then the object to be weighed is placed in the water, the weight of the object being determined by the rise of the water at the grooves. But in that case, the Talmud objects, the original reply falls to the ground since here it is an *act* that takes place, and it is direct, not indirect. Therefore, the Talmud concludes, both Rava and the *Baraita* deal with water weighed in the balance of the scales. The reason the *Baraita* holds the water to be unfit is because the *Baraita*, unlike Rava, is thinking of a man who by using the water as a weight took his mind off the proper use of the water and there is a rule that if such positive absence of mind took place the water is thereby rendered unfit. But this disqualification is certainly not the result of an act but of absence of thought and this is so indirect that Hezekiah agrees that there is no liability by the laws of man.

Rava's disciple, R. Pappa, now raises a fatal objection to Hezekiah from a Mishnah (*Bava Kama* 9: 2). Here the Mishnah rules that if a man stole a coin and this was later taken out of circulation by the government, or he stole *terumah* and it later became contaminated, or he stole leaven and kept it until the Passover so that it was no longer allowed to be used, the thief can still return that which he had stolen, saying: 'Here is your property' (i.e. which I now return to be absolved from my responsibility). Now the law is that a thief can only be exonerated if he returns the object he had stolen in an undamaged state. It follows from the Mishnah that in these three cases the property is considered as being restored in an undamaged state and this can only be, contrary to Hezekiah, because indiscernible damage is not held to be damage in the eyes of the law. The Talmud concludes with *tiyuvta*, 'It is, indeed a refutation.'

The Talmud now asks: 'Shall we say that the point at issue between Hezekiah and R. Johanan is debated by Tannaím?' and a *Baraita* is quoted. Here it is stated that in the three instances recorded in our Mishnah – contaminating *terumah*, mixing *terumah* with *ḥullin* and 'stirring' – R. Meir holds that the perpetrator is liable even if he did it unintentionally, whereas R. Judah holds that he is only liable if he did it intentionally, our Mishnah thus following the view of R. Judah. Now why does R. Meir hold him to be liable even if he did it unintentionally? It can only be because he holds that indiscernible damage is held to be damage in the eyes of the law, whereas R. Judah agrees with the opinion expressed by R. Johanan that according to Biblical law there is no liability and the Rabbinic legislation, as above, covers only intentional damage. To this the Babylonian Amora (fourth-century) R. Nahman b. Isaac replies that both R. Meir and R. Judah agree with the opinion expressed by R. Johanan that indiscernible damage is not damage. In that case why does R. Meir hold him to be liable even if he did it unintentionally. It is because R. Meir holds, as a general principle, that wherever the Rabbis imposed a penalty for an intentional act they extended this penalty to cover even an unintentional act and it is with this general principle that R. Judah disagrees. The rest of the *sugya* is taken up with a discussion of this general principle of whether 'they penalised the unintentional because of the intentional act' – *kanésu shogeg atu mezid*.

The pattern of this section of the *sugya* is:

(1) Hezekiah: 'named damage'; R. Johanan: 'not named damage'
(2) Reasons
  Hezekiah: he is exonerated where the damage is unintentional, in order that he may inform the victim
  R. Johanan: intentional, liable because of Rabbinic enactment
(3) Objection to Hezekiah: Mishnah of priests and *Baraita* on this
(4) Reply: *Baraita* refers to unintentional damage implied in Mishnah

(5) R. Eleazar's objection to Hezekiah: *Baraita* of heifer and water
(6) R. Eleazar's reply: intention the cause and therefore indirect
(7) Objection to this: Rava's ruling regarding weighing
(8) Reply: *Baraita* refers to weighing with water itself
(9) Objection to this: but this is direct and hence original objection remains
(10) Reply: indirect for different reason: taking out of mind
(11) R. Pappa's final objection: a case of thief in Mishnah
(12) Indeed this is a refutation
(13) But shall we say it is debated by Tannaím
(14) No, R. Nahman b. Isaac: debate concerns whether unintentional act penalised.

Although the material is presented in more or less chronological order so far as R. Eleazar, Rava, R. Pappa and R. Nahman b. Isaac are concerned, the more definite pattern is logical, i.e. the reply in (4) cannot be used for (5); replies in (6) to (10) cannot be used for (11). And the framework of the *sugya* has been organised with this progression of thought in mind.

Basically we have here, in fact, two separate *sugyot*: (a) the *sugya* of *heyzek she-eyno nikar*; (b) the *sugya* of *kanésu shogeg atu mezid*. The 'Shall we say' in (13) appears, then, to be no more than a device in order to introduce the second *sugya* (b), which meets the objection of the *Tosafists*, s.v. *tiyuvta*, of stating this after Hezekiah has in any event been refuted. The theme of *heyzek she-eyno nikar* is found, in addition to our *sugya* in *Mo'ed Katan* 13a; *Gittin* 41a; 44b (duplicate of *Mo'ed Katan* 13a); *Bava Kama* 5a. See *Kesef Nivḥar*, part I, no. 49, pp. 86a–87b and *ET*, vol. VII, pp. 702–22.

Thus far we have established that R. Meir penalises even an unintentional act because of an intentional one, while R. Judah refuses to do this. The Talmud now quotes a *Baraita* which seems to suggest that R. Meir and R. Judah hold, in fact, exactly opposite views. The case dealt with in this *Baraita* is that of a man who cooks food on the Sabbath. May the illegally cooked food be eaten? There are three opinions on this in the *Baraita*. R. Meir holds that if the cooking was done intentionally, i.e. the man knew that he was cooking on the Sabbath and knew that it is forbidden to cook on the Sabbath, the food may not be eaten; but if done unintentionally, i.e. the man either did not know that it was the Sabbath or did not know that it was forbidden to cook on the Sabbath, then the food is permitted even on that Sabbath. R. Judah holds that if the cooking was done intentionally it may never be eaten, but if done unintentionally it may not be eaten on that Sabbath but may be eaten after the Sabbath is over. R. Johanan the sandal maker holds that if the cooking was done intentionally neither the man who did the cooking nor anyone else may ever eat it, but if done unintentionally then others may eat it after the Sabbath but never the man himself. Thus here R. Meir is lenient, permitting the food cooked unintentionally to be eaten even by the man himself and even on that Sabbath, whereas R. Judah is strict, forbidding the food to be eaten on the Sabbath itself even if the cooking was done unintentionally. This would seem to contradict the statements in the previous debate where it is R. Meir who is strict, penalising the unintentional act because of the intentional, whereas it is R. Judah who is lenient, not penalising the unintentional act because of the intentional. Or, as the Talmud puts it: 'R. Meir contradicts R. Meir and R. Judah contradicts R. Judah.'

The Talmud first proceeds to resolve the contradiction between the two statements of R. Meir. R. Meir does, in fact, penalise even the unintentional act because of the intentional but only where the intentional act involves a Rabbinic prohibition as in the cases of the first *Baraita*, contaminating *terumah*, mixing *terumah* and 'stirring'. But cooking on the Sabbath is a Biblical prohibition and here R. Meir is content to penalise the intentional act but sees no reason to extend the penalty to the unintentional act. The logic of this position is that Rabbinic law is treated lightly by people and so requires the reinforcement provided by the additional penalising of even an unintentional offence, whereas Biblical prohibitions are viewed strictly in any event and can stand on their own without any additional reinforcement except when the act is intentional. But, the Talmud asks, one of the three instances recorded in the first *Baraita* is the stirring of the libation wine. This is a Biblical prohibition and yet R. Meir does penalise even the unintentional act. To this the reply is given that here R. Meir penalises even the unintentional act because of the great severity of the prohibition, idolatry being the worst of offences. Thus R. Meir does not penalise the unintentional act of cooking on the Sabbath because the offence is Biblical and requires no reinforcement. He does penalise the unintentional acts of contaminating *terumah* and mixing *terumah* with *ḥullin* because the offence is Rabbinic and therefore requires reinforcement. He also penalises the unintentional act of 'stirring', though the offence is Biblical, because this offence is so severe that it does require reinforcement. In other words, R. Meir holds that reinforcement is required in two instances: where the offence is

Rabbinic, because it is so light as to require reinforcement; and where the offence is that of idolatry, because it is so severe as to demand reinforcement. A 'medium' offence, that of cooking on the Sabbath, being Biblical, is sufficiently strong not to require reinforcement on grounds of 'lightness' and, at the same time, sufficiently weak, as it were, not to require reinforcement on grounds of 'severity'.

As for the contradiction between the two statements of R. Judah, this is easily resolved. Contrary to R. Meir, R. Judah holds that the more severe offence, the Biblical offence, requires reinforcement and the less severe, the Rabbinic, does not. Hence in the instances of contaminating *terumah* and mixing *terumah* with *ḥullin*, where the offence is Rabbinic, R. Judah does not penalise the unintentional act, whereas in the instance of cooking on the Sabbath, where the offence is Biblical, he does penalise the unintentional act. But here again the Talmud objects that one of the three instances in the first *Baraita* is 'stirring' and here the offence is Biblical, and yet R. Judah does not penalise the unintentional act. To this the reply is given that the prohibition of idolatry is so severe that people will shun it of their own accord so that no reinforcement is required. Thus according to R. Judah the general principle is that a Biblical prohibition does require reinforcement, hence he penalises the unintentional act of cooking on the Sabbath, whereas a Rabbinic prohibition does not require reinforcement, hence he does not penalise the unintentional acts of contaminating and mixing *terumah*. The exception is stirring the wine. Here the offence is Biblical and yet because it is so severe no extra reinforcement is required. In other words, neither a very severe offence (idolatry) nor a very light one (Rabbinic) requires reinforcement, the one because it is too severe in any event to need reinforcement, the other because it is too light to warrant reinforcement. The 'medium' offence of cooking on the Sabbath is sufficiently severe to warrant reinforcement and, at the same time, sufficiently light to need it.

We have now suggested that R. Meir only penalises the unintentional act where the offence is Rabbinic, not where it is Biblical. A *Baraita* is now quoted. This deals with a Biblical prohibition and yet R. Meir does penalise even the unintentional act. The *Baraita* states that R. Meir holds that if one plants a new shoot on the Sabbath, he may preserve the shoot if he planted it unintentionally but not if he planted it intentionally, when he must uproot it. But if he planted the shoot in the Sabbatical year he must uproot it whether he planted it intentionally (i.e. knowing that it was the Sabbatical year and that it was forbidden to plant during this year) or unintentionally. R. Judah holds exactly the opposite view. If he planted the shoot on the Sabbath he must uproot it whether he planted it intentionally or unintentionally; but if he planted it in the Sabbatical year he is only required to uproot it if he planted it intentionally and he may preserve it if he planted it unintentionally.

Now planting in the Sabbatical year is a Biblical prohibition and yet R. Meir penalises even the unintentional act. The Talmud replies that the *Baraita* appears to be contradictory in any event, since the *Baraita* itself appears to make a distinction between two Biblical offences, that of the Sabbath and that of the Sabbatical year. In fact, the reason for the distinction is stated by R. Meir himself in the continuation of the *Baraita*. R. Meir here declares that the distinction between the Sabbath and the Sabbatical year is based on two factors. The first is: 'Israel counts according to the Sabbatical year but not according to the Sabbath.' This means that one is obliged to count the years of every new shoot because the fruit is forbidden during the first three years (*'orlah*) and even on the fourth year can only be eaten after it has been redeemed (see Leviticus 19: 23–4). Hence it is plausible to suggest that people will count back from the fourth and third years and then they will know that the shoot has been planted in the Sabbatical year. This is why R. Meir forbids it even when planted unintentionally. It is not because he generally penalises even an unintentional act but because if it is here permitted people may conclude that it is really permitted to plant shoots in the Sabbatical year. But with regard to planting on the Sabbath, people do not count back the weeks or days and no one will know that the shoot has been planted on the Sabbath. And R. Meir adds a second reason for the distinction: 'Israelites are suspected of ignoring the laws of the Sabbatical year but not of ignoring the Sabbath laws', i.e. since people treat the Sabbatical year laws lightly, reinforcement is required and therefore even the unintentional act is penalised as it is, according to R. Meir, with regard to the light offences of Rabbinic law. The Talmud then asks, why is this second reason required, since the first seems entirely adequate? The reply is given that on occasion people do count back to the Sabbath. This is because of the law which permits the planting of new shoots 30 days before the Sabbatical year. These 30 days are then counted as a whole year for the purpose of *'orlah*, i.e. the fruit may be eaten after two whole years and 30 days as if three years had passed. Now when people see that the fruit is permitted after only two years they will appreciate that this is because of the 30 days' law. They will then count back these 30 days and discover that the shoot had been planted on the Sabbath. Hence the first reason is not entirely adequate, which is why R. Meir has to produce the second reason.

The contradiction between the two views of R. Meir has now been resolved but there remains the contradiction between the two views of R. Judah. According to R. Judah there is a penalty for cooking on the Sabbath even where the act was done unintentionally because the offence is Biblical; this is consistent with his view in the *Baraita*, which states that according to R. Judah the shoot planted on the Sabbath must be uprooted even if planted unintentionally. But why, then, does R. Judah permit the shoot planted in the Sabbatical year to be preserved, if done unintentionally? The reply is that in R. Judah's district people were very strict with regard to the laws of the Sabbatical year so that here the usual reinforcement of Biblical law is not required. In support the story is told of a man who taunted his neighbour by calling him a proselyte, the son of a proselyte, and the man retorted: 'As least I do not eat the fruit of the Sabbatical year as you do', which shows that for some people the laws of the Sabbatical year were kept so strictly that it was a serious insult to accuse anyone of disregarding these laws.

We have thus far established that R. Meir does impose a penalty on an unintentional act where the offence is Rabbinic. A *Baraita* is now quoted which seems to state the opposite. The rule is that if one eats *terumah* belonging to a priest he must give the priest in return non-sacred food (*ḥullin*) to the value of the *terumah* he had eaten and this becomes automatically *terumah*. The *Baraita* states that if a non-priest had eaten contaminated *terumah* belonging to a priest he must give the priest uncontaminated *ḥullin* which then, as above, becomes *terumah*. But what if he gave the priest contaminated *ḥullin*? There is a debate on this between Symmachus and the Sages as to what R. Meir said. Symmachus states in the name of R. Meir that if the man knew that his *ḥullin* was contaminated when he gave it in payment, his payment is ineffective; but if he made this payment unintentionally, i.e. he was unaware that his payment was made with contaminated *ḥullin*, his payment is effective. The Sages say, however, that according to R. Meir the payment is in any event effective. However, this only means, the *Baraita* goes on to say, that the payment is 'effective' in that the contaminated *ḥullin* then becomes contaminated *terumah*. But in addition, as an extra penalty, he must pay the priest a further amount of clean *ḥullin*. This, being no more than a fine, does not become *terumah*.

So far the Talmud has examined the *Baraita* as it stands. But, the Talmud continues, 'we were puzzled' by this *Baraita*, which is extremely difficult to accept as it stands. If the man ate contaminated *terumah* why should he not be allowed to make payment with contaminated *ḥullin*, which would then become contaminated *terumah*, since this is, after all, what he had eaten? In fact his intention is to go one better, since contaminated *terumah* cannot be eaten at all, whereas contaminated *ḥullin* can be used for food by the priest when he is unclean. (The *ḥullin* may not be eaten by the priest once it has become *terumah* after the payment but the man's intention, at least, is to improve matters.) In reply to 'our' puzzle Rava, 'others say Kadi', explains that the *Baraita* requires to be emended and to read as follows. If he ate contaminated *terumah* he can, in fact, repay any amount, i.e. he need not pay the full value but simply set aside any amount of *ḥullin*, giving this to the priest. On this there is no debate at all. The debate concerns where he ate *clean terumah* and paid with *unclean ḥullin*. Here all agree that if the payment was made intentionally, i.e. with full awareness that the *ḥullin* was unclean, it is ineffective. The debate concerns where the payment was made unintentionally, where he did not know that he was paying with unclean *ḥullin*. The Sages hold that even here the payment is ineffective but Symmachus states that R. Meir holds that here the payment is effective. And, the Talmud concludes, R. Aha son of R. Ika explained that this means that, according to Symmachus, R. Meir does not penalise an unintentional act because of an intentional one. Now here the prohibition of paying with unclean *ḥullin* is Rabbinic, not Biblical, and this contradicts the principle that where the offence is Rabbinic R. Meir does penalise the unintentional act. The reply is that here the man's intention is good. He wishes to make repayment. Here R. Meir would agree that it would be wrong to penalise him for his unintentional act.

There now follows a series of further attempted refutations of the view that R. Meir does penalise the unintentional act where the offence is Rabbinic. The first of these is from a *Baraita* in which it is stated that if the blood of a sacrifice has become contaminated and is then sprinkled on the altar, then if the sprinkling was done intentionally (i.e. the priest being aware that the blood was unclean) the sacrifice is not acceptable (and its meat may not be eaten) but if done unintentionally the sacrifice is acceptable. But according to Biblical law it is acceptable even if the blood is unclean. We have, therefore, a Rabbinic offence and yet the *Baraita* states that there is no penalty for the unintentional act. There is, in fact, no indication that the *Baraita* follows the opinion of R. Meir. As *Rashi* comments, the Talmud could have replied that this follows the opinion of R. Judah but the Talmud seeks to reply even if it follows the opinion of R. Meir. The reply is similar to the previous one. No penalty for an unintentional act is imposed where the motives are good, as they are here, where the sacrifice is for the purpose of finding acceptance in the eyes of God.

The second attempted refutation is from an anonymous Mishnah (*Terumot* 2: 3). An anonymous Mishnah does generally follow the opinion of R. Meir. There is a Rabbinic offence of tithing on the Sabbath and yet this Mishnah states that if the tithing was done unintentionally it is valid. Here again the reply is given that the motives were good, to free the produce from being untithed.

Finally, another clause of the same anonymous Mishnah (*Terumot* 2: 3) is quoted. It is a Rabbinic offence to immerse vessels in order to purify them on the Sabbath, but if it was done unintentionally the immersion is valid. Once again the reply is given that the man's motives were good in that he wished to have clean vessels.

We now revert to a consideration of R. Judah's views. We have thus far established that R. Judah only imposes a penalty where the act was done unintentionally, where the offence is Biblical not where it is Rabbinic. A *Baraita* is quoted dealing with the law of '*orlah*, the fruit of a new shoot forbidden, as above, during the first three years. According to Biblical law if '*orlah* fruit was mixed with ordinary, permitted fruit and the forbidden fruit can no longer be identified, the mixture is permitted if the ratio is two to one of permitted to forbidden fruit. The Rabbis, however, ordained that for '*orlah* fruit to become neutralised a ratio of one to two hundred is required. Furthermore, things of great value and significance can never become neutralised, even at a ratio of one to a thousand. Thus the rule is that a certain species of nut, because of its significance, can never become neutralised. Now the *Baraita* states that if these nuts have been broken so as to lose their special significance, they do become neutralised in a ratio of one to two hundred according to R. Jose and R. Simeon, provided that they have been broken, after they had become mixed, unintentionally, and were not broken intentionally to deprive of them their significance so that neutralisation can take effect. But R. Meir and R. Judah hold that neutralisation cannot take effect, even if the nuts were broken unintentionally. Now here the offence is only Rabbinic since, as above, according to Biblical law there is always neutralisation at a ratio of one to two and yet R. Judah does penalise the unintentional act. The reply is that this belongs in an entirely different category. The reason why R. Judah forbids it here, even when the act was done unintentionally, is not because of a penalty but simply in order to prevent fraud. For if the neutralisation were held to be effective when done unintentionally the fraudulent person would do it intentionally and pretend that he had done it unintentionally.

Finally, the Talmud points to a contradiction between the view of R. Jose stated in this *Baraita*, that where it is done intentionally it is not permitted, and R. Jose's view in a Mishnah ('*Orlah* 1: 6). The Mishnah rules that if an '*orlah* shoot had been planted among other shoots and cannot now be identified all the fruit of all the shoots is forbidden to be gathered since a growing shoot is held to be separate and the law of neutralisation does not come into operation. Once the fruit had been gathered, however, the '*orlah* fruit does become neutralised at a ratio of one to two hundred provided the gathering was not done intentionally, i.e. for the purpose of neutralisation. But R. Jose holds that it does become neutralised even if done intentionally, which contradicts R. Jose's ruling in the other *Baraita* that the nuts do not become neutralised if they had been broken with that intention. The reply is that we have learnt with regard to this case that Rava explained: 'It is an established fact (*ḥazakah*) that no man will allow his whole vineyard to become forbidden because of a single shoot.' As *Rashi* understands the reply, normally the man will mark the forbidden shoot so as to prevent his whole vineyard becoming prohibited. Consequently, unlike the case of the nuts, there is no need for any special Rabbinic rule to forbid intentional neutralisation since the Rabbis do not impose their restrictions in very unusual cases. And, the Talmud continues, when Ravin came to Babylon from Palestine he reported that R. Johanan said the very same thing: 'It is an established fact that no man will allow his whole vineyard to become forbidden because of a single shoot.'

The phenomenon that a fourth-century Babylonian teacher, Rava, should have given the same explanation as that given by the third-century Palestinian teacher, R. Johanan, and, moreover, in exactly the same words, is best understood on the grounds that comments of this kind enjoyed a very wide circulation among the scholars of both Palestine and Babylon, so that Rava, for instance, is not really stating his own original opinion but rather quoting a well-known legal maxim with which he happens to concur. The other Talmudic passages dealing with the theme of *kanésu shogeg atu mezid* are: *Shabbat* 3b; '*Eruvin* 68b and 100a; and *Yevamot* 90a. The *Yevamot* passage is a duplicate of the section in our *sugya* dealing with the payment of *terumah* but the material is presented in a slightly different order to fit in with the theme of that passage. In both passages it is stated that 'we were puzzled', which suggests an earlier *sugya* on which both *sugyot* rely. In the *Yevamot* passage, on the other hand, R. Aha son of R. Ika is quoted as if he was making his original comment there, whereas here our *sugya* records: '*and* R. Aha son of R. Ika said' which appears to suggest a cross-reference, so that our *sugya* depends on that of *Yevamot*. If this is correct, there are three stages here: (1) the original 'we' who were 'puzzled', which means that there had been an early discussion of the difficulties in the *Baraita* and the reply by emendation; (2) the *sugya* in *Yevamot*, which relies on (1) but adds the comment of R. Aha son of R. Ika and generally fits (1) into the new framework of that passage; (3) our *sugya*, which relies on (2) and adapts it to the theme of our passage. For a full discussion of the general theme of *kanésu shogeg atu mezid* see *Kesef Nivḥar*, part III, no. 143, pp. 12a–13b.

The pattern of this section of the *sugya* is:

(1) Debate of R. Meir and R. Judah: regarding contaminating *terumah* etc.
  R. Meir: penalises even unintentional act; R. Judah: penalises only intentional act
(2) Contradiction of R. Meir I: cooking on the Sabbath
(3) Reply: R. Meir only penalises Rabbinic offences not Biblical
(4) Objection: 'stirring' is Biblical
(5) Reply: because of severity of offence of idolatry
(6) Contradiction of R. Judah I: cooking on the Sabbath

(7) Reply: R. Judah only penalises Biblical offences not Rabbinic
(8) Objection: 'stirring' is Biblical
(9) Reply: no need for penalty because of severity of idolatry
(10) Contradiction of R. Meir II: Sabbatical year
(11) Reply: but in any event contradiction between this and Sabbath
(12) Therefore: R. Meir states two reasons: (a) 'counting'; (b) suspicion
(13) Question: why is (b) required, since (a) sufficient
(14) Reply: because sometimes there is 'counting' to Sabbath, hence (a) insufficient
(15) Contradiction of R. Judah II: Sabbatical year
(16) Reply: in R. Judah's district Sabbatical year treated very strictly
(17) Support: story of insult
(18) Contradiction of R. Meir III: payment of *terumah*
(19) Reply: no penalty if man wants to pay
(20) Contradiction of R. Meir IV: sprinkling of blood
(21) Reply: no penalty if man wishes to be accepted
(22) Contradiction of R. Meir V: tithing on the Sabbath
(23) Reply: no penalty if man wishes to tithe his produce
(24) Contradiction of R. Meir VI: immersion on the Sabbath
(25) Reply: no penalty if man wishes to purify his vessels
(26) Contradiction of R. Judah III: breaking nuts
(27) Reply: because of fear of fraud
(28) Contradiction of R. Jose: gathering fruit of plant
(29) Reply: because unusual

It is to be noted that (16) and (17) are found in *Bekhorot* 30a and appear here to be quoted from there, i.e. this small section has been appropriated by the editors in order to fit it in with the sequence in our *sugya*. The sequence of thought in (18) to (25) appears to be: in reply to (18) there is given (19), but this reply – the man wishes to pay – does not apply to (20). Reply: (21). But granted that there is no penalty where he desires atonement, what of (22) where there is no question of atonement? Reply (23): he wishes to put right his untithed produce and this is meritorious since otherwise he may come to eat that which is forbidden. But what of (24), where there is no particular merit in immersing the vessels? Reply (25): nevertheless his motive is positive. If this is correct, it will explain why (see *Tosafists*) (22) is quoted before (24) whereas in the Mishnah (*Terumot* 2: 3) the order is reversed. The *sugya* thus presents the material in a contrived way in order to allow each stage of the argument to follow the previous stage and lead up to the next.

16

Kinyan ḥatzer: acquisition by means of a domain

This comparatively brief *sugya* is *Bava Metzi'a* 10b–11a. The universally-accepted legal principle is that a man's domain can acquire property for him, e.g. if a lost article happened to come into his domain it belongs to him, or if A sells goods to B and deposits them in B's domain, with the intention of both that it should effect a transfer, it does so and neither can retract. This is known as *kinyan ḥatzer*, 'acquisition by means of a courtyard'. That the *ḥatzer* acquires is held to be Biblical. But it is here assumed that this mode of acquisition is not an entirely different one but rather an extension of some other, Biblically-accepted model. There are two possible candidates for the key-mode, as it were. The first is acquisition by the person himself, e.g. by his lifting up the object to be acquired. This is known as *yad*, lit. 'hand'. The second is 'agency', *sheliḥut*, i.e. A appoints B to be his agent to acquire the object on his behalf.

Now it can be argued that *ḥatzer* is 'included' (the term used in our *sugya*), i.e. introduced as a new mode of acquisition in the Torah, as either an extension of *yad* or of *sheliḥut*. If as a mode of *yad*, it means that the Torah provides each person, as it were, with an extension of his own hand; his *ḥatzer* acquiring the object for him as if that object had actually come into his hand. If as a mode of *sheliḥut*, it means that the Torah provides him, as it were, with a kind of automatic agent, his *ḥatzer*, which operates on the same basis as that of his agent acquiring property on his behalf. This is formulated as either *ḥatzer mi-shum yad* or *ḥatzer mi-shum sheliḥut*. The debate in the *sugya* is between the early-third-century Amora, Resh Lakish, speaking in the name of Abba Kohen Bardala, and his contemporary, R. Johanan, speaking in the name of R. Jannai.

The reason why the *sugya* has been inserted here is because there is a preceding statement of Resh Lakish in the name of Abba Kohen Bardala (*Bava Metzi'a* 10a), that statement being relevant to the Mishnah to which it has been appended and which is quoted in the discussion on the statement (*Bava Metzi'a* 10b). Our *sugya* begins, in fact, with: *ve-amar Resh Lakish mi-shum Abba Kohen Bardala*, '*And* Resh Lakish *said further* in the name of Abba Kohen Bardala.' The actual formulation of the debate in these terms – *mi-shum yad* or *mi-shum sheliḥut* – is not that of the protagonists themselves but is editorial and is a typical, abstract formulation peculiar to the Amoraic literature.

Two further points require to be made before proceeding to the *sugya* itself. First, there is a Rabbinic extension of the law of *ḥatzer*, known as 'four cubits', i.e. the four cubits at the centre of which a person happens to be standing operate as his *ḥatzer* during the time he stands there and acquire for him. The second point to be noted is that if the father of a girl who is a minor (*ketanah*) betroths her to a man, she has the full status of a married woman and requires a *get* to release her from the marriage bond. But the *get* has to be delivered into her hand. Unlike an adult woman, she cannot appoint an agent to accept the *get* on her behalf since a minor has no power to appoint an agent. The question discussed in our *sugya* is whether a *ketanah* can acquire the *get* when it is placed by the husband in her *ḥatzer*. If *ḥatzer* operates as *yad* she can, but if as *sheliḥut* she cannot.

The *sugya* begins: 'And Resh Lakish said further in the name of Abba Kohen Bardala: "A *ketanah* has neither *ḥatzer* nor four cubits." But R. Johanan said in the name of R. Jannai: 'She does have a *ḥatzer* and four cubits."' The Talmud asks: 'What is their point of difference?' and replies: R. Johanan in the name of R. Jannai holds that *ḥatzer* is an extension of *yad*. Therefore she has *ḥatzer* just as she has *yad*. But Resh Lakish, in the name of Abba Kohen Bardala, holds that *ḥatzer* is an extension of *sheliḥut*. Since she cannot appoint an agent she has no *ḥatzer*.

The Talmud now asks: 'But is it at all possible for anyone to hold that *ḥatzer* is because of *sheliḥut*?' The objection to anyone holding such a view is stated. A *Baraita*, commenting on the verse: 'If the theft be certainly found in his hand alive . . . he shall restore double' (Exodus 22: 4; *The Torah*: Exodus 22: 3), observes that although the verse speaks of 'his hand' the thief is obliged to pay double even if he stole by means of his 'courtyard', i.e. he closed the gate on an animal belonging to his neighbour that had strayed into his domain. This the *Baraita* derives from the expression: 'found at all', an inclusion expression. It follows that, as the *Baraita* states and derives it from a Scriptural verse, theft by means of a *ḥatzer* constitutes theft and the thief has to pay double, as if he had stolen it himself by his own hand. But this would mean that agency is effective even where a crime is committed and 'we have established the principle' (referring to *Kiddushin* 42b) that the principle of agency does not operate where a crime is committed. This means that if A instructs B to steal something on his behalf the act of stealing is not transferred, as in other cases of agency, to the principal, but the agent, not the principal, is the thief who is responsible in law and he, the agent, not the principal, has to pay double. Now if *ḥatzer* is an extension of *yad*, all is well. But if *ḥatzer* is an extension of *sheliḥut*, how can theft by means of *ḥatzer* render the owner of the *ḥatzer* liable to pay double, since where a crime is committed the agency principle does not operate?

To this a reply is given by the late-fifth-century Babylonian Amora, Ravina, and a different reply is given by his contemporary, R. Sama. Each of these advances a reason why the principle 'no agency where a crime is committed' does not apply to the particular kind of agency provided by *ḥatzer*. Hence the *Baraita*, and by implication the verse on which it relies, affords no refutation of the view that *ḥatzer* is because of *sheliḥut*. It may, indeed, be because of *sheliḥut* and yet the thief, through his *ḥatzer*, is still liable despite the 'no agency where a crime is committed' principle since, for the reason each gives, that principle does not operate in the particular kind of agency that is *ḥatzer*.

See *Gilyon ha-Shas* and *DS*, which indicate that some versions have 'R. Sama bar Rakta in the presence of Ravina in the name of R. Hiyya bar R. Ivo' instead of 'R. Sama', as in our texts. In any event these two are very-late-Babylonian Amoraím, sufficient evidence that our *sugya* in the form we now have it must be very late and this is supported by the 'but we have established the rule' which appears to be a quote from the conclusion of the *sugya* in *Kiddushin* 42b.

Ravina argues that the principle 'no agency where a crime is committed' only applies when the agent himself has an obligation to keep the law and commits the crime if he does not. Here it is held that the principal is not liable since the law against theft is addressed as much to the agent as to the principal and it is, after all, the agent who actually commits the crime, albeit on behalf of the principal. The *ḥatzer*, on the other hand, even if it does operate under the principle of *sheliḥut*, is an agent without obligations. The *ḥatzer* has no obligation to keep the law and here the 'act' of the 'agent' is transferred to the principal, as in all cases of agency where no crime is committed.

The Talmud now seeks to refute Ravina's argument by a *reductio ad absurdum*. No one would dream of suggesting that if a man instructed a married woman to steal or a slave to steal that he, and not they, should be liable. And yet, since neither a married woman nor a slave has property, if Ravina is correct he must be liable and not they. The reply is obvious. The married woman and the slave do have an obligation not to steal and they are, indeed, even obliged to pay. The reason why payment cannot be made is simply because they have no money with which to pay. And a Mishnah (*Bava Kama* 8: 4) is quoted in which it is, indeed, ruled that when the married woman is divorced and so has property of her own and when the slave is freed and so has property of his own, they are obliged to pay.

R. Sama argues for a slightly different distinction. The principle of no agency where a crime is committed only applies where the agent acts voluntarily, where he can please himself whether or not to obey the instructions of the principal. If he then steals it is he who commits the offence, not the principal, since no one compels him to obey the principal's instructions. The *ḥatzer*, on the other hand, even if it is an extension of *sheliḥut*, is involuntary. The *ḥatzer* is, as it were, an agent who cannot help obeying his principal's instructions and here the rule 'no agency where a crime has been committed' does not apply.

We now have two reasons why 'no agency where a crime is committed' does not apply to *ḥatzer*. Ravina's reason is because *ḥatzer* has no *obligation* in law and R. Sama's because *ḥatzer* has no *choice*. The Talmud asks: what is the difference between the two reasons? The reply suggests that there is a practical difference between the two reasons, not with regard to *ḥatzer* (where both reasons apply, since *ḥatzer* has neither *obligation* nor *choice*), but where an agent instructed to commit an offence has no *obligation*, so far as that offence is concerned, but has free *choice*. The Talmud discovers two such instances. The first is when a priest, who may not marry a divorcee (Leviticus 21: 7), instructs an Israelite, to whom this prohibition does not apply, to act as his agent to betroth a woman for him. Here there is no *obligation* on the part of the agent but there is *choice*; no one compels the agent to carry out the priest's instructions. Here according to Ravina the principle 'no agency where an offence is committed' does not apply and the betrothal is valid; but according to R. Sama, since there is *choice* even though there is no *obligation*, the principle 'no agency where an offence is committed' does apply and the betrothal is invalid. The second instance is that of a man, who may not 'round the corners of his head' nor have them 'rounded' for him (Leviticus 19: 27), who instructs a woman, to whom these prohibitions do not apply, to 'round' the corners of the head of a minor (i.e. a male to whom the prohibitions do apply but who, because of his youth, will not prevent it). According to Ravina the principle 'no agency where an offence is committed' does not apply since the woman has no *obligation*. Hence the man who gave the instructions is liable, the woman acting as his agent. But according to R. Sama, since the woman has free *choice* whether or not to obey the man's instructions, the principle of 'no agency where an offence is committed' does apply. Hence there is no agency here and the man who gave the instructions is not liable.

The Talmud now asks: 'But is it at all possible for anyone to hold that *ḥatzer* is not an extension of *yad*', i.e. the previous difficulty has been how anyone could possibly hold that *ḥatzer* is an extension of *sheliḥut* (in view of the principle 'no agency where a crime has been committed') but now a new difficulty presents itself that even if, theoretically, *ḥatzer* can be an extension of *sheliḥut* there is still ample proof that it is, in fact, an extension not of *sheliḥut* but of *yad*.

A *Baraita* is quoted, commenting on a verse which deals with the *get*: 'give it in her hand' (Deuteronomy 24: 3). The *Baraita*, like the previous one quoted, states that 'hand' is not to be taken literally, but from the general form of the statement – *ve-natan*, 'he shall give it' – it is derived that the husband can *give* the *get* to his wife by placing it in her 'courtyard.' This would suggest that *ḥatzer* is an extension of *yad* since the very fact that a *get* can be given by means of *ḥatzer* is derived from a verse which speaks of giving it in her *hand*. The Talmud, therefore, now suggests that both Resh Lakish in the name of Abba Kohen Bardala and R. Johanan in the name of R. Jannai agree that, in the case of *get*, *ḥatzer* is because of *yad*. Consequently, there is no debate on the question of whether a minor can be given her *get* by means of her *ḥatzer*. All agree that she can. When Resh Lakish in the name of Abba Kohen Bardala observes that a *ketanah* has no *ḥatzer* he is not referring to *get* but to acquiring a lost article. His argument is that it does not follow at all that, because a *ketanah* can be divorced by means of *ḥatzer*, in all other instances, such as acquiring a lost article, *ḥatzer*, is because of *yad*. In other instances it is, in fact, because of *sheliḥut* and hence a *ketanah* cannot acquire a lost article by means of her *ḥatzer* and this is what Resh Lakish in the name of Abba Kohen Bardala means when he states that a *ketanah* has no *ḥatzer*. R. Johanan in the name of R. Jannai holds that it is feasible to deduce the law of acquiring a lost article from that of *get*. Since the Torah has informed us that a *ketanah* has a *ḥatzer* for the purpose of *get* this demonstrates that the Torah considers *ḥatzer* to be an extension of *yad*, not of *sheliḥut*, and it would therefore be effective for a *ketanah* even for the purpose of acquiring a lost article.

'If you want I can say', the Talmud continues, with regard to a *ketanah* (a minor who is a female) all agree that just as she can receive her *get* by means of *ḥatzer* so, too, she can acquire a lost article by means of *ḥatzer*. Both agree, according to this version, with the view stated in the first version as that of R. Johanan, namely, since the Torah has informed us that a *ketanah* has a *ḥatzer* for the purpose of *get* it follows that the Torah considers *ḥatzer* to be because of *yad* and hence *ḥatzer* does acquire for a *ketanah* even a lost article. But Resh Lakish in the name of Abba Kohen Bardala argues, granted a *ketanah* has a *ḥatzer* and that this is because of *yad* so that she can even acquire a lost article by means of the *ḥatzer*, it does not follow that a *katan* (a minor who is a male) can acquire a lost article by means of his *ḥatzer* since, in all other instances than that of *ketanah*, *ḥatzer* is not because of *yad* but because of *sheliḥut*. The argument is that since there are minor females who require to have a *ḥatzer* for the purpose of divorce the Torah would not give them this *ḥatzer* in part, but the Torah gives it to them categorically. Hence with regard to *ketanah* we say, since she has a *ḥatzer* for the purpose of acquiring her *get* she has it, too, for the purpose of acquiring a lost article. But R. Johanan in the name of Abba Kohen Bardala argues that since from the case of *ketanah* we learn that *ḥatzer* is because of *yad* it is illogical to treat it as because of *sheliḥut* in the case of a *katan*. Hence, according to this 'If you want I can say', Resh Lakish in the name of Abba Kohen Bardala did not refer at all to a *ketanah* but to a *katan*.

This is one of numerous instances in the Talmud where it is stated that Rabbi A *said*... and the Talmud itself later suggests that he did not in fact *say* it or did not *say* it in these words. At first in our *sugya* Resh Lakish in the name of Abba Kohen Bardala is quoted as *saying*: 'A *ketanah* has neither *ḥatzer* nor four cubits' whereas it now turns out that what he really *said* was: 'A *katan* has neither *ḥatzer* nor four cubits' and the same applies to the *saying* of R. Johanan in the name of R. Jannai. Cf. my article: 'How much of the Babylonian Talmud is pseudepigraphic?' in *JJS*, 28, 1 (Spring 1977), 46–59.

Finally, the Talmud concludes, 'If you want I can say' that in fact there is no debate at all between Resh Lakish in the name of Abba Kohen Bardala and R. Johanan in the name of R. Jannai. They speak of two different cases. Thus Resh Lakish in the name of Abba Kohen Bardala speaks of *ḥatzer* for the purpose of acquiring a lost article, while R. Johanan speaks of *ḥatzer* for the purpose of acquiring a *get*; or Resh Lakish in the name of Abba Kohen Bardala speaks of a *katan* and R. Johanan in the name of R. Jannai of a *ketanah*.

The pattern of the *sugya* is:

(1) Resh Lakish – Abba Kohen Bardala: *ketanah* has no *ḥatzer*
R. Johanan – R. Jannai: *ketanah* has *ḥatzer*
(2) Point at issue: whether *ḥatzer* because of *yad* or *sheliḥut*
(3) Question: *ḥatzer* – theft – but 'no agency where crime committed'?
(4) Reply I: Ravina: only where agent has *obligation*
(5) Question: but what of married woman and slave?
(6) Reply: they do have obligation but no money
(7) Reply II: R. Sama: only where voluntary
(8) Question: what is practical difference between (4) and (7)?
(9) Reply: priest and divorcee – man who instructs woman to round head
(10) Question: but *ḥatzer* in case of *get* derived from *yad*?
(11) Reply I: debate only with regard to lost article
(12) Reply II: debate only with regard to *katan* not *ketanah*
(13) Reply III: no debate – each deals with a different case

The artificial element in this *sugya* is particularly obvious. First there is the strange phenomenon (see *Tosafists*) that in the case of *get* the proof that *ḥatzer* is because of *yad* is from a verse that includes *ḥatzer* in a verse dealing with *yad*. Why, then, does the Talmud not use the very same method to prove it from the original verse of theft where, in exactly the same way, *ḥatzer* is included in a verse dealing with *yad*? Even after the difficulty of 'no agency where a crime is committed' has been disposed of, this same verse can still be used, as the other one is, to prove that *ḥatzer* is because of *yad*. It looks as if this whole section has, in fact, only been introduced in order to discuss not the question of *ḥatzer* but the principle of 'no agency where a crime is committed' and when this applies. Secondly, the final series of replies in the form of 'If you want I can say' effectively contradicts the whole of the opening passage and has been kept to the end so as to provide a startling dénouement to the discussion.

Our *sugya*, in connection with the principle of 'no agency where an offence is committed' is discussed at length in a *Responsum* of Ezekiel Landau, *Noda' Bi-Yhudah, Kama, Even ha-'Ezer*, no. 78. The theme of *ḥatzer* as a mode of acquisition is found in numerous instances in the Talmud but the theme of our *sugya* – whether *ḥatzer* is because of *yad* or because of *sheliḥut* – is also referred to in *Gittin* 21a; 77b; *Bava Metzi'a* 12a. See *Kesef Nivḥar*, part II, no. 66, pp. 23a–25b.

17

Palginan be-dibbura: admission of part of a testimony even though another part of the same testimony is rejected

The *sugya* is *Sanhedrin* 9b–10a and is in the form of a discussion around legal statements of the fourth-century Babylonian Amoraím R. Joseph and Rava. The term *palginan be-dibbura* means literally: 'we (i.e. the Court or the Rabbis) divide up the word (e.g. of a witness's testimony)'. According to the Rabbinic interpretation of Deuteronomy 24: 16, the testimony of a man against his own near relative, his *karov*, is unacceptable, i.e., if a father testifies that his son has committed a crime that testimony is rejected. Again, according to the Rabbinic interpretation of: 'put not thine hand with the wicked to be an unrighteous witness' (Exodus 23: 1), a 'wicked' person, i.e. one who has committed a crime, cannot serve as a witness. Now it is held that a man is a *karov* (a 'near relative') to himself and consequently a man's confession that he has committed a crime is also rejected. If, therefore, a man testified in Court together with another (two witnesses being required in a criminal charge) that he has committed a crime, his own testimony against himself is rejected so that only one witness remains and he cannot be convicted. Supposing, now, A and B testify that C has committed sodomy with A and with A's consent so that A's testimony is, in fact, that he himself is 'wicked'. Obviously, as above, A cannot be convicted on his own testimony, but can his testimony together with that of B serve to convict C? Since his testimony against himself is rejected he is not 'wicked' and, therefore, his testimony that C has committed sodomy is accepted. It can be argued that when A testifies: 'C has committed sodomy with me and with my consent', since that part of it relating to himself, 'with me and with my consent', is rejected the whole of the testimony is rejected. On the other hand, it can be argued that while this part of A's testimony ('with me and with my consent') is rejected, the rest of the testimony ('C has committed sodomy') is accepted so that C can be convicted on the strength of A and B's testimony. If this second line of argument is followed the principle of *palginan be-dibbura* is said to be accepted. The Court rejects that part of the testimony relating to A's own guilt but accepts that part relating to C's guilt.

The *sugya* opens with a statement of R. Joseph dealing with the laws of evidence. This is inserted here because the previous discussions in this section of tractate *Sanhedrin* have to do with questions of evidence in a Court of Law. This first statement of R. Joseph is then followed by a second statement of R. Joseph regarding testimony and this second statement has to do with our question of *palginan be-dibbura*.

R. Joseph's first statement is with regard to the following. It is an accepted ruling that if a person commits an act which makes him liable to the death penalty and to pay compensation, since he is liable to suffer the more severe death penalty he is free from the lesser penalty of compensation. In the technical terms used in our *sugya*, where there are *nefashot* ('souls', 'lives', i.e. the death penalty) there is no *mamon*. If a husband produces witnesses who testify that his wife has committed adultery, their testimony seeks to achieve two things: (a) her condemnation to death; (b) her forfeiture of her *ketubah* (her marriage settlement). According to the law of false witnesses (*zomamim*), these, when their falsehood has been established, have imposed on them the penalty they sought to impose on their innocent victim (Deuteronomy 19:19). Thus if the father of the wife then produced two witnesses to testify that the witnesses produced by the husband are false, these witnesses, although they wished to inflict two penalties on the wife – the death penalty and the forfeiture of her *ketubah* – are only liable to the death penalty and they do not have to pay the value of the *ketubah*. As above, where there are *nefashot* there is no *mamon*. Now the testimony of these second two witnesses – those produced by the wife's father – intends to achieve two things: (a) the death penalty for the first two witnesses – produced by the husband – and (b) the obligation of the husband to pay his wife the *ketubah*, since according to their testimony she is innocent and therefore entitled to her *ketubah*. Now if the husband then produces a third pair of witnesses to prove the second pair false, R. Joseph rules that this second pair have to suffer the death penalty and, in addition, to pay the husband for the *ketubah* from which they sought to deprive him. The reason why the principle 'where there are *nefashot* there is no *mamon*' does not apply here is because that principle only applies where the offence for which there is the death penalty and the offence for which *mamon* is paid are offences against the same person, as in the first case. Here, however, the death penalty is for the witnesses' offence against the first pair of witnesses whereas the *mamon* is for their offence against the husband. This is a case of '*nefashot* to one and *mamon* to another' and R. Joseph declares that in such cases both penalties are imposed.

There now follows R. Joseph's second statement. If A together with B, as above, testifies that C has committed sodomy with A, then if A's testimony is that the act had been done against his will, i.e. he had been raped by C, he is a valid witness and C is convicted on the strenth of A's and B's testimony. But if A's testimony is to the effect that he, A, had been a willing partner to the act, he thereby disqualifies himself as a 'wicked' person (*rasha*') from acting as a witness and there remains only B's testimony, on the strength of which alone C cannot be convicted. Rava, however, as above, holds that *palginan be-dibbura*. A's testimony regarding his own willing participation in the act is disregarded but the rest of his testimony – that C has committed sodomy – is accepted and C is convicted on the strength of A and B's testimony. Thus on the question of *palginan be-dibbura* R. Joseph and Rava disagree. R. Joseph rejects the *palginan be-dibbura* principle, hence since A's testimony regarding his own participation is rejected the whole of the testimony is rejected. Rava, on the other hand, does accept the *palginan be-dibbura* principle, hence while A's testimony regarding his own willing participation is rejected, the rest of the testimony stands that C has committed sodomy and C is convicted on the strength of A and B's testimony.

The question of when exactly the Jewish Courts lost the right to impose the death penalty is complicated (see Excursus xxx: 'The Abolition of Capital Punishment' in Sydney B. Hoenig, *The Great Sanhedrin* (Philadelphia, 1953), pp. 211–13) but it was certainly centuries before the period of the Babylonian Amoraím R. Joseph and Rava. This and all such discussions in the Babylonian Talmud are purely academic. There is, in fact, no evidence that at a time when the ancient Jewish Courts did execute criminals the criminal's confession was rejected.

A second statement of Rava is now recorded. A and B testify that C has committed adultery with A's wife. A's testimony against his own wife is rejected. He is a *karov* to his wife. The wife cannot, therefore, be convicted. But so far as C is concerned there are still two witnesses, A and B, that he has cohabited with a married woman. Thus Rava states that C is convicted on the strength of A's and B's testimony, A's testimony being rejected in part – that C's adultery was with A's wife – but accepted in part – that C had cohabited with *a* married woman.

The Talmud objects that this second case is, in fact, identical with Rava's first case. Here, too, the reason Rava accepts A's testimony is because of *palginan be-dibbura*. Why, then, does Rava repeat his ruling. The reply is that if Rava had not made his second statement we might have supposed that while 'we say a man is a *karov* to himself we do not say a man is a *karov* to his wife'. Therefore, Rava is obliged to repeat the case so as to show that it applies also where A's testimony is not against himself but against his wife.

See *Tosafists*, s.v. *etzel ishto lo amrinan* that, in fact, a husband is disqualified from acting as a witness against his own wife. *Tosafists*, therefore, understand our passage to mean that here, and here alone, we might have supposed that the husband is believed, even against his wife, since his statement that C committed adultery with her is believed.

There now follows a second statement of Rava. If witnesses testify that a man had had intercourse with a betrothed maiden, without specifying which maiden, and they are found to be false, they are executed because they wished to impose the death penalty on the man, but there is no payment of *mamon* for an attempted loss of the *ketubah* since they had not named the maiden. If, however, they did specify 'with the daughter of So-and-so' and are subsequently found to be false, they suffer the death penalty and, in addition, must pay the value of the *ketubah* to the girl's father, to whom the *ketubah* is due. This, as above, is a case of '*nefashot* to this one and *mamon* to another'. As *Rashi* points out, this is different from the first case of R. Joseph (where a husband produces witnesses to his wife's infidelity and they were proved false, where, as R. Joseph states, there is no *mamon*) since there the woman was not merely betrothed, but actually married, so that the *ketubah* is hers and it is a case of *nefashot* to the same person.

A third statement of Rava is now quoted. Two witnesses testify that a man had commited bestiality with an ox and they are subsequently found to be false; they are executed because of their intention to have their victim executed, but there is no payment of *mamon* since no particular ox was specified. If, however, they testify that it was 'with the ox of So-and-so' and are found to be false, then they have, in addition, to pay *mamon* to the owner of the ox, the law being that the ox has to be stoned, and so the false witnesses had intended to deprive the owner of his ox. This, too, is a case of *nefashot* to one [the man against whom they testified] and *mamon* to another [the owner of the ox]. But, the Talmud objects, this is exactly the same as the case of the betrothed maiden. Why, then, does Rava have to repeat it? The reply is that Rava repeats it not because it is necessary to do so for itself but because he wishes to lead into a problem he had set regarding testimony against an ox.

This problem of Rava's is as follows. A and B testify that C had committed bestiality with A's ox. C is certainly to be executed on the evidence of A and B, but is the ox to be destroyed? Here it can be argued that just as we say, in Rava's earlier case, 'a man is a *karov* to himself' so, too, we say 'a man is a *karov* as far as his own ox is concerned', i.e. A's testimony that his ox is to be destroyed is not accepted since this, too, constitutes testimony against himself. Or, possibly, we do accept his testimony regarding the ox and the ox is destroyed. *Rashi* points out that, in fact, a man is not believed normally to testify that his own ox is to be destoyed, since this is a testimony against himself; but here it is possible that the testimony is accepted for if it were not it would have to be because of the *palginan be-dibbura* principle and it is possible that, while this principle is applied so far as A himself is concerned, it is not applied to his testimony regarding his ox. The Talmud concludes that after Rava had set the problem he eventually concluded that A's testimony would be accepted even to destroy his ox and here we do not apply the *palginan be-dibbura* principle. As the Talmud puts it: 'After he [Rava] had set the problem he solved it thus: We do say that a man is a *karov* to himself but we do not say that a man is *karov* so far as his *mamon* is concerned.'

The pattern of the *sugya* is:

(1) R. Joseph I: *mamon* to one and *nefashot* to another
(2) R. Joseph II: A and B testify that C committed sodomy with A and with A's consent; A disqualified, therefore C acquitted
(3) Rava I: *palginan be-dibbura*: C convicted

(4) Rava II: A and B testify that C committed adultery with A's wife: the wife acquitted but C convicted: because *palginan be-dibbura*
(5) Objection: (3) and (4) identical: why repeat?
(6) Reply: in (4) we might have supposed that, since A's testimony is accepted *vis-à-vis* C, it is also accepted *vis-à-vis* the wife
(7) Rava III: *mamon* to one and *nefashot* to another
(8) Rava IV: ox: *mamon* to one and *nefashot* to another
(9) Objection: (7) and (8) identical: why repeat?
(10) Reply: (8) required because of Rava's problem
(11) Rava V: problem: A and B testify that C committed bestiality with A's ox
(12) Rava's solution: ox stoned because A's testimony accepted

The artificial element is particularly obvious with regard to (9) to (12), but it all fits in neatly with the logical sequence of the *sugya*. To be noted especially is the progress of thought from 'a man is a *karov* to himself' to 'a man is a *karov* to his wife' to Rava's problem as to whether he is a *karov* to his *mamon* (his ox).

Other references to *palginan be-dibbura* are: *Yevamot* 25a–b (implied); *Gittin* 8b; *Bava Batra* 134b; *Sanhedrin* 25a (implied). See *Kesef Nivḥar*, part III, no. 135, pp. 48b–50b.

18

Tadir u-mekuddash: which takes precedence: the more constant or the more sacred?

The *sugya* is *Zevaḥim* 90b–91a. The Mishnah (*Zevaḥim* 10: 1) states with regard to sacrifices: 'Whatever is more constant than another takes precedence over the other.' Three examples are given in the Mishnah. (1) The daily offerings (the 'perpetual' offerings) take precedence over the special, additional Sabbath offerings, i.e. the morning 'daily offering' of the Sabbath is offered before the additional offerings of the Sabbath. The daily offerings are 'constant' whereas the additional offerings are limited to the Sabbaths, Festivals and New Moons. (2) If the New Moon falls on the Sabbath, the additional offerings of the Sabbath are offered before the additional offerings of the New Moon, the Sabbath, falling every week of the year, being more 'constant' than the New Moon. (3) The New Year Festival falls on the New Moon of the seventh month. The New Moon additional offerings are offered before the additional New Year offerings, the New Moon being more 'constant'. The term used for 'constant' is *tadir* ('regular'). The next Mishnah (*Zevaḥim* 10: 2) continues: 'Whatever is more sacred than another takes precedence over the other.' Thus the sprinkling of the blood of a sin-offering has to be done before that of a burnt-offering, the sin-offering being more 'sacred' in that it atones for sin. The term used in the Mishnah for 'sacred' is *mekuddash*. The Mishnah goes thus far. The problem discussed in our *sugya* is: which takes precedence where A is *tadir* (more 'constant' than B) but B is *mekuddash* (more 'sacred' than A)? For example, the blood of the daily offering and the blood of a sin-offering are to be sprinkled on the altar. Which of them is to be sprinkled first? The blood of the daily offering is *tadir* (i.e. is more 'constant' than that of the sin-offering) but the blood of the sin-offering is *mekuddash* (i.e. is more 'sacred' than the blood of the daily offering).

The *sugya* opens with the problem set by the anonymous scholars, with the usual formula for this: '*Ibbaya le-hu*', 'They set a problem'. The problem is formulated as: '*Tadir* and *mekuddash*, which of these takes precedence? Does *tadir* take precedence because it is *tadir* or does *mekuddash* take precedence because it is *mekuddash*?', i.e. which is the more significant, the *tadir* principle (so that it overrides the *mekuddash* principle) or that of *mekuddash* (so that it overrides the *tadir* principle)? A solution is attempted (introduced with the usual formula – *ta shema*', 'come and hear') from the first example given in the first Mishnah, that the daily offerings take precedence over the additional offerings of the Sabbath. Now the daily offerings, precisely because they are offered on week-days as well as on the Sabbath, are less sacred than the special, additional Sabbath offerings, which acquire, as it were, the special sanctity of the Sabbath, and yet the daily offerings take precedence. This demonstrates that *tadir* takes precedence over *mekuddash*. The reply is given: 'Is the Sabbath only effective for the additional offerings and not for the perpetual offerings?', i.e. the daily offering brought on the Sabbath also has imparted to it the special sanctity of the Sabbath and thus is different in terms of sanctity from the daily offerings brought on week-days. Thus there is no greater sanctity to the additional offerings brought on the Sabbath than to the daily offerings brought on the Sabbath. Consequently, here the question of *mekuddash* does not arise at all, both possessing the same degree of sanctity. Therefore, the daily offering, being *tadir*, takes precedence. The point at issue here would seem to be whether the 'daily' offering brought on the Sabbath is no more than a 'daily' offering (no different from those brought on week-days and only brought on the Sabbath because the Sabbath is also a day of the week) or whether the Sabbath imparts its sanctity even to the daily offering so that, on the Sabbath, this is, in fact, a special *Sabbath* offering.

The next attempted solution is from the second example given in the Mishnah, that the additional sacrifices of the Sabbath take precedence over the additional sacrifices of the New Moon. Now the additional sacrifices of the New Moon are more 'sacred' than those of the Sabbath since (*Rashi*) the New Moon is called a

'Festival' and (*SM*) there is a special New Moon sin-offering. This demonstrates that *tadir* takes precedence over *mekuddash*. A similar reply is given: 'Is the New Moon only effective for its own additional offerings and not for those of the Sabbath?', i.e. the sanctity of the New Moon is imparted also to the additional Sabbath offerings. Both are thus equally sacred and *tadir* takes precedence.

The next attempted solution is from the third example of *tadir* given in the Mishnah, that the additional sacrifices of the New Moon take precedence over those of the New Year, even though the New Year, as a major festival, is obviously more 'sacred' than the minor festival of the New Moon. This demonstrates that *tadir* takes precedence over *mekuddash*. Again the same kind of reply is given: 'Is the New Year only effective for its own additional offerings and not for those of the New Moon?', i.e. the New Year imparts its sanctity to the New Moon offerings as well as to its own additional offerings. Both are equally sacred and hence *tadir* takes precedence.

A *Baraita* (*Tosefta*, *Berakhot* 6: 1) is now quoted. Here it is recorded that the sanctification benediction – *kiddush* – recited at the Sabbath meal consists of two separate benedictions, the one over the wine and one for the 'day', i.e. praising God for giving Israel the Sabbath, and the former must be recited first because it is *tadir*, i.e. since it is recited not only on the Sabbath but whenever one partakes of wine. Now the second benediction, as the special Sabbath benediction, is more 'sacred' than the first and yet the first takes precedence, showing that *tadir* takes precedence over *mekuddash*. Again a similar reply is given: 'Is the Sabbath only effective for the benediction of the day and not for the benediction of the wine?', i.e. the Sabbath imparts its sanctity to the wine benediction as well as to the benediction of the day; the wine benediction becomes, as it were, not an ordinary wine benediction but a special Sabbath benediction. Consequently, both are equally 'sacred' and *tadir* takes precedence.

A fifth solution is now attempted. The Sages and R. Judah debate (*Berakhot* 28a) which takes precedence, the additional Sabbath prayer or the Sabbath afternoon prayer. The early-third-century Palestinian Amora, R. Johanan, states the rule that the Sabbath afternoon prayer must be recited first since it is *tadir*, this prayer being recited on every afternoon of the year whereas the additional prayer is only recited on the Sabbaths and Festivals. But the additional prayer, as a special Sabbath prayer, is more 'sacred' and yet *tadir* takes precedence. Again the reply is given: 'Is the Sabbath only effective for the additional prayer and not for the afternoon prayer?', i.e. and the afternoon prayer is also a special Sabbath prayer so that both are equally sacred, hence *tadir* takes precedence.

These five attempted solutions to our problem were to prove that *tadir* takes precedence over *mekuddash*. They all failed to establish this. At this stage a proof is attempted that, on the contrary, *mekuddash* takes precedence over *tadir*. This is from a further Mishnah (*Zevaḥim* 10: 6) in the same chapter; in fact, the Mishnah to which our *sugya* is appended! Here the following case is debated. Priests in the Temple have in front of them, for eating, the meat of peace-offerings brought yesterday and the meat of sin-offerings brought today. Which meat is to be eaten first? The Sages hold that the meat of the sin-offerings is to be eaten first, because a sin-offering is more 'sacred' than a peace-offering. But R. Meir holds that the meat of the peace-offerings should be eaten first because, the sacrifice having been brought yesterday, this meat may only be eaten until nightfall, whereas the meat of the sin-offering, the sacrifice having been brought today, may be eaten until tomorrow morning. It is better, according to R. Meir, to ignore the more sacred offering because the demands of the peace-offering are more pressing. It follows that where this reason would not apply, e.g. where both the peace-offerings and the sin-offerings had been brought today, even R. Meir would agree that the sin-offerings take precedence because they are more 'sacred'. But the peace-offerings are more 'constant' since they are brought as free-will offerings, whereas sin-offerings are only brought when sins have been committed. This demonstrates that *mekuddash*, the sin-offering, takes precedence over *tadir*, the peace-offering.

Rava, the fourth-century-Babylonian Amora, retorts that there is no proof at all from this *Baraita*. Rava argues that a clear distinction must be made between that which is 'constant', *tadir*, and that which is merely 'frequent', *matzuy*. *Tadir* refers to that which occurs at regular intervals in a cycle, such as the daily offerings or the Sabbath prayers. It is true that peace-offerings are more 'frequent' than sin-offerings but this does not render them *tadir*. Our original problem, observes Rava, is whether *tadir* takes precedence over *mekuddash* but there is no problem regarding whether *matzuy* takes precedence over *mekuddash*. It certainly does not, which is why the Mishnah implies that the sin-offerings, which are *mekuddash*, take precedence over the peace-offerings, which are only *matzuy*, 'frequent', but not *tadir*, 'constant'.

A *Baraita* (*Sifra*, *ḥova* 1: 6) is now quoted by R. Huna bar R. Judah, through which he challenges Rava's distinction between *tadir* and *matzuy*. We see from this *Baraita* that *matzuy* is referred to as *tadir*. The law is that a sin-offering is only brought for an offence, committed unintentionally, the penalty for which, if committed intentionally, is *karet*, 'extirpation'. But although a failure by intention to bring the Paschal lamb or to be circumcised involves the *karet* penalty, there is no sin-offering for unintentional failure in these instances, the reason being that a sin-offering is only brought for sins of commission and these are sins of omission. Thus both the Paschal lamb and circumcision are excluded from the law of the sin-offering, but in our *Baraita* there is a special verse to exclude the Paschal lamb and another special verse to exclude circumcision. The *Baraita* states that were it not for the special verse to exclude circumcision we could not have derived the exclusion from the verse excluding the Paschal lamb, since the Paschal lamb is less severe than circumcision in that the Paschal lamb is not *tadir* while circumcision is *tadir*. Now circumcision is not *tadir* in the sense of 'regular'. It is only more 'frequent' than the Paschal lamb since circumcision happens all the time, whereas the Paschal lamb can only be brought once a year. Thus circumcision is *matzuy*, 'frequent', and yet the *Baraita* refers to it as *tadir*. This refutes Rava who has argued that *matzuy* does not qualify as *tadir*.

Two replies are given. The first is that when the *Baraita* speaks of circumcision in relation to the Paschal lamb as *tadir* it does not mean *tadir* in time but '*tadir* in commandments', i.e. there are far more injunctions in Scripture regarding circumcision than regarding the Paschal lamb. It is in this sense alone that the term *tadir* is used of circumcision. But when the term *tadir* is used in a time sense it is never used of that which is only *matzuy*, 'frequent'. The second reply (prefaced by: 'If you want I can say') is that circumcision is referred to as *tadir*, even in the time sense, but only when comparing circumcision to the Paschal lamb. That is to say, generally speaking *matzuy* does not qualify as *tadir*, which is why peace-offerings do not take precedence over sin-offerings, even if *tadir* does take precedence over *mekuddash*. Even so the *matzuy* principle does have some significance, though not sufficient significance to override the *mekuddash* principle. Hence, circumcision, which is *matzuy*, cannot be derived from the Paschal lamb, which is not. It is in this sense that the *Baraita* speaks of *matzuy* as *tadir*.

The above is a plausible way of understanding this part of the *sugya*. The objection, however, is why does the *Baraita* refer to *matzuy* as *tadir*? This is probably why *Rashi* offers a different explanation. According to *Rashi* the meaning of this section is that, for something to qualify as *tadir* merely because it is *matzuy*, it must be very frequent in relation to that to which it is compared. Now circumcision is far more frequent than the Paschal lamb, which is only brought once a year, whereas even though it is true that peace-offerings are brought more frequently than sin-offerings they are not sufficiently more frequent to enable their *matzuy* to qualify as *tadir*.

The most puzzling feature of our *sugya* is the repeated attempt at a solution to the problem when the reply given as to why there is no solution in the first instance would seem to apply to all the attempts. (See *Tosafists* s.v. *ta shema*', who raise this question without supplying an answer.) What is the point in attempting what seems to be the same solution five times and in each instance giving what seems to be the same reply in almost identical words? Once the first reply had been given could we not have supplied it ourselves to the other four instances? But the truth is that we have here a beautiful example of how, without stating it explicitly, the Talmudic *sugya* leads from one argument to another. A careful examination of the five instances, demonstrates that the stock reply: 'Is A only effective?' becomes progressively weaker so that the *sugya* is really saying: 'This reply is all very well in case (1) but what of (2)?' and so on. Thus while it may well be accepted, in the first instance, that the daily offering of the Sabbath has imparted to it the special Sabbath sanctity, it is more difficult to see how, in the second instance, the New Moon sanctity is imparted to the Sabbath offerings, since these have nothing to do with the New Moon. And even when it is suggested that these do have imparted to them the New Moon sanctity it is difficult to see how, in the third instance, the New Year sanctity can be imparted to the New Moon sacrifices, since, by definition, New Year is New *Year* and not New *Moon*. And even when this, too, is accepted, it is difficult to see how, in the fourth instance, an ordinary wine benediction can be said to enjoy the special Sabbath sanctity. And even when this is accepted, it is difficult to see how the Sabbath prayer, which is merely an ordinary 'afternoon' prayer, with no connection at all with the additional *Sabbath* prayer (unlike the wine, which has some connection with the second benediction, since they are always recited together), can have imparted to it the sanctity of the additional prayer. (This argument ignores the special nature of the Sabbath afternoon prayer. Evidently, the argument follows the line that the Sabbath afternoon prayer is merely the *daily* afternoon prayer with reference to the Sabbath and with the omission of the petitionary prayers which must not be recited on the Sabbath.) Thus the reply: 'Is A only effective', given in all five instances, is not, in fact, the same reply at all. This helps us to understand why the attempted proofs are presented in this order. They are so presented because only in this way can the reply given be seen to become progressively weaker. Had the final instance been recorded first and the reply given to it where, as above, it is weakest, all the other attempted solutions would be unnecessary because we would have appreciated that if the reply operates successfully in its weakest form it operates *a fortiori* in its stronger forms.

We can now observe the pattern of the *sugya*:

(1) Problem: which takes precedence: *tadir* or *mekuddash*?
(2) Proof that *tadir* takes precedence: daily and Sabbath offerings
(3) Reply: no proof, there both *mekuddash*
(4) Proof II that *tadir* takes precedence: Sabbath and New Moon offerings
(5) Reply: no proof, there both *mekuddash*
(6) Proof III that *tadir* takes precedence: New Moon and New Year offerings
(7) Reply: no proof, there both *mekuddash*
(8) Proof IV that *tadir* takes precedence: benediction of wine and day
(9) Reply: no proof, there both *mekuddash*
(10) Proof V that *tadir* takes precedence: Sabbath afternoon and additional prayer
(11) Reply: no proof, there both *mekuddash*
(12) Proof that *mekuddash* takes precedence: meat of peace-offering and of sin-offering
(13) Reply: there not *tadir* only *matzuy*, Rava
(14) Objection to Rava: Paschal lamb and circumcision
(15) Reply I: *tadir* there means 'in commandments'
(16) Reply II: only in relation to Paschal lamb

We have already observed the neat sequence of thought in (1) to (11). Further to be noted is that (12), the proof that *mekuddash* takes precedence, is on the Mishnah to which the whole *sugya* has been appended. Why, then, was this proof not adduced first? The answer is obvious. This attempted proof that *mekuddash* takes precedence could only have been produced after the other proofs, *from the Mishnah*, had been refuted, otherwise the Mishnah would be in flat contradiction, at first teaching that *tadir* takes precedence over *mekuddash* and then implying here that *mekuddash* takes precedence over *tadir*.

The other Talmudic passages dealing with our theme are: *Berakhot* 28a; 51b; *Shabbat* 23b; *Pesaḥim* 114a; *Sukkah* 56a; *Megillah* 29b; *Menaḥot* 49a. See *Kesef Nivḥar*, part III, no. 154, pp. 39a–40a for a full discussion of the theme. For the question of precedence with regard to the rights of persons see *Bava Metzi'a* 33a–b; *Bava Batra* 9a; *Horayot* 13a–14a.

19

Palga nizka: the nature of the payment of half-damages to which the owner of a goring ox is liable

The *sugya* is *Bava Kama* 15a–b. Based on Exodus 21: 35–6, a distinction is made between an ox that has only gored once or twice and an ox that has gored three times. The former is known as *tam* ('docile', 'tame'), the latter as *mu'ad* ('warned', 'an habitual gorer'). If a *mu'ad* gores another animal the owner of the goring ox has to pay the full amount of the damage but the owner of a *tam* that gores only has to pay a half of the damage. A second distinction between the two is that the owner of a *mu'ad* is liable to make good the damage out of his own pocket, irrespective of the value of his ox, but the owner of the *tam* is only liable to pay out of the value of his ox. If the goring *tam* is not worth half the amount of the damage the owner is not obliged to make good the remainder out of his own pocket. A further law on which our *sugya* is based makes a general distinction between payment that is for the purpose of compensation and payment that is for the purpose of imposing a fine. The former is known as *mamona*, 'money', i.e. an amount to which a victim is entitled because of his loss. The latter is known as *kenasa*, 'a fine', the purpose of which is not to compensate the victim but to penalise the victimiser. For example, if a man steals another's property and is later found out, he has to pay double the amount he had stolen. The payment of the amount he had stolen is *mamona*, to which the victim of the theft is obviously entitled. But the extra amount, to which the victim has no title, since this was not stolen from him, is *kenasa*, a fine imposed as a penalty on the thief. The practical difference between the two kinds of payment is that a man's own admission of his guilt releases him from payment of *kenasa* but not, of course, from the payment of *mamona*. Thus if a thief stole 100 *zuz* and later admits to his guilt, he has to pay only 100 *zuz* and not the other 100 he would have had to pay if he had not admitted his guilt but was found out.

The *sugya* opens with a debate between the late-fourth-century Babylonian Amoraím, R. Pappa and R. Huna son of R. Joshua, regarding the nature of the half-damages to which the owner of a *tam* is liable. R. Pappa holds that this payment is *mamona*. The owner of the ox the *tam* has gored is entitled to this amount as compensation. R. Huna son of R. Joshua holds that it is *kenasa*, a fine imposed on the owner of the *tam*. Thus if the owner of a *tam* admits of his own accord that his *tam* has gored another animal, then according to R. Huna son of R. Joshua he does not have to pay, since there is no payment of *kenasa* where there is an admission of guilt.

The Talmud explains thus the reasoning of R. Pappa and R. Huna son of R. Joshua. The suggestion is made that it all depends on whether it can be assumed that oxen are 'in a state of protection' (*be-ḥezkat shimur*) so far as goring is concerned, i.e. whether it can be assumed that no special protection is required to prevent a *tam*, a docile ox, breaking out to gore. R. Pappa, it is suggested, holds that even a docile ox cannot be assumed to remain permanently docile and the owner is, therefore, obliged constantly to be on his guard. Hence if the *tam* does gore this demonstrates that the owner has failed in his duty to guard it adequately and he should, strictly speaking, be obliged to make good the whole of the damage. Since, however, it is, after all, a *tam*, Scripture lets him off lightly and deducts from his payment half the amount of the damages. R. Huna son of R. Joshua holds that it can be assumed that a *tam* will not gore, so that if it does this betokens no evidence that the owner has failed in his duty to guard it. Strictly speaking, therefore, he should not be liable to pay anything at all; but Scripture does, none the less, impose a penalty to make him take better care in the future, this penalty being the fine of half the damages. In other words, according to R. Pappa the half payment is for the damage done, while according to R. Huna son of R. Joshua it is to prevent damage being done by the ox in the future. Thus according to R. Pappa the payment is *mamona*, compensation for the damage done, while according to R. Huna son of R. Joshua it is *kenasa*, payment to prevent damage being done in the future.

The significance of the debate as thus formulated appears to be this. On the face of it, payment of half the damage is a curious idea. There cannot be any such thing in law as partial responsibility for damages. Either the requisite degree of responsibility has been attained or it has not. The person who is only half responsible is not responsible at all in law. Consequently, in the case of the *tam* where the owner has to pay only half the damage, one is obliged to say that, strictly speaking, the owner is either responsible, and should, therefore, pay the full damage, or not responsible, and therefore should pay no damages at all. And yet Scripture does depart from what the strict law should be, stating that the payment is half the damages. The question, then, is whether this departure is to render the owner liable to pay the half imposed on him (because, strictly speaking, he should not have been obliged to pay *any* damages) or whether the departure is to free him from the other half (because, strictly speaking, he should have been obliged to pay in full). R. Pappa holds that the departure is to free him from payment of the other half, the half he does pay being no departure at all but the compensation demanded by law. R. Huna son of R. Joshua holds that the departure is to impose the half-payment, since strictly speaking, the victim is not entitled to compensation at all.

The Mishnah (*Bava Kama* 1:3), to which the *sugya* is appended, is quoted. The man whose ox has been gored, the man suffering the damage, is known as the *nizzak*. The owner of the goring ox, the man responsible for the damage, is known as the *mazzik*. The Mishnah states that in cases of payment for damages 'both the *nizzak* and the *mazzik* have to pay'. This is a puzzling statement. How can the *nizzak* be said to pay? It is to him that the *mazzik* pays. According to R. Pappa we can well understand the meaning of this clause in the Mishnah. According to him the *nizzak*, where the goring ox is a *tam*, is, strictly speaking, entitled to full compensation so that when he receives only half it can be said that he, as well as the *mazzik*, 'pays'. But according to R. Huna son of R. Joshua the *nizzak*, strictly speaking is not entitled to anything at all. Even the half he does receive is not in the nature of compensation to him but only as a penalty for the mazzik. What sense, then, does it make for the Mishnah to state that the *nizzak* also 'pays'? The reply is that the *nizzak* sometimes 'pays' in that he does not receive even the half damages awarded to him by the Torah. This is what the Mishnah means by the *nizzak* 'pays'. The circumstances are where the carcass of the *nizzak*'s ox deteriorates after it has been killed so that by the time the Court pronounces its verdict its value is considerably less. It is the *nizzak*, not the *mazzik*, who has to bear this loss. If, for example, the ox was worth 200 *zuz* before it was gored and the carcass is now worth 40 *zuz*, the amount of the damage is 160 *zuz* and, since the goring ox was a *tam*, the owner, the *mazzik* , has to pay 80 *zuz*. But supposing, before the verdict of the Court is declared, the carcass so deteriorates that it is now worthless. We might have supposed that the total damage is now 200 *zuz* and the *mazzik* should be obliged to pay 100 *zuz*. But the law is not so. The damages are assessed as at the time of the killing of the ox and any further deterioration is not taken into account, the *nizzak* suffering the loss. This is the meaning of the *nizzak*, too, having to 'pay'.

An objection is now raised that this law – that the *nizzak* bears the loss through deterioration of the carcass – is, in fact, derived from an earlier Mishnah (*Bava Kama* 1 : 1) as is stated in a *Baraita* (*Bava Kama* 10b) commenting on this earlier Mishnah. Why, then, repeat it here if this is what our Mishnah means? The reply is that a repetition is, indeed, necessary to demonstrate that this law applies both to *tam* and *mu'ad*. It does not follow that because the *nizzak* has to bear the loss through deterioration in the case of *tam* that he has to bear it in the case of *mu'ad*, since, it might have been argued, *tam* is, in any event, treated more leniently than *mu'ad*. Conversely, it does not follow that because the *nizzak* has to bear the loss through deterioration in the case of *mu'ad*, which is treated, in any event, more severely, he should certainly have to bear the loss in the case of *tam*. For it may well be that precisely because *mu'ad* is treated more severely, in that the *nizzak* receives the full amount of damages, it is right that he, the *nizzak*, should bear the loss through deterioration. In the case of *tam*, on the other hand, the *mazzik* is let off lightly in having to pay only half the damages and here, it might be argued, he should at least be obliged to bear the loss of deterioration, paying half of that as well. Consequently, two statements are required to show that both in the case of *tam* and of *mu'ad* it is the *nizzak* who bears the loss through deterioration.

A further proof is now attempted from the next Mishnah (*Bava Kama* 1 : 4) which states: 'What difference is there between *tam* and *mu'ad*? *Tam* pays half the damages from itself (i.e. from the value of the ox, not from the owner's pocket, if the ox is not worth half the damage) whereas *mu'ad* pays full damages from the *aliyah* ('upper storey', i.e. from the owner's possessions kept in the upper storey of his house)'. Thus the Mishnah only records two differences between the law of *tam* and *mu'ad*. But according to R. Huna son of R. Joshua there is yet another difference: that *tam*, as *kenasa*, does not pay on the owner's admission whereas *mu'ad*, as *mamona*, does. The reply is that the Mishnah could have, indeed, recorded this further difference but chose simply to omit it, not because it is an invalid distinction but simply because the Mishnah does not list all the differences, only some of them. But, the Talmud objects, 'What else has he omitted that he should omit this?', i.e. the argument that the Mishnah simply omits a case it could have recorded is only valid if there is, at least, one other case it omits by choice. If there is only one omission, this argument cannot be accepted. The logic of this is that, if the Mishnah omits two or more cases, it can be said that the Mishnah is not bent on listing all the examples but simply recording some of them. But if the Mishnah only leaves out a single instance, listing all the others, this shows that the Mishnah is bent on listing all the instances and it would then be arbitrary for the Mishnah to omit a single instance. The reply is that there is, in fact, yet another omission. If a *mu'ad* kills a human being the owner has to pay 'ransom', *kofer* (see Exodus 21: 28–30), but if a *tam* kills a human being the owner does not have to pay even half the *kofer*. Consequently, since there is no law of *kofer* for *tam*, two further differences between *tam* and *mu'ad* have been omitted: (1) that *tam* is *kenasa* and *mu'ad mamona*; (2) that there is *kofer* where the ox is *mu'ad* but not even half-*kofer* where the ox is *tam*. The Talmud concludes, however, that this second omission is not really an omission at all, since the Mishnah may agree with the opinion of R. Jose the Galilean, who holds that the owner of a *tam* does have to pay half-*kofer*.

See *Rashi*, who states that the distinction between the full *kofer* of *mu'ad* and the half-*kofer* of *tam*, according to R. Jose the Galilean, is no omission, since this distinction is embraced by the one made in the Mishnah, that *tam* only pays half-damages whereas *mu'ad* pays in full. It is only according to the opinion of the Sages, who disagree with R. Jose the Galilean and hold that there is not even half-*kofer* in the case of *tam*, that this constitutes a *further* distinction. See *Tosafists*, s.v. *i mi-shum ḥatzi kofer*, that the Talmud means, according to R. Pappa that there is only a single omission – that of *kofer* – and this will not do; to which the reply is that the Mishnah follows the opinion of R. Jose the Galilean. For further Talmudic examples of the idea of omission and that it is illogical to omit only a single instance, see *Ta'anit* 13b; 14a; *Sukkah* 54a; *Yevamot* 21b; 73a; 84b; *Ketubot* 41a; *Kiddushin* 16a; 40a; *Nazir* 38b; *Sotah* 16a; *Bava Kama* 10a; 43b; 62b; *Makkot* 21b.

A further attempt at proving the case is made from a Mishnah (*Ketubot* 3: 9) in which instances are given of where payment is demanded even on the strength of one's own admission (because it is *mamona*) and of where no payment is demanded (because it is *kenasa*). The payment of thirty shekels when an ox gores and kills a slave (Exodus 21: 32) is held by all to be *kenasa*. Thus the Mishnah states: '[If a man declares:] "My ox killed So-and-so", or "My ox killed the ox of So-and-so", he pays on the strength of his own admission. [But if he declares:] "My ox killed the slave of So-and-so" he does not pay on the strength of his own admission.' Now the Mishnah states that when a man declares: 'My ox has killed the ox of So-and-so' it refers even to where the ox is a *tam*. This show that the payment of half-damages in the case of *tam* is *mamona*. No, is the reply, the Mishnah does not refer to *tam* but to *mu'ad*. But in that case, the Talmud objects, why does the Mishnah have to give the instances of the ox killing the slave as an example of no payment because of the owner's admission; he could have found an example, that of *tam*, in the case of the killing of an ox? The reply is given: 'The whole of the Mishnah deals with *mu'ad*, i.e. the Mishnah wishes to inform us that it is *kenasa* where the ox kills a slave, even if the ox is a *mu'ad*.

Another proof is now attempted from the conclusion of this same Mishnah (*Ketubot* 3: 9). This reads: 'This is the rule: Wherever the amount to be paid is greater than the damage done, there is no payment on the strength of one's own admission', i.e. because it cannot be compensation since the victim is not entitled to a greater degree of compensation than the loss he has suffered. The implication of this Mishnah is that the payment is *kenasa* where the payment is *greater* than the damage done, but where it is *less* than the damage done (i.e. in the case of the half-damages of *tam*) it is not *kenasa* but *mamona* and this supports R. Pappa. To this the reply is given, the implication is not that where the amount is *less* it is *mamona* but rather that where it is *the same* it is *mamona*. In that case, objects the Talmud, why does the Mishnah formulate it in the misleading way: 'Whenever the payment to be made is greater', which seems to exclude where it is less? Let the Mishnah formulate it as: 'Wherever the payment is not *the same as*' and this would only exclude where it is *the same as* but not where it is either *greater* or *less*. It follow from the formulation in the Mishnah that only where it is *greater* is it *kenasa*, but where it is not *greater*, i.e. where it is either *the same as* or *less*, it is *mamona*.

The Talmud concludes: *tiyuvta*, 'This is, indeed, a refutation.' But the Talmud continues immediately: 'And the law is in accordance with the opinion that half-damage is *kenasa*.' To this the Talmud objects: *tiyuvta ve-hilkheta*, '"It is, indeed a refutation", and yet "And the law is"!', i.e. how can the law be in accordance with the view of R. Huna son of R. Joshua since he has just been refuted? The reply is that the alleged refutation can itself be refuted. This is because there is another case – that of *tzerurot*, 'pebbles' – where all agree that although only half the damage is paid it is *mamona* not *kenasa*. If an animal, while walking along in the normal way, causes 'pebbles' or some other object to spring from under its feet and these break a vessel, there is a tradition, said to go back to Moses at Sinai, that only half the damage is to be paid even though it is *mamona* (since the reason given above why the half-damage of *tam* is *kenasa* does not apply here). Consequently, the Mishnah speaks only of where the amount paid is *greater* than the damage done. If the Mishnah were to state, wherever the damage is not *the same as* it would have implied that wherever it is *less* it is *kenasa* and while it is perfectly true that the half-payment of *tam* is *kenasa* it is not true that the half-payment of *tzerurot* is *kenasa*. Thus R. Huna son of R. Joshua is not really refuted and it is perfectly logical to declare that the law follows his opinion.

The pattern of the *sugya* is:

(1) Half-damage of *tam*: R. Pappa: *mamona*; R. Huna son of R. Joshua: *kenasa*
(2) Reasoning: whether oxen are assumed to gore
(3) Proof I for R. Pappa: Mishnah; the *nizzak* also pays
(4) Reply: refers to loss through deterioration
(5) Objection: this stated previously
(6) Reply: two statements required, one for *tam* and another for *mu'ad*
(7) Proof II for R. Pappa: only two differences in Mishnah between *tam* and *mu'ad*
(8) Reply: there is a further difference but omitted
(9) Objection: what else omitted?
(10) Reply: half-*kofer* also omitted
(11) Elaboration on this: R. Jose the Galilean
(12) Proof III for R. Pappa: Mishnah *Ketubot*; no payment on strength of admission where ox gores ox
(13) Reply: this refers to *mu'ad* not to *tam*

(14) Objection: then why state case of slave, state case of *tam*
(15) Reply: all deals with *mu'ad*, ox and slave
(16) Proof IV for R. Pappa: Mishnah *Ketubot*: only where *greater* is it *kenasa*
(17) Reply: does not exclude where it is *less*
(18) Objection: then should have stated: where it is *not the same*
(19) *Tiyuvta*, indeed refuted
(20) 'and the law is that it is *kenasa*'
(21) Objection: since refuted, how can law follow this opinion?
(22) No refutation because *less* of *tzerurot*

The sequence is clear. Proof after proof is attempted for R. Pappa's view and against that of R. Huna son of R. Joshua until the final, total refutation of R. Huna son of R. Joshua's opinion. It is possible that (20) to (22) are the result of later editorial work, but if we are correct that the *sugya* is so contrived that it leads to the dénouement in the total refutation of R. Huna son of R. Joshua it is possible, even plausible, to suggest that this, too, is part of the contrived *sugya*. That is to say, the impression is first created that all the arguments favour R. Pappa and none R. Huna son of R. Joshua, so much so that R. Huna son of R. Joshua is, in fact, finally refuted conclusively and yet, when all seems lost, the surprise conclusion is recorded that the law follows the opinion of R. Huna son of R. Joshua and the refutation is itself refuted.

The next section of the *sugya*, beginning: 'And now that you say' through to the end, does appear to be a later editorial addition, supplied at a later date after the whole of the *sugya* had been completed. This whole section, in fact, consists of practical rules in the same vein as that used by the earliest Codifiers in post-Talmudic times. On the phenomenon of 'And now' as a Saboraic addition, see Lewin, *Rabbanan Savorai ve-Talmudan*, pp. 154–6. It should be noted that *Ketubot* 41a–b is an exact duplicate of our *sugya*, including the final section, i.e. the later editorial addition. It has been inserted in *Ketubot* on the Mishnah quoted in the *sugya*. The theme of half-damage is a '*Bava Kama*' theme, dealt with, in fact, in the previous pages of this tractate. It seems certain therefore, that originally the *sugya* belonged here and was later duplicated in *Ketubot* by still later editors. There are thus at least three distinct stages of reduction to be observed: (1) the original *sugya* up to (22) as above; (2) the addition of: 'and now that you say' and the rest of the material until the *sugya* ends where it now ends; (3) the appending by still later editors of the whole of (1) and (2) to the Mishnah in *Ketubot*. There are cross-references to the debate in our *sugya* in *Sanhedrin* 3a and *Shevu'ot* 32a.

The final section begins with: 'And now that you say, half-damage is *kenasa*, if a dog devours lambs or a cat devours chickens, it is unusual and payment cannot be enforced in Babylon.' The meaning of this is that the half-damage of *tam* does not only apply to a goring ox but to any malicious or unusual damage done by any animal. This is known as *keren*, 'horn' (see *Bava Kama* 2a–3b). Now in Talmudic times only the Palestinian Amoraím had full ordination, *semikhah*, and only they, not the Babylonian teachers, were empowered to impose fines, though they could, of course, render decisions in cases where compensation was called for (*mamona* but not *kenasa*). If, therefore, the final ruling had been that the half-damage of *tam* is *mamona*, the Babylonian Courts could have enforced payment by the owner of the dog or the cat. But 'now that you have said' that half-damage is *kenasa*, then the owner of the dog or cat cannot be compelled to pay by the Babylonian Courts, who have no *semikhah* and cannot, therefore, impose fines. This only applies, however, the Talmud continues, to large lambs or chickens. If they are small it is 'usual', so that it is not *keren* at all and full payment would have to be made and this can be enforced in Babylon. Furthermore, the Talmud adds, even where it cannot be enforced, if the *nizzak* manages to obtain for himself some of the *mazzik*'s property to the value of half his damages, he can hold on to this and the Courts are not empowered to take it from him. Again, if the *nizzak* declared that he wished to be given time to submit his case to a Palestinian Court, he is given the time and if the *mazzik* then refuses to have the case submitted to the Palestinian Court he is placed under a ban until he agrees to do so. In any event he is placed under the ban until he gets rid of the vicious dog or cat. In this connection the saying of R. Nathan is quoted: 'How do we know that one should not keep a vicious dog or an unsafe ladder in the house? Because Scripture says: "thou bring not blood upon thine house" (Deuteronomy 22: 8).'

20

Patur mi-diney adam ve-ḥayyav be-diney shamayim: cases where there is liability in the eyes of God even though the human Courts cannot enforce payment

The *sugya* is *Bava Kama* 55b–56a. There are instances of loss and damage to another where, for various technical reasons, the law cannot enforce payment but where, nevertheless, there is a moral obligation to pay. This is called: *patur mi-diney adam ve-ḥayyav be-diney shamayim*, literally, 'exempt from the laws of man but liable by the laws of Heaven'. Actually the term denotes something more than a moral obligation to pay. It is rather that there is a legal obligation to pay, only it is one that cannot be enforced by the Courts.

The *sugya* begins with a *Baraita* which reads as follows: 'R. Joshua said: There are four things which, if a man does them, he is exempt from the laws of man but is liable by the laws of Heaven and these are they: He who breaks down a fence before his neighbour's animal (and the animal escapes and is lost); he who bends his neighbour's corn into the path of a fire; he who hires false witnesses to testify; and he who can testify on behalf of his neighbour but fails so to do.' In each of these cases the Courts cannot enforce payment, since the loss is caused indirectly and the law only demands compensation where there is a direct act of injury or damage to property. Thus where a man breaks down a fence and the animal escapes and is lost his act is indirect, but since otherwise the neighbour's animal could not have escaped he is liable by the laws of Heaven. Similarly where a man sees a fire spreading but in such a way that it will pass by his neighbour's corn and he bends the corn so that it will eventually catch fire, this, too, is indirect since at the time he bends the corn the fire has not yet reached that spot. In the third case, the man causes his neighbour a loss by hiring false witnesses to testify that his neighbour is liable when, in fact, he is not. Here, too, the loss is caused by the witnesses who are his indirect agents. Finally, in the fourth case, he does cause his neighbour a loss by failing to testify on his behalf, but it is an indirect cause.

See *Rashi* who refers to *gerama bi-nezakin*, 'causing damage', i.e. 'indirect damage'. On this subject see *Kesef Nivḥar*, part I, no. 43, pp. 75b–77a and *ET*, vol. VI, pp. 461–97. On the concept *patur mi-diney adam ve-ḥayyav be-diney shamayim* see *ET*, vol. VII, pp. 382–96. The *Baraita* quoted in our *sugya* is *Tosefta*, *Shevu'ot* 3: 1–3 but there the order is different and, instead of *patur mi-diney adam ve-ḥayyav be-diney shamayim*, reads: 'Four are not liable to pay by law but Heaven does not forgive them until they pay.' It would seem that our *sugya* has paraphrased the *Tosefta* using a form that fits in with the needs of our *sugya*'s argument, e.g. the cause of the animal is mentioned first (unlike in the *Tosefta*, which mentions the case of testimony first because this is the *Shevu'ot* context) because this is the previous theme treated in this section of *Bava Kama*

The Talmud now examines each one of these instances in turn. First the Talmud examines the case of the man who breaks down the fence in front of his neighbour's animal. The Talmud observes that this cannot refer to a sound fence, i.e. to one that otherwise would not have fallen in, since then the man would be liable even by the laws of man, at least for his destruction of the fence, even though here, too, he would be exempt for the loss of the animal since this is still indirect causation. The reply is that the *Baraita* deals with a shaky fence that would, in any event, have fallen in.

This follows *Rashi* and *Tosafists* but see *Meíri* and *ha-Gra* who show that other commentators understand the question to be, if the fence is sound the man ought to be liable by the laws of man even for the loss of the animal, i.e. because to break down a sound fence so that the animal will escape is considered to be *direct*, not indirect, damage.

The Talmud now examines the second instance in the *Baraita*, that of the man who bends his neighbour's corn in the path of a fire. The Talmud asks, why should the man not be liable to pay by the laws of man if the fire will reach the corn even if fanned by a normal wind? The significance of the question is that according to the law (Exodus 22: 6; *The Torah*: Exodus 22: 5) as interpreted by the Rabbis, if a man lights a fire in his own field and the fire, fanned by a normal wind, spreads to his neighbour's field and does damage there, the man who lit the fire is liable to pay for the damage. Now if the fire, in our case, can reach the corn when fanned by a normal wind, the man who bent the corn so that the fire will now reach the corn ought to be liable by the laws of man.

This is, in fact, the case mentioned in Scripture of *esh*, 'fire', since there is surely no difference between putting the fire in the way of the corn (the Scriptural case) and putting the corn in the way of the fire (our case, see *Tosafists*). The reply is given that the *Baraita* speaks of fire that cannot travel by a normal wind, only by an abnormal wind. Consequently, there is no liability by the laws of man but there is a liability by the laws of Heaven. R. Ashi gives a different answer, interpreting the *Baraita*'s reference to 'bending' the corn in a novel way. According to R. Ashi the *Baraita* does not mean that the man simply 'bent' the corn so that it came into the path of the fire for then, indeed, he would be liable by the laws of man, as above. 'Bending' the corn means that he covered the corn, already in the path of a spreading fire, with a sheet, thus 'bending' it under the weight of the sheet. Now the law is (Mishnah, *Bava Kama* 6: 5) that a man who lights a fire, as above, which spreads to do damage is only liable if the corn and so forth that is burnt is uncovered. If it is 'covered', *tamun*, 'hidden', there is no liability. Consequently, if A kindled a fire that spread when fanned by a normal wind he is liable for any damage it causes to B's corn. But if, before the fire reached B's corn, C covered the corn with a sheet, A is exempt from paying, since the corn is now *tamun*. Thus C's act has the effect of causing B to suffer loss, since B cannot now claim damages from A. C's offence is that he introduced a technicality by means of which B loses his case. For this there is no liability by the laws of man, since, after all, it was the fire kindled by A that did the damage, but there is liability by the laws of Heaven and, according to R. Ashi, it is to this that our *Baraita* refers.

The third example given in the *Baraita* is now examined, that of the man who hires false witnesses. The Talmud objects that if he hired these false witnesses to obtain money for himself then, when they are found to be false, he must return the money he has obtained through false pretences. Consequently, here he is liable according to the laws of man. The reply is that he hires the witnesses to testify falsely on behalf of another (i.e. who has died in the meantime or has vanished, *Tosafists*). By hiring the false witnesses he has caused his neighbour to lose money yet, since this is indirect, there is no liability according to the laws of man but there is by the laws of Heaven.

Finally, the fourth case in the *Baraita* is examined, that of the man who can testify on behalf of his neighbour but fails so to do.

Now according to the Rabbinic interpretation of: 'if he do not utter it, then he shall bear his iniquity' (Leviticus 5: 1), if *two* witnesses refuse to testify they commit a sin, since in monetary matters the evidence of two witnesses is required. But if one witness refuses to testify, this Biblical sin is not incurred since the testimony of a single witness can only succeed in imposing an oath on the person against whom the testimony is given. The Talmud asks, when the *Baraita* speaks of a man failing to testify does it refer, in fact, to two witnesses, each of whom refuses to testify? If it does then 'It is obvious' that each is liable by the laws of Heaven (*Rashi*) since this is stated explicitly in the Scriptural verse: 'if he do not utter it, then he shall bear his iniquity'. The reply is that the *Baraita* speaks of a single witness. A has a claim on B and asks C to testify on his behalf, which C refuses to do. Now even if C does testify all his testimony can succeed in doing is to compel B to take an oath and it is possible that B will then swear falsely. On the other hand, B may not wish to swear falsely so that C, by refusing to testify on A's behalf, may be causing A a loss. Therefore, there is no liability according to the laws of man (there is no liability according to the laws of man even if two witnesses refuse to testify, as above) but there is liability according to the laws of Heaven. This is not, however obvious and requires to be stated, since this case, of a single witness, is not covered by the Biblical text.

The Talmud now raises a new difficulty. R. Joshua in the *Baraita* refers to only four cases which are 'exempt by the laws of man and liable by the laws of Heaven'. But, the Talmud proceeds to ask, there are, in fact, other examples of this rule. Why, then, does R. Joshua only refer to these four? The Talmud proceeds to list these further examples of cases 'exempt by the laws of man and liable by the laws of Heaven'. All these are from Tannaitic sources, *Baraitot* and in one case a Mishnah.

This is the list as given in the Talmud.

(a) If a man does work with the red heifer or the purifying water (Numbers 19) and by so doing renders them invalid and thus causes their owner a loss, he is exempt by the laws of man but liable by the laws of Heaven (see *supra*, p. 148).

(b) If a man places poison in front of his neighbour's animal and the animal eats it and dies, he is exempt from the laws of man but liable by the laws of Heaven. This is indirect damage, since the animal may not have eaten the poison but there is, none the less, complete liability by the laws of Heaven.

(c) If a man gives a flaming torch to an imbecile or a minor and they take it and set a haystack alight the man who gave them the torch is exempt by the laws of man (because it is indirect) but liable by the laws of Heaven (Mishnah, *Bava Kama* 6: 4).

(d) If a man gives his neighbour a sudden fright, i.e. by shouting into his ear and the like, he is exempt by the laws of man, since this, too, is considered to be a case of indirect injury, but he is liable by the laws of Heaven.

(e) A man's jar broke in the public domain or his camel fell down there and he failed to remove them and they did damage. According to R. Meir he is liable even by the laws of man, but the Sages hold that he is exempt by the laws of man and liable by the laws of Heaven.

Thus there are five further examples of '*patur mi-diney adam*' etc., so why does R. Joshua in our *Baraita* only record four and omits these? The reply is that there are, indeed, more examples and R. Joshua is not bent on listing all possible examples. What R. Joshua means by his examples is that even with regard to these four there is a liability by the laws of Heaven. R. Joshua has to state this because there are sound arguments in all these four cases for holding that in these there is no liability at all, not even by the laws of Heaven. The Talmud then proceeds, case by case, to show what these arguments are.

It hardly needs saying that, historically speaking, the problem raised by the Talmud here is artificial. R. Joshua may have had his reasons for only referring to these four. He may, indeed, have known only these four. One of them is, in fact, debated by R. Meir and the Sages and, for all we know to the contrary, R. Joshua may have held the same view as that held later by R. Meir. The truth is that we have here an example of purely artificial *sugya* in which the question, 'why these four only', is raised for the sole purpose of developing the argument that in these instances a good case can be made out for exempting the man even by the laws of Heaven. See *SM*, who raises the question about R. Meir and suggests that the 'Sages' who disagree with R. Meir are to be identified with R. Judah, the usual anonymous protagonist of R. Meir, and that the reading in our *Baraita* is not R. Joshua but R. Judah. This is forced and, in any event, in the *Tosefta* texts the reading is R. Joshua.

As stated, the Talmud now proceeds to show why it could have been argued in these four cases that the man is not even liable by the laws of Heaven. In the case of breaking down the fence, since we have established that it must be a case of a shaky fence, it could have been argued that there is no liability at all, not even by the laws of Heaven, since the fence is due to be demolished. In the second case, that of the man who bends his neighbour's corn in the path of the fire, since we have established, according to the first reply above, that the fire only travels by means of an abnormal wind, the man might have argued: 'How could I have anticipated that an abnormal wind would bring the fire to the corn?' And according to R. Ashi's reply, that the man 'covered' the corn, it might have been argued that his intention was not malicious in spreading the sheet but rather was to prevent the fire getting at the corn. Though, in fact, by covering the corn, he rendered it *tamun*, we might have argued that he is not liable even by the laws of Heaven (see *Tosafists*). In the case of a man who hires false witnesses, we might have argued that the hirer can say to the witnesses: 'Where there are the instructions of the master and the (opposite) instructions of the disciple, whose instructions should one obey?', i.e. God instructs witnesses not to testify falsely and they should not have heeded the opposite instructions to give false witness. If they did, it is the witnesses who should bear the full load of the guilt and the hirer, we might have said, is not even liable by the laws of Heaven. Finally, in the case of the witness who refuses to testify, since we have established that it is a case of a single witness, then there is no guarantee that his testimony would have had any effect, since, even if he did testify, the man against whom he testified might have sworn falsely and have been acquitted. Hence we could well have argued that through his refusal to testify he does not incur liability even by the laws of Heaven. Thus in all four cases there is a strong argument for exempting the man even by the laws of Heaven, which is why R. Joshua sees fit to mention these four cases, to inform us that he is liable by the laws of Heaven.

The plan of the *sugya* is:

(1) Joshua's statement:
- (a) breaking the fence
- (b) bending the corn
- (c) hiring false witnesses
- (d) refusing to testify

(2) In (a) let him be liable for the fence by laws of man?
No, (a) refers to shaky fence

(3) In (b) let him be liable as 'fire' by laws of man?
No, abnormal wind or (R. Ashi) 'bending' means *tamun*

(4) In (c) let him be liable for the money he has gained illegally?
No, he hires the witnesses not for himself but for another

(5) In (d) if there are two witnesses it is obvious since Biblical?
No, it speaks of a single witness

(6) Why does R. Joshua only list these four; there are also:

(i) red heifer
(ii) poison
(iii) torch sent by imbecile
(iv) giving another a fright
(v) the jar or camel in the public domain

(7) These four are necessary because we might have thought no liability here at all, not even by laws of Heaven because:

(a) *since the wall is weak*, as above
(b) *since the wind is abnormal*, as above or (R. Ashi) *since he could have covered it with good intentions*
(c) *since it is not for himself and he does not have the money* the full guilt should be borne by the witnesses
(d) *since a single witness*, as above

As soon as one studies the construction of this *sugya* one sees immediately that the replies given in (7) to the question in (6) only make sense after R. Joshua's four cases have been qualified in the way they have been in (2) to (5). In other words (2) to (5) pave the way for the solutions in (7) and this can only mean that the whole *sugya* has been constructed as a unit with a degree of artificiality but one that gives power to the sequence of argument. This is an excellent illustration of the Talmudic *sugya* as a literary unit, contrived, but all the more effective for it. All this must be the work of editors subsequent to R. Ashi since R. Ashi's interpretation and the alternative one in (3) have been utilised as bricks in the complete edifice. The mnemonic referring to the list in (6), given in brackets in 56a, is probably post-Talmudic but this list may originally have been independent of our *sugya*. It is perhaps not without significance that all five items in the list are quoted elsewhere in *Bava Kama* and it is just possible that they may have formed originally a '*Bava Kama*' collection.

21

Maḥal 'al kevodo maḥul: renunciation of honour by one to whom it is due

The *sugya* is *Kiddushin* 32a–b. It deals with the question, how far does the honour and respect due to certain persons extend? According to Rabbinic teaching there are four persons it is a religious obligation to honour: a father (and mother); a teacher (*rav*); the Prince (*nasi*), the leader of Palestinian Jewry, mainly of the House of Rabban Gamaliel; and the king (*melekh*). Now although to pay these honour is a religious injunction yet the honour is paid to another human being. Consequently, it can be argued that if that person is prepared to renounce the honour due to him, there is no longer any obligation to pay him honour, or, it can be argued, it does not lie in his power to renounce the honour since, after all, it is a religious obligation. Renouncing the honour is referred to as: *maḥal 'al kevodo*: 'he renounces his honour'. If he can renounce it, then we say: *kevodo maḥul*, 'his honour is renounced'. If he cannot, then we say: *eyn kevodo maḥul*, 'his honour is not renounced'. The *sugya* is based on a ruling by the third-century Babylonian Amora, R. Hisda. With regard to the father and the teacher the question was of practical significance in R. Hisda's day. With regard to the Prince and the king the whole question was purely academic. The *sugya* has been inserted here because this section of tractate *Kiddushin* considers the rules of honouring parents.

The *sugya* opens with a saying of R. Isaac bar Shila in the name of R. Mattena in the name of R. Hisda: 'If a father renounces his honour his honour is renounced but if a teacher renounces his honour his honour is not renounced.' The reason for the distinction is because the honour due to the teacher is really not because of his own person at all but because of the Torah he teaches and it does not lie within his power to renounce the honour due to the Torah. But R. Joseph disagrees with R. Hisda and holds that even a teacher can renounce the honour due to him. R. Joseph quotes in support: 'And the Lord went before them' (Exodus 13: 21), i.e. God is Israel's Teacher and yet He renounced His honour by leading them and, as it were, serving them. To this Rava, R. Joseph's pupil, objects that there is no proof whatsoever from this verse. The whole world belongs to God and the Torah belongs to God. It is all for His glory and He can renounce His due. But the Torah is not the teacher's, so that he should be able to renounce it. Yet Rava, it is said, later changed his mind, arguing that a teacher can renounce the honour due to him because the 'Torah is his.' Rava quotes the verse: 'And in his Torah doth he meditate day and night' (Psalm 1: 2).

Rava's interpretation of the text is better understood by the parallel reference in '*Avodah Zarah* 19a where Rava says that at first it is the Torah of the Lord and then (i.e. after a man has mastered his studies) it becomes 'his Torah'. Rava interprets the verse: 'But his delight is in the Torah of the Lord; And in *his* Torah doth he meditate day and night', i.e. the personal pronoun refers, not to God as in the plain meaning, but to the student. The Torah becomes 'his Torah' and the teacher can, therefore, renounce the honour as due to *him*.

We have thus established that, eventually, Rava came to hold that a teacher can renounce the honour due to him. But, the Talmud objects, it once happened that at the wedding feast of Rava's son, Rava handed a cup of wine to R. Pappa and R. Huna son of R. Joshua and they rose before him (to pay him respect) but when he handed the cup to R. Mari and R. Phinehas son of R. Hisda they did not rise before him. Rava took offence and declared: 'Are these Rabbis Rabbis and those Rabbis not Rabbis?', i.e. R. Pappa and R. Huna son of R. Joshua are also scholars and yet they paid Rava honour by rising out of respect; why, then, did R. Mari and R. Phinehas remain seated? Now this shows that Rava objected to the failure of the two Rabbis to pay him the respect due to him as their teacher even though, by handing them the cup of wine in the first place, he had demonstrated that he had renounced the honour due to him and, according to Rava's own eventual decision, if a teacher renounces his honour, his honour is renounced. Furthermore, it once happened that R. Pappa, Rava's pupil, who, presumably, agrees with Rava's decision, was serving drinks at the wedding feast of his son, Abba Mar, and he handed a cup of wine to R. Isaac son of R. Judah and when the latter did not rise before him he took offence. All this shows that even when a teacher renounces his honour his honour is not renounced. The reply is: 'Nevertheless, they should have paid him some token of honour', i.e. even though, it is true, a teacher can renounce his honour, the disciple, while accepting this, should pay his teacher some small token of respect, such as rising before him.

There is now reported the saying of the fifth-century Babylonian Amora, R. Ashi. R. Ashi said: 'Even according to the authority who holds that if a teacher renounces his honour, his honour is renounced, if a Prince renounces his honour his honour is not renounced', i.e., because it is not his to renounce, unlike the teacher whose Torah, as Rava has said, is his own. An objection is raised to R. Ashi's statement. A *Baraita* is quoted where it is stated that R. Eliezer and R. Joshua and R. Zadok were reclining at the wedding feast of Rabban Gamaliel's son and Rabban Gamaliel was handing round the drinks. When he handed the cup to R. Eliezer he refused to accept it but when he handed the cup to R. Joshua he did accept it. R. Eliezer said: 'What is this, O Joshua! Shall we recline and allow Rabban Gamaliel to serve us with drink?' R. Joshua replied: 'We find that a greater one than he served others. Abraham was the greatest one of his generation (i.e. he was the equivalent in his day of the *nasi*, as Rabban Gamaliel was) and yet of him it is written: "and he stood by them" (Genesis 18: 8). And perchance you might say that they appeared to him as angels. They only appeared to him as Arabs. So, as for us, shall not Rabban Gamaliel stand by us to serve us drinks?' R. Zadok thereupon said to them: 'For how long will you leave aside the honour of God and discuss the honour of His creatures? The Holy One, blessed be He, causes the winds to blow. He makes the vapours (*nesiim*) ascend. He brings down dew. He causes the soil to yield its produce. And He prepares a table before every one (on earth). And as for us, shall not Rabban Gamaliel stand by us and serve us drinks?.' Thus we see that the Sages argued that Rabban Gamaliel could renounce his honour and this refutes R. Ashi's contention that when a *nasi* renounces his honour is not renounced. The reply is given: 'But if it was stated thus was it stated', i.e. R. Ashi did not say what he is reported to have said. The true version of R. Ashi's saying is: 'Even according to the authority who holds that a Prince who renounces his honour, his honour is renounced [presumably referring to R. Joshua and R. Zadok], a king who renounces his honour, his honour is not renounced. As it is said: "Thou shalt in any wise set him king over thee" (Deuteronomy 17: 15).' His fear must be 'over thee', i.e. and, therefore, a special injunction exists to the effect that a king cannot renounce his honour.

It should be noted that: 'As it is said: Thou shalt in any wise set him king over thee' is a quote from the Mishnah (*Sanhedrin* 2: 5), cf. Abraham Weiss, *le-Ḥeker ha-Talmud*, p. 58. In our *sugya*, at first, R. Ashi refers to the *nasi* and it is only after the objection from the Rabban Gamaliel narrative that R. Ashi's statement is emended to read: 'Even according to the authority who holds that a Prince who renounces his honour, his honour is renounced, a king who renounces his honour, his honour is not renounced. As it is said: *thou shalt in any wise set him king over thee.* His fear must be upon thee'. Thus when in *Ketubot* 17a, *Sotah* 41b and *Sanhedrin* 19b the Talmud quotes *this version* in the words: 'As R. Ashi said' it presumably means that in those instances we have a quote from our *sugya*! In other words after our *sugya* had been completed there are cross-references to it in the other tractates. It is also just possible, however, that the cross-references are not to our *sugya* but to the original and correct version of R. Ashi. But if this is so then it means that in our *sugya*, at first, an incorrect version was recorded in order for the *sugya* to lead on from father to teacher to *nasi* and eventually to king! It is perhaps significant that the word for 'vapours' (*nesiim*) is also the plural of 'prince' so, possibly, there is a pun here: 'God causes the *princes* to rise to greatness', i.e. if He can renounce His honour, how much more so the *nasi* to whom He has given greatness!

The pattern of the *sugya* is:

(1) R. Hisda: *father* can renounce his honour; *teacher* cannot renounce his honour
(2) R. Joseph: even *teacher* can renounce his honour: *And the Lord went before them*
(3) Rava objects: is the *Torah* his?
(4) Rava's reply: yes, the Torah is his and he can renounce his honour
(5) Objection: but in that case why did Rava take offence and why did R. Pappa take offence?
(6) Reply: because some small token of respect should have been paid
(7) R. Ashi: even if *teacher* can renounce his honour, *nasi* cannot renounce his honour
(8) Objection: narrative of Rabban Gamaliel and the Sages
(9) True version of R. Ashi: even if *nasi* can renounce his honour, *king* cannot renounce his honour

It is clear that the *sugya* has been so constructed that it leads from the lesser to the greater – from *father* through *teacher* and *nasi* to *king*.

For this purpose, as above, the Talmud first quotes the incorrect version of R. Ashi, which it then refutes in order to lead to the climax: that even if in the other three cases there can be renunciation there cannot be in the case of the king. Since the whole *sugya* depends on the two versions of R. Ashi, it must have been edited some considerable time after R. Ashi's death.

On the face of it there appears to be a contradiction in the *sugya*. Thus at the beginning Rava refutes the argument, from the fact that God led the people, that a teacher can renounce his honour and yet in the narrative later R. Zadok proves his case from the fact that God serves 'everyone'. But the distinction is an obvious one. The proof from God leading them was, if God as Teacher can renounce His honour, how much more so a human teacher? To this Rava retorts that God can renounce His own honour but the teacher cannot renounce God's honour. But in R. Zadok's application it is not to God's honour that he refers but to the honour of the *nasi*. To this it is perfectly reasonable to argue that if God can renounce *His* honour how much more so can a human Prince renounce *his* honour?

22

Conclusions

We have examined a number of *sugyot* in some detail, each forming a unit complete in itself. These have been chosen, however, as altogether typical of the Babylonian Talmud as a whole so that it is possible to draw from them conclusions regarding the literary constructions and methods of argumentation of this apparently unsystematic work.

With regard to literary style, it must first be noted how futile it is to expect the kind of elegance usually associated with a work of literature (not, at least, in the Halakhic portions constituting the major part of the Talmud). The vocabulary is severely limited, consisting, in the main, of technical terms; the presentation of the material is cryptic, with hardly any spelling out of the meaning; there is no conscious striving for rhyme, rhythm or alliteration; and wherever punctuation is required it has to be supplied vocally by teacher and student, who 'sing' rather than 'read' the Talmud.

Yet the Talmud does have a literary style of its own, provided by the ordering of the material in a dramatic way. It is a style not of words but of ideas. The arguments and debates are so arranged that there is a building up of the discussion step by step until the climax is attained. Information is withheld until it can be given at the appropriate stage for drawing the threads of the argument together, as if the editors are saying: We have been leading you, the student, into tortuous paths and you have gone astray. Now we will show you the true path and all will become clear. The student is led to side first with one protagonist then with another until all the pros and cons have been exhausted. Even the digressions from the main argument have been planned so as to give the impression of spontaneity, much as a dramatist will use interruptions of the main plot in order to prevent the stereotyping of his play and its characters.

Repeatedly throughout the Talmud this element of contrivance can easily be discerned once more than a surface reading is attempted. Take the *sugya* on the Scriptural derivation of the probability principle (pp. 50–63). Ten Amoraím, over a two-hundred-year period, are recorded as endeavouring to prove, each in his own way, that Scripture permits reliance on probability. But, as we have seen, these proofs are not arranged in any chronological order but in a sequence in which the objection which can be advanced against the first proof cannot be advanced against the second; the further objection to this cannot be levelled against the third, and so on. The words used for 'R. Y. *said*' are not in Hebrew but in Aramaic, the language used by those responsible for providing the framework of the *sugya*. We do not have, in other words, the actual formulations of the original teachers who advanced the ten attempted proofs but a paraphrase by the editors. It is as clear as can be that the final editors have collected the ten proofs, originally independent of one another, and then arranged these to provide a dramatic sequence. In a word, this *sugya* and all the others are structured. (We are still in the dark as to the actual process through which the material from different ages and places came into the hands of the editors. Did the various generations actually transmit the sayings or is there an element of artificiality in it all?) It is not beyond the bounds of possibility that ten proofs, neither more nor less, are given because ten is a 'sacred number', as in the Decalogue and other Jewish institutions! In any event the *sugya* is far more than a mere recording of differing opinions. It is a literary unit in its own right.

Or take the *sugya* on the inability of mental reservations to invalidate a transaction (pp. 101–9). The *sugya* first gives an illustration of case law and then proceeds to a suggestion of what might have been in the mind of the teacher when he rendered his decision. The editors do not declare that they know the arguments by which Rava arrived at his decision that mental reservations do not count. The question, 'How does Rava know this?', implies that the editors have no tradition regarding the reasoning for Rava's decision. All they had was the decision itself. Moreover, the suggested reasoning is conveyed in the form of proof and refutation and then further proof typical of every Talmudic *sugya*. The first attempted proof is from the case of the man who has to be coerced into bringing the offering he had promised to bring. This shows that mental reservations are irrelevant, since otherwise there is a mental reservation even though, under coercion, the man states his willingness to bring the sacrifice. No, the argument continues, in that case the man may actually give his unreserved consent, albeit through coercion, because he really does wish to have the atonement that the bringing of the sacrifice will afford him. The second attempted proof is from the case of the man who is compelled to give a bill of divorce to his wife. Here the idea of consent without reservations does not apply, since here no atonement through the bringing of a sacrifice is involved. No, but here, too, there are no mental reservations since the man does wish to obey the law and the law demands that his wife should obtain her release. The third proof is from the Mishnah to which the *sugya* is appended. Here mental reservations are undoubtedly present, since there is no question of atonement or of obedience to the law and yet the reservations are ignored, which proves Rava's case.

A less contrived presentation – but that would not be the way of Talmud – would have been simply to make the suggestion at once that Rava derives his ruling from the Mishnah, the third attempted proof being quoted directly, the others simply ignored, since they are not conclusive in any event. But the Talmud is not interested solely in how the teacher arrives at his decision. The skilful working up of the material is the essence of the Talmudic presentation. What we have in this, and in all the other *sugyot* we have examined, is the telling of a story, as it were, in which, as in any good story, the dénouement comes in its right place. It is only in the final pages of the detective story that all the false clues are shown to be such and we learn that 'the butler did it'. In fact, the *sugya* does not allow even this third proof to stand. The clinching argument is from tractate *Me'ilah* and, in fact, as we have noted, in the Talmud to *Me'ilah* there is what appears to be a cross-reference to our *sugya*. Our *sugya* is appended to the third proof, which has taken us at least three-fourths of the road we have to traverse in order to obtain complete certainty.

Occasionally, as in the *sugya* on effects taking place simultaneously (pp. 75–82), the editors state explicitly that the argument is a step-by-step one. Here the steps in the argument from things that can be done by halves, to things that can be done in error, to things that can be done neither by halves nor in error, is all stated by the editors as part of their total construction. In the far more usual scheme, however, it is left to the reader to supply the step-by-step element, which he can easily do once he has grasped the nature of the Talmudic style.

To turn now to the conclusions to be reached regarding the Talmudic form of argumentation as a result of our investigation, we have noted in the first chapter the various moves open to the protagonists. In each of the *sugyot* described these moves are employed as the need arises, contributing to the liveliness of the debates. The student comes to feel that the Babylonian Amoraím are there with him in his room. He hears their voices, at times raised in vehement protest at a faulty conclusion, at other times haltingly exploring the admissibility of an alternative view to their own, and, again, at times giving assent, grudgingly or with brave acceptance, to the refutation of their deeply-held propositions. With their skills in presentation, the editors have brought about an uncanny sense of student participation in the debates which took place so long ago. It is no accident that the subsequent debates among the commentators on what the Talmud means in this or that passage are conducted in the Talmudic way as if the Talmud did not receive its final editing at all, but continued down the ages in the Yeshivot.

Yet for all the formal structuralism of the Talmudic *sugya*, the reasoning processes themselves are conveyed in no more than a few words. The student is expected to elaborate on these in order that their full meaning may be grasped. There is generally only a skeleton, to be clothed with flesh by acute, penetrating commentary. The danger is ever present, of course, of reading into these cryptic texts meanings their authors never intended. It is really a matter of becoming attuned to the mental processes of the Amoraím, of putting oneself into their universe of discourse, of acquiring the ability to anticipate their views. In the traditional Yeshivot this capacity to think the thoughts of the Amoraím after them, to delve into the profundities beneath the surface texts of the Talmud (the Gemara, as the Talmud came to be called) is known as 'having a Gemara head' or having a head for Gemara. It is partly art as well as science. We repeat that this whole area of Talmudic thinking has been largely ignored by modern scholarship, just as the Talmudists of the old school have been indifferent, on the whole, to the kind of question, raised by the moderns, of authorship, historical background, form and textual criticism. In this book we have tried to combine the two approaches, considering the literary problems without losing sight of that which gives the Talmud its force and appeal, the meaty argument in itself.

Let us examine some of the illustrations of legal maxims quoted in the *sugyot* to see how the bare statements require to be filled out if their meaning is to be grasped. In the *sugya* on probability (pp. 50–63) two different types are noted: (1) 'where the majority is before us'; (2) 'where the majority is not before us'. The rule that the majority be followed in a Court decision or that, where nine shops sell *kasher* meat and one forbidden meat, any meat found is assumed to come from the nine shops and is *kasher*, is called a 'majority that is before us'. Where the meat of an animal whose internal organs have not been examined is allowed to be eaten, it is said to be on the basis of a 'majority that is not before us'. That the Torah relies on a 'majority before us' does not entitle us to conclude that it relies on a 'majority that is not before us'. On a superficial reading the distinction is a purely formal one. In the one case the 'majority' is actually present – the members of the Court are here and the nine shops are here – whereas the majority of healthy animals is not actually present when the meat of this particular animal is being considered. But the Talmud gives no hint of the logic behind the distinction. Why should it matter whether the majority is present or absent? It all becomes abundantly clear once it is appreciated that in the words they use the editors are thinking of two kinds of probability, as we have noted. The 'majority that is before us' is a purely mathematical probability. If the Torah relies on it that can only be a procedural matter. That nine shops sell *kasher* meat does not mean that the Torah informs us that any meat is actually *kasher*, only that, even if it is not, it may be eaten by reliance, as a procedure, on the probability principle. In the other case of 'majority not before us' the probability that the animal is *kasher* is based on empirical investigation. The majority of animals examined are found to be healthy and not to suffer from a disease that renders their meat forbidden so that in any individual case it can be assumed that the animal is healthy and *kasher*. Here, where the 'majority is not before us', if the Torah does permit us to rely on probability it is a different type of probability on which we are to rely, that the animal is not only procedurally *kasher* but actually *kasher*. In the one case the probability principle is only applied as a matter of law. In the other case it is sought to apply it as a matter of fact. Obviously, the second type cannot be derived from the first. The reasoning is clear, but only after the precise but elusive formulations of the Amoraím or the editors have been translated into the language of abstract thought.

That mental reservations cannot be allowed to invalidate a contract (pp. 101–9) is formulated as: 'words in the heart are not words'. The word for heart (*lev*) denotes in Hebrew the whole inner being of man. The Amoraic formulation means that while the reservation has remained unexpressed in speech it is too intangible to revoke a verbal or written contract. Only verbal explication is sufficiently forceful, psychologically speaking, to denote real resolve. Otherwise, the mental reservation is too inchoate, too vague and uncertain, for it to be taken into consideration by the law, since the person who has this unexpressed reservation is not sufficiently definite about it when it contradicts his actual words or those of his bond. Similarly, when the Talmud wishes to suggest that a legal procedure is no test of veracity (so that, as on pp. 168–73, the testimony of a witness against himself is rejected by the law while the same testimony is accepted in relation to others), the way the Talmud expresses this is simply by saying 'we divide his words'. Again, when the Talmud discusses whether or not mere designation for a purpose is considered in law as if that purpose has been achieved, the way this is put is whether designation is or is not 'a thing' (pp. 122–32). That is to say, is the act of designation sufficiently substantial to count in law or is it too insubstantial; is it a 'thing' or is it not a 'thing'? This is a general principle, which is why the Talmud can consider in the same *sugya* such apparently unconnected items as designation of a cloth for a shroud and the designation of hide for *tefillin*. The question involved does not have to do specifically with the law of a corpse or of *tefillin* but with the general principle of whether mere designation counts. This Talmudic method of comparing diverse cases because they conform to a general principle can be observed in all the passages examined in this book.

In the *sugya* on the conveyancing of a thing not yet in existence (pp. 64–74), the term used for what we would call unrealised assets is 'a thing not yet in the world'. A distinction is made in the *sugya* between two types of unrealised assets. Where these, although not yet realised, can be realised (literally, 'it is in his hand') by the person seeking to transfer them, the transfer can more readily be accepted in law than where he has no power to realise them (literally 'they are not in his hand'). No reason for the distinction is given by the Talmud. If unrealised assets cannot be transferred in law, why should his ability to realise them make any difference? For that matter, the Talmud does not tell us why it is held that realised assets cannot be transferred. The later commentators explain it all in this way and what they have to say is very convincing. The reason why a transfer of unrealised assets is doubtful is because, while a man may have full resolve to sell or otherwise transfer to another something he has, his resolve to sell assets as yet unrealised is too weak for him to have the requisite degree of assent the law requires for a valid transaction. But where he himself has the power now to realise those assets his resolve is sufficiently strong (since it depends solely on him) to make his decision to sell or otherwise transfer them capable of being recognised by the law.

A similar type of reasoning would seem to be implied in the *sugya* on retrospective specification (pp. 24–33). Where a man instructs the scribe to write out a bill of divorce for the wife who will first emerge through the door, the bill of divorce (the *get*) is valid, it being considered as if the later specification was present at the time of writing. But, it is suggested, there may be no retrospective specification if the man's instruction to the scribe was to write the *get* for whichever wife the man will later decide to divorce. The wording of the distinction is, in the first case the later specification 'depends on others' (i.e. on the wife to emerge first through the door), while in the second case it 'depends on him' (i.e. on his later decision to divorce wife A rather than B). No reason is given for this bald distinction. In both cases there is lack of specification at the time the instructions were given and the *get* written by the scribe. If in the one case retrospective specification operates why should it not operate in the other? *Rashi* follows the standard method of amplification in order to make the distinction clear. Where the later specification depends on others, the husband has done all the specification he wishes to do. He has decided to leave it to others and this is in itself a sufficiently strong form of specification. But where the lack of specification is due to the husband's own indecision, there is so little specification at the time when the instructions were given that no amount of later specification by him can be allowed to operate retrospectively.

It can be seen from all the *sugyot* examined in this book that the task the Amoraím set themselves was to give abstract expression (although in very concrete formulation requiring, as we have just noted, further elaboration in abstract terms) to the individual formulations and cases of the Tannaím. The earlier, Tannaitic method of discourse is to consider particular cases. The Amoraím examined these particular cases in order to see whether or not a general, abstract principle of the law can be discerned. Thus the Tannaím speak of a man divorcing the wife who will first emerge through the door and of a man who wishes to drink out of a jar of wine from which he later gives the tithes. The Amoraím subsume these otherwise distinct cases under the heading of retrospective specification (pp. 24–33).

A feature of the Amoraic literature, insufficiently noted by many scholars but which can be seen from our investigation, is the purely academic and theoretical nature of a good deal of the material discussed. It is a moot point, for example, whether polygamy was widely practised during the Amoraic period but, even if it was, it is inconceivable that the case of a man instructing the scribe to write out a bill of divorce for whichever of his wives, *both with the same name*, emerges first through the door can ever have come before the Courts to be decided as a matter of practical law. Reliance on probability is everywhere accepted, but the whole question of how this principle is derived from Scripture has no practical consequences. There was no capital punishment in the Amoraic period so that all the passages dealing with this subject are about pure legal theory, as are all the debates and discussions on the sacrificial system, abolished long before the Amoraic period. Other than the love of learning for its own sake, what practical advantage could have resulted from the discussion of the man who betroths one of two sisters without specifying which of them he betroths? Even when the discussion centres around an actual case, as in the instance of mental reservations, the discussion itself is for its own sake, with no practical consequences. Unless this element of study of the Torah for its own sake, of occupying the mind with the word of God in much the same way as the pure scientist may be indifferent to the practical use to which his work may be put, is recognised, there is total failure to understand the Talmud. The

Talmud is not a Code of Law, although it became the basis and the final court of appeal for all the later Codes. The Rabbis were, of course, observant Jews and the Talmud does contain much practical law. But the main thrust both of the Amoraím and of the final editors of the Talmud is in the direction of pure legal theory – naturally, the legal theory as contained in the divine word they sought mightily to explicate.

Finally, it must be noted that all the passages considered in this book belong to the Halakhah, the legal element in the Talmud, which is after all the largest component in this gigantic work. Considerations of space dictated that the Aggadic element – the religion, history, folklore, medicine, science, legends and stories of the saints – be omitted. In the Aggadic passages there is, naturally, more poetry, less prose; more appeal to the emotions, less to the intellect; more attention to literary composition, less to acute analysis. Nevertheless, no hard and fast distinction between the Halakhic and Aggadic passages can be drawn. It can be shown that the type of argumentation exhibited in the Halakhah is not entirely absent from the Aggadah and, as we have seen, a striving for literary effect is present throughout the Halakhah.

In summary, then, the following are the conclusions we can be said to have reached.

(1) The Talmudic *sugya*, in its present form, is a complete literary unit. To affirm this does not preclude the existence of earlier strata in the *sugya* as we now have it. Indeed, form criticism has succeeded in detecting such strata in many a *sugya*. But there is abundant evidence that the earlier material has not been left intact. Rather it has been reshaped and adapted to the requirements of the *sugya* as we now have it, so as to form a unit complete in itself.

(2) This reshaping of the *sugya* has not been done haphazardly but with consummate skill. The argument is made to proceed step by step leading, with dramatic effect, to a climax. The presentation of the material in the form of question and answer, argument and counter-argument, affirmation and refutation, suggestion and rejection, all produce a vivid effect, as if the student is present while the debates are taking place and encourage his own participation in them.

(3) The Talmud is a literary work. Literary recasting of this kind can only have been achieved by creative literary effort. If any doubts remained about the literary form of the Talmud they have

surely been removed by the kind of investigation undertaken in this book.

(4) The teachers who provided the literary units, those whom we have called, for want of a better word, the editors, must have flourished at the end of the fifth century and the beginning of the sixth. That this is so can be seen from the fact that the framework for which they were responsible includes, frequently, elaborations of teachings stemming from early and mid-fifth-century Amoraím. Nor can it be maintained that the sections containing these elaborations alone are late, the others early. The amount of later material and the uniform style of the framework are sufficient evidence for the view that if some of the material of the framework is late all of it is late.

(5) The actual identity of the editors cannot now be determined. Their number is unknown, as are the methods by which they worked. Did they have something like a card-index? From the difference in vocabulary it seems certain, as both mediaeval and modern scholars have maintained, that some tractates were compiled in different places and schools from others. Yet, despite the slight differences, the literary form is virtually the same throughout the Talmud, which seems to suggest that at this period there existed a uniform Babylonian method of presentation. It remains puzzling that the Talmud contains not a hint of how it was put together or how it succeeds in giving the impression of having all come from a single hand. The conventional term Saboraím for the post-Amoraic teachers can still be accepted, provided the vast extent of their work as the actual creators of the Talmud is acknowledged. A further problem is posed by the existence of later work, differing markedly in style from the rest of the framework material. There was sound tradition in the middle ages that, for instance, the opening passage of tractate Kiddushin is a later addition and there are other such passages, as well as obvious later glosses on the framework. It would seem, therefore, that at least two kinds of Saboraic material are found in the Talmud. The first and by far the most important of these is the creative framework itself – the Talmud proper. The second consists of the comparatively small amount of later Saboraic material added to *sugyot* already completed. It cannot be denied, nevertheless, that the problems around this whole question remain unsolved.

(6) As for the Talmudic argument itself, this is an extremely

complex form in which various moves are open to the protagonists; in the light of what has been said previously we should rather say, the alleged protagonists, it all being the work of those who provided the framework. In the course of a single *sugya* there may be found, for instance, an appeal to authority; a rejection of the appeal on the grounds that the two cases are different or the authority quoted not followed because there is a rival authority to be relied on; a request for further information; a statement of two possible opinions and reasoning about which of them is correct; objections on logical grounds; and other forms of argument sketched in the first chapter of this book.

(7) A major portion of the Talmud consists of precise, legal definitions. These are, however, expressed in the concise and concrete form of Hebrew and Aramaic. It is the task of the commentator and student to translate these into the terminology of logical analysis, getting behind the actual formulations in order to discover their true meaning. Perhaps it can be put this way: the Talmud is a literary work but different from every other literary work in that its verbal exposition by those who study the work is indispensable to the form itself. Here it is true that the medium is the message and the message the medium.

Glossary

Aggadah: the non-legal material in the Talmud

Amora, Amoraím: 'interpreter'; 'interpreters'; name given to the post-Mishnaic teachers (from the beginning of the third century to the end of the sixth century) in Palestine and Babylon

Baraita: 'outside teaching'; a teaching from the period of the Tannaím but not included in the official Mishnah

Gaon, Geonim: 'excellency'; 'excellencies'; the Jewish leaders and teachers in Babylon who followed the Saboraím

Gemara: 'text', originally the text of a Talmudic passage, later used as a synonym for the Talmud as a whole

get: bill of divorce

Halakhah: the legal material in the Talmud

kasher: 'fit'; the meat of an animal fit for food

lulav: 'palm branch', used in the Tabernacle rituals (Leviticus 23: 40)

mezuzah: piece of parchment on which the Shema' is inscribed, affixed to the doorposts (*mezuzot*) of the house (Deuteronomy 6: 9)

Midrash: Rabbinic exposition of Scripture

Mishnah: the official digest of Judaism compiled by Rabbi Judah the Prince at the end of the second century

mitzvah: 'commandment', a precept of the Torah

perutah: a copper coin, the smallest coin of the realm

piggul: 'abomination', a sacrifice rendered unfit by an unlawful intention on the part of the priest

Saboraím: 'expounders', name given to the immediate post-Talmudic teachers

sefirat ha-'omer: the counting of the days from Passover to Pentecost (Leviticus 23: 15–16)

Shema': 'Hear, O Israel' (Deuteronomy 6: 4–9; 11: 13–21), the Jewish declaration of faith recited twice daily

shofar: ram's horn sounded on the festival of the New Year (Leviticus 23: 24; Numbers 29:1).

Sifra: a Rabbinic Midrash to Leviticus

Sifre: a Rabbinic Midrash to Numbers and Deuteronomy

sugya: a complete Talmudic unit
sukkah: 'booth', the tent-like structure in which Jews dwell during Tabernacles (Leviticus 23: 42)
Tanna, Tannaím: 'teacher', 'teachers', who flourished in Palestine in the first two centuries and whose views and opinions are found in the Mishnah, *Baraita* and *Tosefta*
tefillin: 'phylacteries'
terēfar: a diseased animal, the meat of which is forbidden
terumah: the tithe given to the priest
tevel: untithed produce
Tosefta: 'Supplement' to the Mishnah
tzitzit: 'fringes', worn on the corners of garments (Numbers 15: 37–41)
Yeshivah: school or college in which the Talmud is studied
zuz: a coin, the equivalent of a denar

Bibliography

Only works referred to in the book are listed.

GENERAL

Texts

Mishnah, ed. C. Albeck, Jerusalem–Tel-Aviv, 1957
Talmud Bavli, edn. Vilna, Romm, various printings
Talmud Yerushalmi, ed. Vilna, Romm, various printings; edn. Krotoschin, 1886
Tosefta, ed. M. S. Zuckermandel, Pasewalk, 1881
Sifra, ed. I. H. Weiss, Vienna, 1862
Sifre, ed. M. Friedmann, Vienna, 1864; ed. L. Finkelstein, Berlin, 1939
Midrash Rabbah, edn. Vilna, 1878
Avot de-Rabbi Natan, ed. S. Schechter, Vienna, 1887
Midrash Tehillim, ed. S. Buber, Vilna, 1891
Midrash Tanḥuma, ed. S. Buber, Vilna, 1913
Pesikta de-Rav Kahana, ed. S. Buber, Lyck, 1868
Yalkut Shim'eoni, Warsaw, 1877
The Mishnah, translated by H. Danby, Oxford, 1933
The Babylonian Talmud, translated into English under the editorship of I. Epstein, Soncino Press, London, 1948
Iggeret de-Rav Sherira Gaon, ed. B. M. Lewin, Haifa, 1921
Maimonides, *Yad ha-Ḥazakah*, Amsterdam, 1702
Sefer ha-Mitzvot, Warsaw, 1883
Kovetz Teshuvot ha-Rambam, ed. A. Lichtenberg, Leipzig, 1859
Moreh Nevukhim, Lemberg, 1886, English translation: *The Guide of the Perplexed*, by S. Pines, Chicago, 1963
Jacob ben Asher, *Turim*, Warsaw, 1886

Encyclopedias/Dictionary

Encyclopedia Judaica, editors in chief: Cecil Roth and Geoffrey Wigoder, Jerusalem, 1972

Entziklopedia Talmudit, ed. S. J. Sevin, Jerusalem, 1947–
Jewish Encyclopedia, general editor: Isidore Singar, printed by Funk and Wagnalls, New York–London, 1925
Eliezer ben Yehudah, *Thesaurus: Complete Dictionary of Ancient and Modern Hebrew*, Jerusalem, 1959

Commentaries

Isaiah Horowitz, *Sheney Luḥot ha-Berit* (*Shelah*), Amsterdam, 1649
Joshua ha-Levi of Tlemcen, *Halikhot 'Olam*, edn. Warsaw, 1883
Malachi ha-Kohen, *Yad Melakhi*, Jerusalem, 1976
Mevo ha-Talmud, attributed to Samuel ha-Naggid, in Vilna, Romm, edn. of Talmud, after tractate *Berakhot*
Samson of Chinon, *Sefer Keritut*, ed. J. Z. Roth with commentary, New York, 1961; ed. S. B. D. Sofer with commentary, Jerusalem, 1965

Introductions

Albeck, C. *Mevo ha-Talmud* ('Introduction to the Talmud'), Tel-Aviv, 1969
Goitein, Baruch Benedict, *Kesef Nivḥar*, Jerusalem, 1964
Meilziner, M. *Introduction to the Talmud*, 4th edn. with new bibliography by Alexander Guttmann, New York, 1968
Strack, H. *Introduction to the Talmud and Midrash*, Philadelphia, 1945

Variant readings

Rabbinovicz, R. *Dikdukey Soférim* (Latin title: *Variae Lectiones in Mishnam et in Talmud Babylonicum*), New York, 1960

SPECIAL WORKS

Ashkenazi, Bezalel. *Shitah Mekubbetzet*, Lemberg, 1837 and various editions
Bacher, W. *Exegetische Terminologie der jüdischen Traditionsliteratur*, translated into Hebrew: '*Erkhey Midrash* by A. Z. Rabbinowitz, Tel-Aviv, 1924; *Agada der Tannaiten*, translated into Hebrew: *Aggadot ha-Tannaím* by A. Z. Rabbinowitz, vol. II, Berlin, 1922
Berlin, N. Z. J. *Meshiv Davar*, Warsaw, 1894
Bloch, J. L. *She'urey Halakhah*, Tel-Aviv, 1958
Daube, David. 'Rabbinic methods of interpretation and Hellenistic rhetoric', *HUCA*, 22 (1949), 239–64
De Friess, B. *Meḥkarim be-Sifrut ha-Talmud*, Jerusalem, 1968
Edels, Samuel. *Ḥiddushey Maharsha*, commentary in Vilna, Romm, editions of the Talmud
Eger, Akiba. *Gilyon ha-Shas*, marginal notes in Vilna, Romm, editions of the Talmud
Elijah Gaon of Vilna. *ha-Gra*, marginal notes in Vilna, Romm, editions of the Talmud

Engel, J. *Lekaḥ Tov*, Warsaw, 1892
Epstein, J. N. *Mevuot le-Sifrut ha-Amoraím* (Latin title: *Prolegomena Ad Litteras Amoraiticas*), ed. E. Z. Melamed, Jerusalem, 1972
Feigensohn, S. *Homat Yerushalayim*, in Vilna, Romm, editions of *Talmud Yerushalmi*, beginning
Friedman, Shamma. *Perek ha-Ishah Rabbah be-Bavli*, Jerusalem, 1978
Ginzberg, Louis. *The Legends of the Jews*, Philadelphia, 1925
Goodblatt, David. *Rabbinic Instruction in Sassanian Babylon*, Leiden, 1975
Guttman, M. '*Sheélot Akademiot ba-Talmud*', *Dvir*, I (1923), 38–87; 2, (Berlin, 1924), 101–64
Halevy, I. *Dorot ha-Rishonim*, Berlin–Vienna, 1922
Halivni, David. *Sources and Traditions* (in Hebrew): vol. I, Tel-Aviv, 1968; vol. II, Jerusalem, 1978
Heller, Aryeh Laib. *Shev Shema'tata*, Jerusalem, 1957
Higger, M. *Otzar ha-Baraitot*, vol. x, New York, 1948
Hirschensohn, C. *Berurey ha-Middot*, New York, 1929–31
Hoenig, Sidney B. *The Great Sanhedrin*, Philadelphia, 1953
Hoffman, David. *Melammed le-Hoíl*, New York, 1954
Hyman, A. *Toledot Tannaím ve-Amoraím*, Jerusalem, 1964
Jacobs, Louis. *Studies in Talmudic Logic and Methodology*, London, 1961
TEYKU: The Unsolved Problem in the Babylonian Talmud, London–New York, 1981
'Are there fictitious Baraitot in the Babylonian Talmud?', *HUCA*, 42 (1971), 185–96
'Hermeneutics', *EJ*, vol. VIII, pp. 366–72
'The "*qal va-ḥomer*" argument in the Old Testament', *BSOAS*, 35, 2 (1972), 221–7
'How much of the Babylonian Talmud is pseudepigraphic?', *JJS*, 28, I (Spring, 1977), 46–59
Kagan, Meir Simhah. *Meshekh Ḥokhmah*, Jerusalem, n.d.
Kaplan, Julius. *The Redaction of the Babylonian Talmud*, New York, 1933
Klein, H. Articles on 'Gemara' and 'Sebara', *JQR*, New Series, 38 (1947), 67–91; 43 (1953), 341–63; *JSS*, 3 (1958), 363–72 and printed, together with other articles, as *Collected Talmudic Scientific Writings of Hyman Klein*, introduction by A. Goldberg, Jerusalem, 1979
Kroch, J. L. *Ḥazakah Rabbah*, vols I–XI: ed. P. J. Kohn, 1927–61 (vols I–IX publ. in Leipzig; vol. X publ. in London; vol. XI publ. in Jerusalem); vol. XII: ed. A. Krauss, Jerusalem, 1963
Krochmal, Nahman. *Moreh Nevukhey ha-Zeman*, ed. S. Rawidowicz, 2nd edn., London–Waltham, Mass., 1961
Landau, Ezekiel. *Noda' Bi-Yhudah*, New York, 1973
Lauterbach, J. Z. 'Talmud hermeneutics', *JE*, vol. XII, pp. 30–3
Lewin, B. M. *Rabbanan Savorai ve-Talmudan*, in memorial volume for Rabbi A. I. Kook, *Azkarah*, vol. IV, Jerusalem, 1937, pp. 145–208
Lieberman, Saul. *Hellenism in Jewish Palestine*, New York, 1950
Maimon, J. L. *Abbaye ve-Rava*, Jerusalem, 1965

Medini, H. H. *Sedey Ḥemed*, ed. A. I. Friedmann, New York, 1962
Meíri, Menahem. *Bet ha-Behirah*: to *Gittin*, ed. K. Schlesinger, Jerusalem, 1974; to *Kiddushin*, ed. A. Sofer, Jerusalem, 1963; to *Bava Kama*, ed. K. Schlesinger, Jerusalem, 1973; to *Makkot*, ed. S. Sterlitz, Jerusalem, 1965
Neusner, Jacob, ed. *The Formation of the Babylonian Talmud: Studies in the Achievements of Late Nineteenth and Twentieth Century Historical and Literary-Critical Research*, Leiden, 1970
Ostrowsky, M. *ha-Middot she-ha-Torah Nidreshet ba-Hem*, Jerusalem, 1924
Raábad. Strictures of R. Abraham ben David of Posquirês on Maimonides' *Yad*, printed together with the work in most editions
Ramban. Commentary of R. Moses ben Nahman, Nahmanides to Talmudic tractates, Jerusalem, 1928
Ran. Commentary of R. Nissim Gerondi on tractate *Nedarim*, in Vilna, Romm, editions of the Talmud
Rashba. Commentary of R. Solomon Ibn Adret on Talmudic tractates, Brünn, 1798, Warsaw, 1883 and various editions
Rashi. Standard commentary on the Talmud by R. Solomon Yitzhaki, printed at the side of the text in practically all editions
Riban. Commentary on part of tractate *Makkot* in Vilna, ed. by R. Judah ben Nathan
Ritba. Commentary on tractates of the Talmud by Yom Tov Ishbili, various editions
Rosh. Digest of the Talmudic Arguments by R. Asher b. Yehiel (*c*. 1250–1327), printed in the Vilna, Romm, editions of the Talmud
Rubinstein, S. M. *le-Ḥeker Siddur ha-Talmud*, Kovno, 1932
Schechter, S. *Studies in Judaism*, Philadelphia, 1945
Schwarz, A. *Der Hermeneutische Syllogismus in der Talmudischen Litteratur*, Karlsruhe, 1901
Die Hermeneutische Antinomie in der Talmudischen Litteratur, Vienna, 1913
Die Hermeneutische Quantitätsrelation in der Talmudischen Litteratur, Vienna, 1913
Skopf, Simeon. *Sha'arey Yosher*, Warsaw, 1928
Soloveitchik, Hayyim. *Ḥiddushey Rabbenu Ḥayyim ha-Levi*, with notes by Rabbi A. I. Karelitz, entitled *Ḥazon Ish*, n.p., n.d.
Talmage, Frank E. *David Kimhi The Man and His Commentary*, Harvard University Press, 1975
Taviob, I. H. '*Talmudah shel Bavel ve-Talmudah shel Eretz Yisrael*', in his *Collected Writings* (in Hebrew), Berlin, 1923, pp. 73–88
Tenenblatt, M. A. *The Formation of the Babylonian Talmud* (in Hebrew), Tel-Aviv, 1972
Tosafists. Standard glosses to the Talmud from the French and German schools, printed together with the text in most editions of the Talmud
Urbach, E. E. *Ḥazal*, Jerusalem, 1969
Vidal Yom Tov of Tolosa. *Maggid Mishneh*, Commentary on Maimonides' *Yad*, printed in most editions

Weiss, Abraham. *Hithavut ha-Talmud Bishlemuto* (English title: *The Babylonian Talmud as a Literary Unit*), New York, 1943
le-Ḥeker ha-Talmud, New York, 1954
Weiss, I. H. *Dor Dor ve-Doréshav*, New York–Berlin, 1924
'Survey of Talmudic methodologies' (in Hebrew) in *Bet Talmud*, vol. I, Vienna, 1881, pp. 26–31, 53–60, 85–9, 105–12, 153–9, 181–4; vol. II, Vienna, 1882, pp. 1–8